GETTING UNSTUCK

Also by Dr. Joy Browne

Dating for Dummies

The Field Experience (contributor)

It's a Jungle Out There, Jane

The Nine Fantasies That Will Ruin Your Life
(and the Eight Realities that Will Save You)

Nobody's Perfect:
How to Stop Blaming and Start Living

The Used Car Game

Why They Don't Call When They Say They Will

❦ ❦ ❦

All of the above are available at your local bookstore,
or may be ordered by visiting:
Hay House USA: **www.hayhouse.com**
Hay House Australia: **www.hayhouse.com.au**
Hay House UK: **www.hayhouse.co.uk**
Hay House South Africa: **orders@psdprom.co.za**

GETTING UNSTUCK

8 Simple Steps to Solving Any Problem

Dr. Joy Browne

HAY HOUSE, INC.
Carlsbad, California
London • Sydney • Johannesburg
Vancouver • Hong Kong

Published and distributed in the United States by: Hay House, Inc., P.O. Box 5100, Carlsbad, CA 92018-5100 • Phone: (760) 431-7695 or (800) 654-5126 • Fax: (760) 431-6948 or (800) 650-5115 • www.hayhouse.com • **Published and distributed in Australia by:** Hay House Australia Ltd., 18/36 Ralph St., Alexandria NSW 2015 • Phone: 612-9669-4299 • Fax: 612-9669-4144 • www.hayhouse.com.au • **Published and distributed in the United Kingdom by:** Hay House UK, Ltd. • Unit 202, Canalot Studios • 222 Kensal Rd., London W10 5BN • Phone: 44-20-8962-1230 • Fax: 44-20-8962-1239 • www.hayhouse.co.uk • **Published and distributed in the Republic of South Africa by:** Hay House SA (Pty), Ltd., P.O. Box 990, Witkoppen 2068 • Phone/Fax: 2711-7012233 • orders@psdprom.co.za • **Distributed in Canada by:** Raincoast • 9050 Shaughnessy St., Vancouver, B.C. V6P 6E5 • Phone: (604) 323-7100 • Fax: (604) 323-2600

Design: Julie Davison

Library of Congress Cataloging-in-Publication Data

Browne, Joy
  Getting unstuck : 8 simple steps to solving any problem / Joy Browne.
     p. cm.
   ISBN 1-56170-946-8 (hardcover) • ISBN 1-4019-0057-7 (tradepaper)
   1. Problem solving. I. Title.
   BF449 .B76 2002
   153.4'3—dc21

                                   2002003502

ISBN 1-4019-0057-7

06 05 04 03   6 5 4 3
1st printing, August 2002
3rd printing, September 2003

Printed in the United States of America

CONTENTS

❦   ❦   ❦

Please note:
All of the stories and case studies in this book are true.
All names have been changed for confidentiality purposes.

❧ Preface ❧

I assume at this moment that you're going to read the entire book that follows. You'll be thoughtful, fair, open-minded . . . and you'll be convinced that you truly want to become unstuck and get on with your life. But, if by some chance, someone you barely know or like bought you this book and you really enjoy being stuck, I'm willing to help you do with your life as you please, even though I don't agree with your decision. So, if you want to be stuck, I'll teach you how to be really, *really* stuck—we're talking major adherence here—in 13 simple, self-defeating steps.

1. Look for someone to blame. By blaming, you'll always be looking over your shoulder, stuck in the past. Make blame crucial to your life. Don't be shy. Be willing to blame everyone—your parents, ex-lovers, kids, bosses, and high school classmates. Blame your height, weight, color of your hair, country of origin, neighborhood, ethnicity, shoe size, diet, and the fact that you didn't get a pony when you were seven. Blaming, by definition, means you're forever stuck in the past, which will make you feel safe—unhappy, but safe.

2. Host frequent pity parties for yourself, ensuring that your blame is always fresh and active. Who needs stale blame? Make sure you share with *everyone* (from your co-workers to complete strangers at airports, grocery stores, and bus stops) how really lousy your life is and how you're the victim of a universal conspiracy.

3. Never listen to anybody. Other opinions? *Ha!* They're only going to confuse you! You know how miserable you want to be. Don't let anybody encroach on that. People may want to talk you out of it, offer a logical explanation, an escape plan, or worst of all, their own tale of woe. Ignore them.

4. Use words such as "never" and "always." "Coulda, woulda, shoulda" are also helpful in staying stuck. Not only will they bolster, feed, and nourish the misery quotient, these words will also make it virtually impossible for anyone to disagree. And if some smart aleck does dare to offer a counterexample, remember the previous lesson: "Never listen to anybody."

5. Rely on the "If you loved me, you'd know" method of communication. In other words, never give information to the enemy (anyone who disagrees with you). However, if some rascal uses this on *you,* point out to them that you're not a mind reader (swearing is always appropriate here)! Together, this one-two punch will ensure rotten communication and enable you to continue feeling victimized.

6. Make any problem an obstacle. Combine small problems into big ones, and big ones into giant, unsolvable monsters. For example, if you wake up with a headache, assume that it's brain cancer contracted from a tainted water supply due to your mother's negligence and a money-grubbing doctor who missed the early symptoms—all of which assures you an early, untimely, lonely, imminent death. And if some lout tries to bring you an aspirin suggesting a hangover, remember lesson #3.

7. Assume often and negatively, making yourself as miserable as possible. Make sure to always include the basics—that nobody likes or understands you, that nobody has ever had it as bad as you, and that everyone is out to get you.

8. Try to be in control of all situations at all times. All other people are nincompoops who will only hurt you if given half a chance. You have to make sure that you're *always* in charge—never let your guard down for even one second.

9. Minimize your effort. And I don't mean just verbally—actually *do* as little as possible. Hard work is for chumps. Cheat, cut corners, do whatever you can to slide by—just don't get caught!

10. Go for the jugular. Winning is everything. Mercy, cooperation, and caring are for suckers. And don't ever forget that the world owes you.

11. Be dependent. Make someone take care of you, and never ever take care of anybody else. You deserve to have an easy life. Don't worry about returning favors—it's your rightful reward to have other people take care of you and revolve their lives and schedules around you.

12. Act impulsively. Never think through what you're doing, and never explain. If things don't work out—and they won't—just go on the defensive. Say things like, "The devil made me do it," "Mother didn't raise me right," or "It's not my fault if nobody [listens, understands, tries, cares . . . take your pick]."

13. Believe that you're different from everybody else. No one has *ever* felt or understood what you're going through, so trying to communicate is just a big, fat waste of time. In fact, when you come right down to it, no one really understands you at all or even speaks your language. It's you against the world.

Feeling better? Worse? If you're stuck in the middle, either reread this chapter or take a chance—live a little! Start with Step One and try an entirely new approach to your life. Good luck!

❧ ACKNOWLEDGMENTS ❧

Writing books never gets easier, at least for me. Every one has its own unique pleasures and pains, but *Getting Unstuck* was a venture into spanking new territory for me. My acknowledgments start, as this book did, with my agent and friend, Joni Evans. Joni said, "It's time; get to it," and "There's someone I want you to meet . . . ." Enter Reid Tracy and Danny Levin of Hay House, who asked, "Can you explain to people how you think?"

"Don't know," I cheerfully replied.

Thanks, then, to that anonymous, annoying seatmate I had on a subsequent transcontinental flight, since it was either write the entire outline of this book on cocktail napkins, or engage in clever repartee with him. Voilà—a book born on cocktail napkins.

The women Furman—Elena and Leah—allowed me to voice my book. When I made no sense, their befuddled looks guided me. Thanks as well as for the neat typing, shortened paragraphs, and willingness to holler when my really cool idea was clear to me but no one else.

My assistant, Elizabeth Wipff, helped me keep track of drafts and revisions and manned the phones when we were trying to track down a correction. And then there's the adorable, efficient, cheerful editor Shannon Littrell, who was willing to arm wrestle me firmly and persuasively—and improved the book immeasurably for it.

I acknowledge and appreciate and adore every one of you for helping to polish, refine, define, and birth *Getting Unstuck*.

❦ INTRODUCTION ❧

What if I told you that you'll never again have to involve yourself in one of those stomach-turning, mind-numbing, relationship-ending arguments where everybody goes away feeling defeated, unhappy, and miserable? Don't misunderstand me: I'm not proposing that we turn all of the world's inhabitants into Stepford wives and husbands or zombie employees and bosses. I'm not even suggesting that we bring an end to conflict and disagreement—just to nastiness, unhappiness, and defeat as a *by-product* of disagreements. Hey, not only is this possible, it's doable. The way I plan to do this is by teaching you to ask the right question; get to the point; use time to your advantage; problem-solve without hostility; escape the sticky, messy past; and get on with your life.

For nearly two decades, I've been fielding questions on my daily syndicated call-in talk program from folks who basically wanted me to tell them that they were right and whoever was making them unhappy was rotten, depraved, uncaring, and deserving of a harsh, unspeakable cruel punishment. Often, my callers have been exceptionally skilled at disguising this motive, but when it comes right down to it, isn't that what we all want deep down inside—comfort, sympathy, and to be told *we're* right?

However, as most callers to my show soon learn, my task isn't to dole out sympathy and make people feel good about feeling bad. That isn't the reason I get out of bed every morning, brush my teeth, take a shower, and prepare to talk to nine million people about their problems. No, I want to do more than just chat or allow y'all to bend my ear—my goal is to help my callers live better lives by actually *solving* their own problems. And I have less than six minutes (on average) to do so. I can hear you skeptically muttering right now: "How can she possibly help an absolute stranger solve a problem in minutes without so much as seeing them? Yeah, yeah, I know she's a trained clinical psychologist, but still . . . "

Congratulations—you're absolutely right to be doubtful. Your heart wants to believe, but you know all about those books that claim everything and promise platitudes—'60s slogans repackaged for the 2000s. You've bought so many self-help tomes over the years that you could practically open your own bookstore . . . and not a single one of them (with the possible exception of one of mine) has made you happy. Well, guess what? You can relax.

That's right, inhale deeply and breathe a great big sigh of relief, because I'm not going to make you happy, and this book isn't going to change your life—*you'll have to do that all on your own.* You won't find any magic or instant solutions in this book—just effective problem-solving techniques that I've unearthed, learned, evolved, and developed during my many years of practice. This method comprises simple, straightforward steps that you can put to use whether you're trying to resolve the biggest or the smallest of your own issues.

Taking That First Step (or Let's Get Moving)

I've written several other books about how to deal with specific situations—but this time, my publisher asked if I could teach people to think like *I* think. At first, I wasn't so sure. But then it occurred to me that the dean of a medical school had once asked me to teach physicians to do what I do. He wrote, and I quote, "If you've given it any thought, this will probably be a breeze; if not, it's probably not worth the effort." Always curious as to how things work (and double-dog-dared challenged), I rose to the occasion to figure out my own unique technique.

I began with the basics. On the radio program, the process starts with my screener asking the caller, "What's your question for Dr. Browne?" If a caller can't come up with a question, then as much as I might like to chat, they probably won't get on the air, because the first clause in the "contract" I have with my callers is *they must admit that they have a problem.* They've got to be willing to admit to me (as well as themselves) that something in their lives just isn't working and that they're *stuck* in the past—unhappy, unfulfilled, embarrassed, and unable to move on. They must also be willing to ask me for help, which is no easy task considering that this process entails picking up the phone, getting a busy signal, trying time and time again until my screener finally answers . . . and then being put on hold. Heavy. So how, in a couple of minutes, can I get a caller up and running, confident in their ability to not only *do* something, but do it *right?*

The first step in getting somebody unstuck is for both of us to look at the muck and believe that there *is* a way out. This is known in the trade as a *solution.* Without a stated problem, my caller and I aren't sharing a point of reference—a common starting point. I'm a professional problem solver, not a psychic. I can't divine a problem out of thin air (or even superimpose one on a reluctant caller), and without a shared problem, we'll *never* share a solution.

So getting unstuck is the idea of being able to move from a past dilemma to a current action. This rests on five basic assumptions— assumptions that underlie the premise of the book you're about to read. They are:

1. **Solutions exist:** If not, why bother?

2. **Solutions are knowable:** They can be found if you know where to look.

3. **Solutions are useful:** I'm not a philosopher—I'm a psychologist, and I'm pragmatic.

4. **Solutions are feasible:** As in possible and doable; pie in the sky need not apply.

5. **Solutions work for everyone:** If you're willing to give up the notion that somebody has to win and somebody has to lose, problem solving gets much more challenging, a lot more fun, and much less hostile.

I'm not offering sorcery, magic wands, or a promise to absolutely put an end to all disagreements. Instead, I propose a new and radically different approach to resolving conflict: by declaring victory and moving on, surrendering and moving on, or admitting defeat and moving on—but mostly by *moving on*, getting unstuck from the past, and getting on with your life. This approach doesn't involve eating crow, walking out, blowing up, or losing (or even winning). I'm talking about shifting the focus from winning to *solving,* thus making every conflict into a win-win proposition, a way to evaluate our own behavior through lessons not wars, by learning not vanquishing, and most important, by *moving*—not getting bogged down, wigged out, defeated, or embarrassed. Bottom line: *getting unstuck.*

Getting Unstuck in 8 Simple Steps

As I mentioned before, the part of the contract that I make with callers is my determination to help. And by "help," I mean giving them something they didn't have when they began the phone call, something that will make them better able to function or understand or accept—something that is, first and foremost, useful. As it turns out, this certain something is actually made up of eight principles that, taken together—or even separately—form the basis of each and every bit of advice I've ever doled out. These are the principles that turn mountains into molehills and that make up the substance of this book. They are, as follows:

1. **Time Shifting:** Figure out where you are.

2. **Patterns:** Remember where you've been.

3. **Self-Awareness:** See yourself.

4. **Perspective:** See your world.

5. **Building Blocks:** Find and use the right materials.

6. **Goals:** Have a direction; know what you want.

7. **A Toolbox:** Determine the dozen crucial skills that allow you to see the big picture clearly.

8. **Interactions:** Know that the behavior you can control is your own, but other folks live here, too.

About This Book

Before we dig in, I want to take a moment to familiarize you with the format of this book. As you'll notice, every chapter kicks off with a problem, a specific story that I find more compelling than a theory (and I assume that you folks will feel the same way). Not only does this mimic the fact that every caller on my program begins with their story, but that a theory is a lot more comprehensible when using a down-to-earth example instead of a generalized abstraction. In my world, the specifics are people and their problems, so every one of the eight steps to getting unstuck starts with a real person's dilemma. Whether or not you have the exact same problem, you can follow along, get involved, enjoy a bit of distance, and *bingo!*—I bet you'll clearly understand how each step relates to you by the end of the chapter.

The second reason I begin each chapter with a specific problem is because it literally puts us both on the same page. We're starting at the same time and at the same point. When someone calls me on the radio, I always have a name, an age, the town they're calling from, and their question. This book is written in the same way: We discuss a specific problem, which embodies the concepts about to be set forth in the chapter; next, we talk about the step that goes into solving the problem; and then I give very specific examples of how to take the necessary step.

I'm a "tell-you-what-I'm-going-to-tell-you, tell-you, and tell-you-what-I-told-you" kinda girl. I'll start off by telling you everything that's going to be in each chapter, then I'll elaborate on the specifics and introduce you to helpful exercises. At the conclusion, I'll do two things that may be different from what you're used to. The first of these is called "Playing Doctor" (no, not *that* kind of doctor!), and it's my way of helping you track how much you've learned from each chapter.

Now I was trained as a scientist, and as such, one of the things you're taught to do is take whatever you've learned in the classroom and try it out in a lab to find out how theory translates into practice. Since I can't take all of you into my lab, I've made you temporary doctors. In the "Playing Doctor" sections, I'll give you specific examples and let you find your own solutions. Then, I'll tell you whether your answers were right or wrong, and why.

At the tail end of each chapter, you'll find a mini-conclusion called "Shrink Wrap" (get it? I'm a "shrink," and this is a wrap-up (or rap) of the chapter . . . aren't I punny?). Like actual shrink-wrap, this section will be very clear, enabling you to see through to the "meat" of the chapter. And that, in a nutshell, is the format of each of the eight chapters

You may have noticed that I've also included a chapter called "Conclusions." Well, these aren't really *conclusions* in the classic sense of the word. Since each chapter has a "Shrink Wrap," the conclusion chapter would be pretty boring if all it did was recapitulate what you've already learned. Instead, the chapter is a kind of "goodie bag."

Let me explain: When I go to a ritzy seminar or fancy corporate retreat, I'm just delighted when I'm handed a container of nifty little gifts as I'm walking out the door (yeah, I know they also have them for Academy Award presenters, but I haven't done that yet . . . so let's stay real). Usually the people that put on the seminar or retreat will give the participants "loot" that serves as a reminder of the event itself *and* contains things that can be used in everyday life. That's what I've done for you in this chapter. The "Conclusions" chapter is my goodie bag for you: a compact collection of practical, useful tools that you can use. My editor said, "Ooh, I loved the last chapter, with all these little prizes that I didn't expect." So be prepared to be surprised. (Anticipation makes the surprise cooler—no fair peeking!)

So now you know everything about the book, except why I called it *Getting Unstuck*. Originally, I wanted to call it *Playing Doctor*, but everybody thought that was a little too sexual (which is probably why I liked it), so that got vetoed. Other people wanted to call it *Problem Solving 101*, which it certainly is, but talk about your boring title. So at one point I was sitting around thinking about titles, and I said to Danny Levin, my initial contact at Hay House, "Well, how about if we just call it *Unstuck*?" And he came back with, "How about *Getting Unstuck*?" Now I don't know if you know about the politics of getting your books published, but when your major contact says, "Let's add a gerund," you add a gerund. Hence the title: *Getting Unstuck*. (**Author's note:** My editor feels that not everybody knows what a "gerund" is, but I love this word. Put simply, a "gerund" is just a verb used as a noun. So, if I say, "Running is good for you," "running" is a gerund. Now that we've cleared that up, back to the book.)

Let me be perfectly honest with you: *Getting Unstuck* isn't going to make you deliriously happy immediately. But it *will* teach you to be effective and focused—not because you've memorized some catchy slogans, but because you've learned a new way to think about conflict, problem solving, moving on, and getting unstuck.

You've probably heard the tale about the hungry man who comes to Confucius, begging for food. Confucius begins to carve a fishing rod, and the amazed, disgruntled, and hungry man asks what he's doing. Confucius replies that a benefactor can feed someone, taking care of their hunger for the day; or he can teach them to fish, enabling them to feed themselves forever. Those who learn to fish can become well fed, independent, and potentially helpful to others. *Prepare to learn to fish, not get fed.*

You can expect to experience some of the reactions I get from my callers—sometimes they're thrilled with me, sometimes furious.

They're often thoughtful, amused, curious, unclear, and repentant—but they're usually polite and willing to reconsider the patterns in their lives that just aren't working anymore.

My job is to do my best to listen and respond, carefully and thoughtfully; I take comfort in realizing I'm only responsible for *my* behavior, not anybody else's. Along the way, I try to practice empathy, diplomacy, kindness—charm, even humor occasionally. Once the basics are in place, I'm seldom angry and almost always confident that I can deal with disagreements without anyone hanging up or walking away hurt. You've heard of Krazy Glue—well, this is Unstuck Sanity.

So, without further ado, turn the page . . . and learn how to be a better parent, spouse, friend, employee, employer, son, daughter, and significant other by letting go of past regrets, hurt feelings, and even ancient triumphs. The past is truly history—learn from it and move on. The future is fantasy—*today* is what you've got. The steps will all be revealed to you page by page. Let's get unstuck.

STEP 1:
❧ TIME SHIFTING ❧

[**Author's Note:** For the rest of this book, I will address each caller directly, just as I do on my show. However, since Bob is our first example, he'll be treated a little bit differently. I'll let you read his problem, but I won't give him an answer directly. Instead, I'll show you how his problem breaks down for the purposes of this chapter.]

> *I've been married to the mother of my two grown children for almost 25 years. My wife and I haven't had sex in a year, and I think it's because I'm gay. I've never actually had sex with a man, but I feel that I've been lying to myself all these years. At the same time, I can't imagine tearing my family apart.*
>
> — Bob, 48, Gloucester, MA

Bob is a classic example of someone who's really, really stuck—he's so used to feeling good about feeling bad that he's victimizing himself. If he really has spent the last 25 years feeling as he does today, it's unlikely that he's been: (a) happy; (b) a good husband; or (c) a good father—how could he when he's constantly looking back at what might have been?

Bob feels trapped by circumstances, while being unwilling to ask himself these crucial questions:

1. Am I gay?
2. What do *I* want?
3. What are my trade-offs?

Is questioning his sexuality a way of creating a gay alter ego in order to escape his marriage, feel closer to men, or irritate an overbearing father? Or has Bob simply repressed his sexuality for decades? Who knows? Well, Bob needs to, but by wallowing in his questions instead of whittling them down, he's not moving any closer to a plan that might make him happier. Bob's got to let his past go and contemplate a future where he can be happy long enough to decide what he wants to do. Coming out of the closet and leaving his wife, finding a way to contentedly stay in his marriage, or even seeking a therapist and sorting out his sexuality are all impossible until Bob lets go and elects to *move.* When he decides that he wants to stop concentrating on what *was,* Bob can focus on what *is* and will finally be able to help himself.

What's Your Question?

Most of us spend way too much time being consumed by stuff that's already happened. Obsessing about the past is never going to change it; and while it allows us to see where we've been, the past isn't a roadmap for the future. Psychology pioneer William James said that human beings are the only species that can contemplate their own death . . . which means that we're constantly aware that the meter's running, so to speak.

How we see ourselves with respect to our beginning and our eventual end personalizes how we see time. In essence, time is really like a river. As human beings, we want to divvy this flow into distinct elements—years, months, weeks, days, hours, minutes, and seconds. We're superimposing a structure on something that isn't structured but flowing. The fact that our days on this planet are numbered and we know it makes time seem like the single most valuable commodity we have. This notion can be useful and positive, propelling us forward and giving our lives structure so we don't feel as if we're bobbing around rudderless on a stormy sea. On the other hand, our perceptions of time can also overwhelm and work against us in the same way that it's working against Bob. He's stuck in a little eddy that's going 'round and 'round, while everyone else is moving on. In fact, Bob's been spinning around in circles for so long that he doesn't even realize he's not moving forward. People can spend their entire lives trapped in whirlpools such as these. Here's where I come in.

Think about it—every one of my callers knows their history better than I do. If their answers were to be found in their past, they wouldn't need my help. And if I let them dwell on the past, I wouldn't be of any help either. So, the first and most important service I provide for my callers is to get them unstuck. I do that by asking: "What's your question?"

Listeners of my radio program will no doubt recognize those three little words as my signature line. Demanding a question is my version of a wake-up call, a splash of cold water, and, occasionally, a smack upside the head to get the caller to snap out of it. I've posed this query to everyone from Gina, whose brother-in-law had committed suicide; to Michael, who was distraught over his wife's request for a trial separation after six years of marriage; to Gerald, a widower who merged his family with that of a widow after a one-week courtship; to Holly, whose friend was always drinking fancy wine and then wanting to split the check 50-50.

It's no coincidence that almost all of my callers elicit this same question from me. The very act of calling a radio psychologist means that someone recognizes that they're caught in the sticky past. My task is to encourage my unhappy caller to escape by shifting from past to present immediately, to bring them into the here-and-now by asking: "What's your question?" (Or if I have to get *really* strict: "What's *today's* question?")

Tell me what it is you want—not what's bothering you. *What's your question*, not *what's your problem*. I first grasped the full importance of "What's your question?" during a seminar I gave in a packed high school auditorium in Portland, Maine. After patiently waiting until the question-and-answer period began, a tall, blond, bespectacled man stood up. Identifying himself as "John, 35 years old," he promptly embarked upon a tale of woe concerning his ex-wife's dysfunctional family, their arguments over sex, money, work, raising the kids, etc. I waited patiently for him to take a breath so I could calmly and sympathetically inquire what his question was.

Undeterred, John launched into a description of the horrors of his wife's divorce lawyer, the difficulties of visitation and custody fights, her increasing demands for money . . .

"Is there a question in here?" I asked with a smile.

Next, John told me about his son's problems with school and a questionable diagnosis by the school psychologist of Attention Deficit Disorder (ADD), the kids' fighting with each other, their seeming dependency on their mother . . .

"And your question is?"

"Well, I'd like to see my kids every other weekend, and she's always filling up their time so that I can't see them, and she's dating this guy . . . "

"Question, question," I cheerfully insisted.

"It's just a matter of trying to get her to stop taking out all her jealousy and hurt on me. She's just like her mother, her whole family never liked me, we never should have . . . "

By now, the once sympathetic audience of 3,500 was chanting along with me: *"What's the question? What's the question?"*

I had no mute button; I couldn't cut to a commercial; and while John was obviously very unhappy and felt enough urgency to expose himself and his plight in front of his friends and neighbors, I wasn't getting him anywhere.

A woman high up in the balcony apparently felt the same sense of frustration and concern that I did, for she impatiently hollered out, "How should I deal with my ex-wife?!"

The audience applauded wildly. John blushed and began to go back to his seat.

I waited until the noise had died down and calmly, yet firmly, said, "Nope, lady—that's *your* question. John, your question might be, 'How do I get over the divorce?' or 'How do I get on with my life?' or 'Does home schooling make sense for my son?' or 'Should I sue for custody?' or 'Is my child support really getting spent on the kids?' or 'Will I ever be happy again?'"

Looking rather pitiful, John took a deep breath and finally managed to come up with not only a question but his very own answer, too: "Do you think it's too soon for me to date? What do you think? Guess so . . . " he trailed off. The audience went wild.

I hugged him, and John sat down a wiser man with some direction in his life. Admittedly, not all of his problems were solved—I'm sure his wife's family is still dysfunctional, his kids still squabble, and his son may still have a learning disorder—but John truly cleaned up his act before our very eyes and launched himself into his new life. And although he was right that it was way too soon for him to start dating, that day John took a giant step toward leaving the past behind. All of this magic happened by getting to the question.

A question is a focus, a statement of uncertainty. I understand that all of us, like John, have a history that's by turns interesting, compelling, sad, and funny, but *it's already known.* To get unstuck, something has to change, and that's the thing about the past—it's unchangeable. That little fact, however, doesn't deter most people from dwelling on their histories. If I had a dollar for every person who's called just to vent their frustrations about what was to me, you'd find my name alongside Bill Gates and Warren Buffett on the World's Richest People list.

Staying stuck may make us feel virtuous—"I don't want to hurt my [fill in the blank with *wife, family, mother, friend, partner, child, teacher, doctor, cocker spaniel, credit rating*]." But such self-sacrificing behavior only looks good on paper. In real life, not taking responsibility for our actions is a pain in the neck to live with. We become grouchy, demanding, and expect gobs of gratitude. Then we wind up feeling ill-used by and resentful of all those who have innocently taken us up on what we proffered. Misdirected anger, hostility, and passive-aggressive behavior ensue. And when people turn on us—which they inevitably will if we persist with this destructive course of action, or rather, *inaction*—we end up feeling like martyrs. We're full of good intentions that have been thwarted and misunderstood by the entire world—but really, all we're doing is playing the same old victim role.

Taking the time to figure out what they want out of life and then attempt to act upon it is empowering and productive; victims invariably insist that they would, could, or should make a change if only the circumstances were a little different. But understand this: We can't control what happens to us; we can only control our behavior.

If you're in hell, don't stop. When something's bothering you, instead of staying stuck and bemoaning your cruel fate, shift your focus to what can be done to change the situation. This simple time shift from past to present will have a positive impact on your life and the world around you, and will improve your life immediately.

The focus of this chapter, then, is to find *your* question—that is, how to get unstuck from the past and time-shift into your present. I'll show you how to:

- move out of the past once and for all;

- play your choices forward (I'll explain what this means later); and

- come back from the future.

Move Out of the Past

Okay, now we're cookin'. Once you've boiled the problem down to one question, we can understand what the focus is right now, this moment, today! *Ta-dah!* Getting from the murky, unyielding past to the present might be confusing, but at least something can be *done* about it. On my radio program, this sort of time shift into the present allows me to move the caller from passive victim (stuck) to active problem solver (unstuck). The moment you can formulate a question or state a need, you're in charge. You've overcome the victim mentality by owning up not only to responsibility, but to a plan, an action, a movement.

Responsibility. . . . Think about that word for a minute. What does it mean to be responsible? The word is a conjunction of the words *response* and *able.* Able to respond. People phone my program when they're unable to respond to events in their life. They're unhappy, anxious, and stuck. Life is dealing them some serious blows, and they feel powerless. Stuck in this victim's frame of mind, many callers have made an unconscious decision to dwell on the injustices of the past instead of working toward a better future. The first and most important thing I can do for a person is to help them reclaim their power— or their responsibility—to restore the ability to respond, to act!

The ancient Stoic philosophers had responsibility down to a science. Living my motto: "We can't control what happens to us, we can only control our behavior," the Stoics were known for keeping their cool in the face of great pressure . . . because they had one-track minds. They were constantly thinking *What's my next move?* And that, folks, is exactly the philosophy that I attempt to impart from the get-go.

"Living in the moment" may not sound like a revolutionary philosophy, but you'd be surprised how few people actually do it. Judging by the calls I field every day, we as a species are much more comfortable complaining about past events than trying to make a change for the better—be it in our personal or public lives. Just look at the gobs of people who complain about the state of education, health care, and welfare in this country, as opposed to the number who actually *do* something—anything—to change the status quo.

This same inertia is sadly apparent in our personal lives. Henry David Thoreau said a sad, memorable mouthful when he wrote, "The mass of men lead lives of quiet desperation." The sense that everybody else is as sad, lonely, and passive as we are may be a comfort or may make us feel superior or less lonely but, man, what a downer! If you agree with Thoreau, it's about time you stopped wallowing and asked yourself: "What can I do *now* to make my life work better?"

When I was in graduate school, studying to be a clinical psychologist with the plan to go into private practice, I was taught a relatively passive style of listening to people recite their troubles. The radio work gave me the insight to understand that insight alone isn't sufficient—you've got to *do* something to feel better about your life and yourself. Self-esteem is just what it says—your feeling good about what you *do* as a path to feeling happy about who you *are*. Thoughts don't make us who we are—actions do.

Play It Forward

Now that we've looked at the first part of time shifting, the acknowledgment of a problem and the search for a solution, let's establish the second part, which revolves around moving into the future. I call this step "playing it forward."

Playing it forward is an incredibly helpful tool. The concept is as simple as understanding that each and every one of our actions carries consequences. When we shift forward to assess various possibilities, we can begin to understand the effects our behavior will have. Then our choices and decisions are based on something other than blind luck. Our perceptions may not always be accurate, but at least they're not random. If they're flawed, we can return to our assumptions and reevaluate them, instead of feeling victimized by a cold, cruel world.

※ ※ ※

Sometimes, playing it forward can give us the serenity to accept the inevitable, or a kick in the butt to avoid the otherwise inevitable. Cynthia's dilemma illustrates this perfectly.

> *My 20-year-old son and his 18-year-old girlfriend want to get married. They've been dating for two years but have only been exclusive for one. I think they're rushing things—but the girlfriend's parents are so dead set against this marriage that*

I'm afraid they're just pushing the two of them closer together.
How do I tell my son that I don't think he and his girlfriend
should get married so soon without alienating them?

— Cynthia, 42, Elgin, IL

Let's look at your possibilities here, Cynthia. Life is like a game
of chess: For every move you make, your opponent makes a counter-
move. In order to get what you want and win the game, you can figure
your opponent's reactions into your moves by playing situations
forward. Everyday problems can benefit from the same degree of
intense scrutiny and concentration as well.

You've already played one scenario forward by assessing the
strategy of your would-be daughter-in-laws' parents. If you tell your
son and his girlfriend that you think they're rushing into marriage,
they're going to feel offended and become defensive. I agree, we
don't want to set up a Romeo-and-Juliet situation here. The last thing
you want when you're trying to keep two people focused and sane is
to unite them against a common enemy. Fending off parental assaults
on their plans would allow the couple an opportunity to bond over
their anger with a common foe, which could spur them on to a
speedy marriage just to spite everybody. Cynthia, telling your son
not to get married is not only unlikely to work, but it's an approach
that may provoke the lovebirds to find a justice of the peace the first
chance they get.

Doing absolutely nothing may be tempting, but it's dangerous.
By playing the situation forward, we know that neither objecting to
the wedding nor supporting it won't serve your interests *or* the kids'
in the long run. Since these two options represent polar opposite ends
of the spectrum, our goal is to find a middle ground—something
between outright condemnation and hearty support.

You're going to hate what I'm going to suggest, and I'm going
to get huge amounts of mail, but let's deal with the problem
realistically. Since it sounds as though their relationship is already
sexual, I'd say the following to your son and his intended: "I love
you both and I know you love each other. I'll bribe you to postpone

the wedding for a year—I'll help you set up housekeeping so you can live together while you get to know each other and plan a lovely wedding. Just make sure you're practicing effective birth control."

Offer to give them a generous gift, such as a great wedding reception, a honeymoon, or help with a down payment on their first home. Just make sure that they understand you're not against their relationship and that your only concern is that they're still quite young to marry. If they're not living together yet, tell them that this might be something they want to try prior to getting married. Worst-case scenario, they get married . . . maybe these are the kids who *can* put together a successful marriage in spite of their youth.

❦ ❦ ❦

Offering her son and his girlfriend a desirable incentive to postpone the wedding is a viable solution for Cynthia—especially when one considers that every other course of action will only serve to hasten the young couple's impending marriage, and possibly drive them away from their parents completely.

Back from the Future

Having just discussed moving out of the past and playing it forward, two aspects of time shifting that I use most often, I now want to address a third, less common (but just as important) part of the time-shifting concept: coming back from the future.

Not all of my callers are stuck in the past. Some actually do know what they want and would be ready to act were it not for one small hitch. I call this the vicious "what-if cycle." In the process of playing it forward, many people find themselves paralyzed by either the sheer number of possible outcomes, or their fear of the worst-case scenario, what I cheerfully refer to as "analysis paralysis." For instance, your daughter is caught stealing candy from the school cafeteria and you tell her to return it, but then you get an attack of the "what-ifs": (1) What if she gets expelled? (2) What if she winds up resenting you for the rest of her natural-born life? (3) What if she's so emotionally disturbed by the idea that she develops a crippling psychological complex? And so on.

Left unchecked, the game of "what if" can be as much a trap as never asking the question at all. Action without thought of consequences is childish, but thinking too much and acting too little is old-fogey city—armchair quarterbacking. At times like these, we tend to become immobilized. In effect, we wind up thinking too hard and acting too little. Life is unpredictable, but you can raise the likelihood of a happy outcome by playing the odds. Rephrase the above questions to instead ask: (1) What are the chances that your daughter would get expelled? (2) What are the chances that she'll wind up resenting you all her livelong days? and (3) What are the chances that she'll be psychologically damaged? You see, here's where your knowledge of the situation's circumstances comes into play.

One of my favorite sayings is, "When you hear hoofbeats, think horses, not zebras." This means that when you're unsure, play the odds—go for the most probable scenario first, with the least probable bringing up the rear. Maybe it's because we all have a little drama queen (or king) in us, or maybe it's because we've learned fear at Mommy's knee, but most of us tend to do exactly the opposite of this technique by scaring ourselves silly with catastrophic visions of the worst-case scenario, brought to us in living color and stereophonic sound.

While we're on the subject of horses and statistical probability, think of possible outcomes as thoroughbreds in a race: Some are longshots, others are sure things. In horse racing, the oddsmakers do the research and figure out each horse's chances, but in real life, you get to do the analysis and be your own handicapper. Let's go back to the example of the candy-stealing daughter. What kind of school does your daughter attend? What kind of constitution does she have (that is, is she a nervous or unusually tense child)? In the end, you might just decide that, knowing what you do about your daughter, the best way to handle the little sticky-fingered rascal is to ban her from watching TV for two weeks.

Then again, you might fall into the "what-if cycle," getting so caught up in your fears of the worst-case scenario that you decide to forget about the entire thing, letting your daughter off the hook because of your fears rather than her behavior. Opting to do nothing out of fear or indecision *is* in reality a decision, but it's not one guaranteed to result in optimum outcomes for either you or your daughter. When you're tempted to do nothing—that is, when you find yourself in hot water, remember that a frog will patiently sit in a pot of water as it heats on the stove, until it's boiled to death. Whether the little dickens is tolerating the intolerable because it's happening slowly or simply hoping for the best, the passive frog is toast. Awaiting a better future but unwilling to do anything about it, the frog pays the ultimate price. But *you* don't have to.

You will get unstuck if you can accept that the past is gone and the future is a dream—one is history, the other mystery. *All we can change is the present.* Focusing on the future to the exclusion of the present is incredibly dangerous. What's more, escaping present pain by fantasizing about a terrific future allows for no real, actual pleasure—ever. Once again, our frog friend provides a rather grotesque example of this: Fantasizing about cooler climes or yummy flies, he's so focused on an imaginary future that he invalidates his present, and consequently, has no real future at all.

Don't misunderstand me. I'm not implying that you should abandon thinking about the past or planning for the future—just don't spend most of your time on what's already done or yet to be. The past can be a valuable source of insight (I am a psychologist, after all), but spending more than 10 to 15 percent of your time thinking about what's already happened isn't going to get you anywhere. Remember, the value of insight lies entirely in its potential to effect positive, constructive action. There's no such thing as insight for insight's sake—sooner or later, you've got to do something, move, and get on with it.

By the same token, I don't recommend spending more than 15 to 20 percent of your time on thinking about the future. Goals and plans are wonderful sources of inspiration. They can guide our actions and motivate us to overcome obstacles, but, as Thomas Edison once said,

"Genius is 1 percent inspiration and 99 percent perspiration." You can plan and dream all you want, but you'll eventually have to expend time and energy to see your plans and goals through to completion.

Learn from the past, keep an eye on the future, but devote most (65 to 75 percent, let's say) of your time to active problem solving—emphasis on *active*. Concentrating on the present is the only way to change the past or improve the future. Pam's dilemma offers a perfect opportunity to do just that.

❧ ❧ ❧

I've been experiencing problems conceiving, and have been seeing an infertility specialist for almost three years with no success. Most days I can handle it, but as the years go by, I get scared and begin to wonder if I'm doing the right thing. I can't believe how much time has gone by since I first started trying to conceive. It's gotten to the point where this is all I think about! How do I deal, and what do I do?

— Pam, 31, Bloomfield Hills, MI

I'll tell you what *I'd* do in your case—and definitely talk this over with your husband and your fertility doctors, because they're probably not going to agree with me. As a psychologist, a woman, and someone who has also gone through some fertility issues of her own, I advise that you take a year off from trying and don't think about it at all. Don't take your temperature, don't take any drugs, just take the year off. I'm not suggesting that doing this will help you get pregnant; it's just that you need a chance to figure out what you *really* want to do here.

You've spent the last three years working on fixing what's going on below your waist; now it's time to pull back a little and work on what's going on above your neck. Three years of dreaming about and working toward your future as a parent has made it nearly impossible for you to grasp what's going on in your head right now. At this point, you're not even sure whether you want to continue with the fertility treatments, adopt a child, or just forget about the entire parenting thing altogether.

Take the year off to live in the moment and enjoy your life with your husband. You'll see—a year from now, you'll be thinking more clearly. That's when you'll be able to decide how to proceed. In the meantime, do an emotional cleansing of your palate. Say, "For a year, I'm not going to think about babies, I'm not going to worry about babies, I'm not going to plan parenting, I'm not going to do *anything*. I'm just going to let the universe do with me what it will for the next year. I'm going to enjoy my marriage and my life and see where I am a year from today."

There are times when you just have to let go—this is one of those times. You can always renew your effort to conceive in a year, if that's indeed what you still want to do. For now, embrace a belief in destiny and suspend any active yearning for children. There are lots of ways to deal with nurturing feelings, whether by adoption or foster parenting, being everyone's favorite aunt, getting involved in a field that deals with children, or adopting a pet.

❦ ❦ ❦

As you may have noticed, Pam's situation lends itself perfectly to exploring the time-shifting concept of coming back from the future. We often become so fixated on our dreams, goals, and aspirations that we experience what's commonly referred to as "tunnel vision." We're so focused on reaching the light at the end of our chosen tunnel that we never look around to see that there are different tunnels with lights of their own all around the periphery.

By no means is tunnel vision limited to people with fertility issues. Starving artists, chronic dieters, and long-distance lovers provide three examples of people who live in and for the future. For example, starving artists—be they actors, musicians, painters, or writers—often spend much of their lives wishing for greatness and recognition. If their ambition is strong enough, many of these dreamers wind up neglecting other paths to personal fulfillment while striving to attain their ultimate goals. They pass up jobs, educational opportunities, and even family lives for fear of cutting themselves off from their aspirations.

The same can be said of the person who's forever trying to attain some sort of physical ideal by losing weight. Focusing on their new and improved physique as a prerequisite to happiness, they exclude the possibility of gaining satisfaction while this one goal remains unmet. They shop for an ideal self instead of buying clothes that fit; they remain on house arrest instead of going out with friends, lest they be judged unfavorably due to their size; in short, while they work to wow the world in the future, they miss out on a lot of opportunities to make themselves happy in the here-and-now.

Long-distance relationships offer another case in point. Because so little time is spent together, the couple's emphasis is always on the next time they meet, even when they actually are together. The pair often finds themselves thinking about the future even as they attempt to enjoy their precious few moments in each other's company. By ignoring any chinks in their perfect relationship armor by falling back on what they're used to doing—planning the next time. The couple are never enjoying or learning from the here-and-now. It's moments like these that make one wonder exactly how much of the relationship is real and how much is the fantasy of some imaginary bliss.

All three situations resemble Pam's case in that one accomplishment—be it career success, weight loss, or a long-term commitment—comes to represent a magical cure for all of life's ills, something that, once attained, will make and keep these individuals happy for the rest of their days. In the end, however, it's who people are and what they need and do *today* that really matters. After a long period of concentrating all their energy and strength on gazing into a crystal ball, these people need to take a breather to figure out if their dreams are still their own . . . or just remnants of who they were three, ten, or twenty years ago.

❧ ❧ ❧

Playing Doctor

Now that you've read my advice and absorbed the reasoning that went into it, can you play therapist? This is your chance to test your knowledge about time shifting. Test your understanding of this chapter on Jason.

(If you take the quiz only to find that you're still hung up on time, take a break, and then in a week or two, reread this chapter. Being stuck is common but futile—you want to learn how to work at making your life your masterpiece.)

> *I just decided to break off contact with my father. My mother left him many years ago because he was physically abusive. Recently, he remarried, and my wife and I had grown very close to his new wife. But once again, my father turned violent and abusive—now my stepmom is divorcing him also. I can understand how someone young and immature could act out like that, but at his age? I'm afraid that he's mentally unstable and might get abusive with my wife and kids. I don't want him in my life anymore, but people are telling me that I'm doing the wrong thing. Am I?*
>
> — Jason, 37, Baltimore, MD

1. As the doctor, your first question to Jason should be:

   (a) Do your kids like their grandfather?
   (b) Has your father ever been violent with your kids?
   (c) Does your wife agree with you?
   (d) Was your father ever physically abusive with you?

First things first: You've got to blast Jason out of the past. Choice "a" isn't going to do it—the question has no bearing on whether Jason should sever all relations with his father. Choice "c" is also irrelevant since this is ultimately Jason's decision. Choice "d" is a popular answer, as it illustrates the problem many of us have with staying in the past, but it focuses on old wrongs and doesn't address the issue at hand. The only answer that immediately and directly affects Jason's decision is "b": Has your father ever been violent with your kids? Now, *that's* a consideration that must be taken into account first and foremost.

2. Assuming that Jason answers "no" to your first question, you would then tell him to:

   (a) Confront his father about all the pain he's caused the family.
   (b) Stop returning his father's calls altogether.
   (c) Keep seeing his father in the hope that one day they'll be able to have a good relationship.
   (d) Try to be honest, and reason with his father.

Jason's relationship with his father doesn't have to be an all-or-nothing proposition. In this chapter, we've talked a lot about finding a middle ground and playing forward our options. Which piece of advice would help Jason find a middle ground with his father and achieve the most desirable end? Well, let's see which choices would not.

Choice "a" would relieve Jason of his frustrations for the time being, but it wouldn't endear him to his father and they'd have no hope of improving their relationship at all. Jason's anger might lessen, but his father would likely be gone for good. Jason and his father may want to sort out some old wrongs, but not under the guise of doing what's best for the kids. Kids aren't poker chips.

Choice "b" would leave both Jason and his father without a place to go, accomplishing nothing. Life by temper tantrum is expensive and frustrating. Similarly, choice "c" will only disappoint Jason in the long run. The fact is that if his father's behavior remains unchecked, he's unlikely to change for the better.

The correct answer is "d." Honesty mixed with reason is the best course of action here. Jason could say, "Look, Dad, your anger gets out of control. I can't count on you to be stable or nonthreatening with the kids. If you can control yourself, you can see them with either me or my wife present." Depending on the situation, Jason could even go a step further and suggest that his dad see a counselor or attend anger-management meetings. This way, Jason's father would know how serious a menace he is perceived to be by his loved ones and would have the opportunity to change for the better. Meanwhile, Jason would be able to work on his relationship with his father, but with a measure of control that he'd never had before. By separating his personal, childhood hurts from his children and their needs, he can work out a stable basis for Grandpa to interact with the grandkids, which could be a jumping-off point for Jason to do some business with Dad about his own concerns. But this will only happen if Jason is willing to leave his past behind by deciding what he wants from his father *now!*

Shrink Wrap

Getting stuck in the past isn't sinful, just silly. We've all done it at some point in our lives. But just because no one is immune to life's curveballs—or the feelings of frustration, confusion, and powerlessness that accompany them—this doesn't mean that we need to give in to painful and destructive emotions. In this chapter, I've shown you how to shift time to make it work for you by using the following principles:

- **If you're stuck, admit it.** When you find yourself obsessing about a problem, that means you're stuck in the past. So admit it and . . .

- **Focus.** Ask yourself what you want. Say, "If I were calling Dr. Browne, what would my question be?"

- **Get unstuck.** Return to the present moment by contemplating possible solutions to your problem and answer your own question.

- **Move ahead.** Think about all of your potential solutions and play them forward to their inevitable conclusions.

- **Think horses, not zebras.** The most probable outcome is just that—stay away from worst-case scenarios.

- **Don't get ahead of yourself.** Steer clear of getting caught up in an endless "what-if cycle," and don't forget to reevaluate your goals once in a while. Remember, don't stray too far into the future lest you stay too long.

STEP 2:
❧ PATTERNS ❧

I'm a 31-year-old gay man and have had three unhealthy relationships in a row. My friends tell me that I'm attracted to the wrong type of man, and I agree. I keep falling for these guys who end up not loving me back—somehow I get off on it and I can't figure out why. It just sort of seems that whenever there's a guy who's interested in me, I'm not interested in him. I think it's the challenge of it all, but it's happened to me so often, and my friends are getting tired of hearing about it. Might this have something to do with my anxiety disorder?

— Mike, 31, New York, NY

Mike, being attracted to someone who doesn't know you're alive proves that you're normal. Unfortunately, both men and women—whether straight or gay—do this with amazing regularity and consistency. All of us are insecure enough to believe that if somebody doesn't like us, they must have superior perception. Like Groucho Marx said: "I don't care to belong to any club that will have me as a member." Many of us end up living Marx's maxim, so when we find someone to love who doesn't love us back, it becomes a real challenge to make them do just that. Usually, this is because we've picked a withholder or someone who just doesn't like us at all. The sad fact is that even if we work really hard to get these people to love us, the challenge is over, so we're no longer interested in them. This sort of rat race doesn't get anybody anywhere.

Mike, why don't you try getting to know somebody on a nonsexual basis first? (I know, I sound like your great-aunt Charlotte). You have friends—why not focus on the two you think are the sexiest? Don't have sex with them; just start looking at them in a more romantic way. Try getting to know them on a more emotionally intimate basis so that when you're ready to have sex with one of them, you'll actually care about this person, and you'll know that they care for you, too.

Your anxiety disorder has nothing to do with this, Mike. Make sure that you don't spend a lot of time talking about why it's fun to do what you're doing—you know it isn't. This kind of nonsense is a thrill at the beginning, but then you crash and burn, and you're knee-deep in misery again. Feeling good about feeling bad defines "nincompoopicity!"

The difference is like taking a roller-coaster ride and rowing a boat. A roller coaster is exhilarating, but it's just going to end up making you nauseated and giving you a headache, and you'll end up back where you started. Rowing a boat, on the other hand, is more work, but it will still get you from one place to another. You'll also have more control as far as where you're going and how long it takes you to get there . . . and you won't get sick. Mike, I hope for your sake that you give up roller coasters and start to row your own boat to happiness.

❦ ❦ ❦

This chapter is all about breaking free of destructive patterns. By definition, *patterns* are things that we do over and over again, usually without awareness, such as: eating ice cream in times of stress, gaining weight, and proceeding to go on a fast in order to quickly shed some pounds; dating folks who are overbearing because we're looking for someone just like one of our parents; or hanging out in bars to meet people whenever we relocate because that's what we did before we went into a 12-step program. These unconscious ways of behaving survive because we never shed any light on them by asking, "What am I doing? Have I done this before? Does it work? Has it *ever* worked?"

If you've adopted a pattern that's successful—congratulations! It ain't broke, so no fixin' is necessary. But if you find yourself cycling through an unsuccessful pattern over and over again, the time has come to interrupt it in favor of a new, useful way of coping. This chapter will give you the keys to making patterns work *for* you rather than *against* you. You'll learn to do this by:

- recognizing patterns;

- breaking the cycle;

- finding a safe place; and

- using general patterns to your advantage—you've been there and done that already, so there's no need to do it again.

Recognizing Patterns

We all have a variety of different patterns that characterize our lives. Since most of them work perfectly well, there's not much motivation to take notice of them. If, for instance, acting nice and friendly whenever you're introduced to someone helps you make friends, then you probably wouldn't even notice the behavior as a pattern—you'd just go on doing what you've been doing.

Patterns become problematic when they cease to work or start to function negatively. Let's say that your outgoing manner, which used to win you so many friends, was suddenly met with hostility. How long would it take for you to stop and reevaluate it? Most of us react to breakdowns in operation defensively. Instead of changing the pattern, we seem to switch off our logic and dig in, contrary to common sense. We believe our ability to reason differentiates us from animals, but even a rat can run circles around us when it comes to effective, goal-oriented behavior.

At one point in my career, I ran laboratory rats through a maze to demonstrate learning theory: An animal will randomly search through various possibilities until it encounters a reward and will eventually return to it. Learning occurs after an initial behavior is consistently rewarded (with cheese, in the case of rats) and is based on how long it takes for the "subject" to consistently find the reward after it's been moved to the new place. Animals eventually stop going to the old place and find a new, rewarding one. They learn. Human beings, however, will continue to go to the old place, time and time again, long after the cheese has been removed—because it worked once, it's the "right" thing to do, everyone else does it that way, or our parents taught us to do it like that—all rationalizations for irrational behavior. But wait: there's no cheese here!

Patterns . . . they can either be a prison, keeping us trapped within their rigid confines; or a refuge, keeping us safe, comfortable, and on the right track. Mike, our unrequited-love addict, has hopefully recognized a pattern that's making him miserable. He's only interested in men who aren't interested in him. While the chase gives his life meaning, it's ultimately doomed to fail and make him unhappy. In Greek mythology, Zeus sentenced Sisyphus, the king of Corinth, to an eternity of rolling a massive boulder up a hill in Hades. Each time Sisyphus reached the top of the hill, the boulder would roll back down, and he'd have to renew his efforts. Mike, and the rest of us who are stuck in unproductive patterns, are Sisyphusian. But Sisyphus had no choice—he was condemned to repeat the same pattern forever. You, however, have a choice. Once you realize that you're hurting, you can stop and ask yourself, "Have I been here before? Do I really want to continue rolling this stupid rock up this hill?"

The good news about patterns is that once you start looking, they're relatively easy to recognize—that's why they're called *patterns* (think of the plaid, houndstooth, or leafy trellis varieties). If you hear yourself saying, "My boss always takes credit for my work," or "My mom always underestimates me," you've hit upon a pattern of behavior. Whenever you're using the words "always," "often," or even "seldom," make a mental note. These words are earmarks, asterisks that say, "Wait a minute! I've been here before!" If you *have* been here before, then you already know how the situation will play out—the question is, will you like the outcome? And if the answer is, "Well, it's not me, it's my boss/mother," then you have to say, "I can't change someone else's behavior, I can only change my own. If my boss/mother is always acting a certain way, and I'm always responding the same way, I may not be able to change my boss/mom, but I can change how *I* behave." In other words, if you hate button "a," but every time you press button "b," button "a" pops up, for heaven's sake, stop pressing "b"!

Once you look for and recognize a pattern, you can *change* it, and that's the point. You can recognize and analyze your patterns 'til the cows come home, but your time will have been wasted if you can't get beyond your patterns. After all, why would you want to be aware of the fact that you're miserable all the time if you can't do anything about it? The answer is, you wouldn't . . . and that's exactly why I was so tough on Mike. He recognized a pattern, but he didn't want to move on.

Discovering What's Behind Your Patterns

Patterns fall into two basic categories: those that work and those that don't. A highly functional, fully working pattern is an amazing thing, but chances are you won't recognize it until it stops working. In the grand tradition of the squeaky wheel, we're prone to mainly noticing errors, so we write off everything else as "normal." For instance, at this moment, I'd be willing to bet that you're not thinking about how great it is that your breathing is regular. You're probably not even aware of or thinking about your breathing at all. But if I catch you at a time when you're hyperventilating, your breathing will be *all* you think about!

Similarly, if dating emotionally unavailable men had worked for Mike, he wouldn't have needed to call my program to complain about it. And yet, he told me that this is the third time he's become involved in a relationship with a disinterested party. A three-year-old need only touch a stove once to realize that it's hot and that hot = bad because hot hurts. Unfortunately, 31 years haven't been sufficient for Mike to figure out that he's taking his third ride on the same roller coaster, while hoping to wind up in a different place—this time without a queasy tummy. Newsflash, Mike: It's bad. It hurts.

Mike's pattern of dating hasn't resulted in a satisfying relationship. Why persist in the same behavior, then? Well, let's examine Mike's assumptions:

- He assumes that he wants a relationship.

- He assumes that he knows what a relationship entails.

He may be wrong on one or both counts. Either Mike isn't seeking a relationship defined by longevity, serenity, or happiness, or his notion about how to achieve a meaningful relationship isn't realistic. Something here is out of whack—either his means or his end. If he believes love is weak knees, fireworks, and sweaty palms, then he may be confusing infatuation and teenage crushes with a true, lasting, adult relationship. He may not be ready for a serious commitment, so he pursues unavailable men as an escape hatch. Maybe Mike doesn't think he's worthy of love and figures that chasing the unattainable will keep him too busy to ever look in the mirror. When Mike *becomes* serious about *being* serious, he'll find the courage and motivation to assess his unproductive behavior so that he can figure out something that might actually work. If he's willing to discover the reasons behind his pattern, he can finally begin to deal with it on a conscious level. Either he'll stop looking for a relationship, or he'll try dating someone who returns his feelings and will come to view relationships or himself or his love object in a new light. Whatever the outcome, he will have broken the pattern that leaves him feeling so down in the dumps and unhappy, not only about his prospects but himself.

Let me take a moment here and offer some advice to all who have ever decided to date someone beneath your standards, on the assumption that if it doesn't work, at least it won't hurt so bad: *Don't do it.* The only thing that hurts worse than breaking up with someone whom you feel you deserve is being dumped by someone you don't even like: "How dare he not call me so I could tell him I'd never go out with him again!" Breaking up stinks, so make sure that you're at least going out with someone who's worth the risk.

❧ ❧ ❧

While Mike is an example of someone pursuing a pattern that has never worked, other people have more problematic patterns to contend with—those that used to work but don't anymore. Take, for example, an engineer who rises to the level of middle management. She may assume that if her talent and creativity got her this far, then they should take her all the way to the executive level, but she may be looking at a pattern that works in one situation, not all. She might have the makings of a talented engineer, but she doesn't necessarily possess the tools for being the "people person" that management demands. When her old pattern no longer works, she'll probably become cranky, more withdrawn, and reliant upon skills that are no longer relevant, and she'll become incensed and frustrated in the process. Instead of altering her behavior to reflect the changed situation to get what she wants— whether by learning corporate politics, improving management skills, or realistically assessing if she even wants to be in management—she continues to disregard the evidence. And all the while, she justifies bashing her head against a wall with the motto that "Life isn't fair!" rather than seeing the tracks of her outdated pattern.

One of the reasons Emma Engineer seems so bullheaded is her dearly held assumption that if it worked once, it will always work, and that nothing changes. Highly unlikely. The energy it requires to play in the big leagues, delegate authority, or learn a new way of behaving at work may be considerable for someone who's accustomed to being promoted based on their productivity alone. In the end, however, it would be better to spend more energy on something new and difficult that actually works, than less energy on something that doesn't.

❧ ❧ ❧

Breaking a once-useful pattern that has since ceased to work is difficult. During my freshman year at Rice University in Houston, Texas, most of our class had been either number one or number two in their graduating high school classes. Needless to say, most of my peers were in for a huge disappointment—not just because there was only room for one student at the top, but because to remain competitive, the students who'd been accustomed to coming in first would have to change study patterns *and* self-images that had worked for the last 12 years of their lives. They'd have to modify their views of themselves as the top students in their class and the smartest people in any given room. Talk about a shock to the system—at the sight of their first C, many panicked. At the sight of more Cs, some stopped trying to improve their grades in favor of improving their social life (translation: they gave up), some maintained a C-average and were miserable about it (a.k.a. head-bashing behavior), and still others learned new ways of studying and met their goals (or changed their pattern). No question as to which took the most work but was the most profitable in the end. Lest you worry, cute little me was in the upper 10 percent, so I figured that since I was dumber than most, I'd be prom queen. Imagine my chagrin at finding out the prom queen was actually *number one* in our class—sigh.

Breaking the Cycle

> *Before I was adopted, my biological grandfather molested me. Now whenever I hear my adoptive father's voice, I lose it. I get hysterical. I start yelling and screaming at him for no reason, and then I realize that I'm overreacting. Can you help me stop this?*
>
> — Beth, 46, Wichita, KS

Beth, people get so caught up in patterns that they lose perspective. We become completely enmeshed in the emotions triggered by the pattern. Even though your adoptive father wasn't the one who molested you, you're upset with him. It's not that I'm unsympathetic, but even if someone smacked you upside the head every night until you were ten years old, that was 36 years ago, so why would *you* continue to smack *yourself* upside the head? Patterns laid down when we're young are deep, but not set in stone. Rather than allowing yourself to react to every man the same as you would to the one man who hurt you, why not begin choosing other ways to behave, ways that don't involve getting frightened and acting frantic? The hysteria, the yelling, the tears . . . all of that may have meant survival at one point when you felt powerless to reason with your grandfather and his unwanted attentions. But you *have* survived, Beth. Now you have options—and becoming completely overwhelmed by your feelings is just one of them. As you change your behavior, you can also change your feelings rather than succumb to them.

Feelings just happen, but that's why we have a big, fancy cortex that sits atop everything else. When a child says, "Mommy, I hate you," a parent feels angry and hurt, but seldom says, "I hate you, too," smacks the kid, or decides to run away from home. Instead, most parents begin the laborious process of trying to figure out why the child is lashing out. Are they retaliating for the hurt they felt at being told no, at being ignored, or at something else the unwitting parent may have done? The parent can then take their adult hurt feelings and use them to understand the child, the situation, and themselves better.

Beth, you can become the parent to your hurt child. You're not responsible for feeling hurt or angry or sad, but you *are* responsible for how you act. You can extract yourself from your feelings and organize. You can move out of your feelings and into your intellect. Ask yourself, "Am I willing to continue acting and feeling so out of control? Can I differentiate between then and now, between my grandfather and my father? Do I want to talk to my dad about this? Can I ask my dad to behave in a way that doesn't remind me of my grandfather—such as to change his aftershave, to let me hug him before he hugs me, or to stop calling me his 'Little Princess'? Can I make myself aware of my associations?"

❧ ❧ ❧

Beth's pattern of getting overwhelmed, stressed, panicked, and ultimately defeated isn't uncommon. Changing a pattern takes concerted effort. However, by correcting her views of herself as a powerless child and her father as an authority figure, Beth can stop feeling frightened. She can then choose to join an incest survivor's group or find a therapist. Beth has options that can't change her past but can alter her future. She doesn't have to surrender to misery or continue a pattern that has outlived its usefulness.

Find a Safe Place

Now just because I've started this chapter with a discussion of destructive patterns, don't assume that all (or even most) patterns are bad. In and of itself, a pattern is neither good nor bad, it just *is*. The way a pattern affects your life is what carries a positive or negative connotation. The trick is to recognize and interrupt patterns that are unproductive, and to organize and implement those that will move you toward your goals. If it worked once, it might be worth trying; if it doesn't, try something else.

For instance, I once had a man call me looking for dating advice. He blamed his fear of rejection for keeping him out of the dating game.

I asked him, "What do you do for a living?"

"I'm a salesman," he replied. *Bingo!* There isn't a salesman alive who doesn't deal with rejection on a daily basis. All this man needed to do was approach dating with the same fearless mentality with which he approached his clients.

"View potential dates as leads, and at yourself as the product," I told him. "Then sell, sell, sell! But remember that every call isn't going to be a sale, and every sale isn't going to be a bonanza."

We've spent our entire lives learning patterns to get us through a variety of situations. And yet, we're constantly confronted with new situations that make us feel helpless. Instead of throwing up our hands in disgust and saying, "I don't know what I'm going to do!" we need to rely on our reservoirs of effective past behavior, which can be tapped when confronted with an unfamiliar scenario. *Start with what you know.* It's likely that at some point in your life, you've faced a situation that's similar if not identical.

For example, in my own life, when I first moved to New York several years ago, I found myself with half my income but double the expenses. Stressed, anxious, and alone, I decided that I'd do what I always did in tough times—join a gym. Great idea . . . except with my luck, I stumbled into one populated by professional ballet dancers. Every time I went in there, I found myself surrounded by these anorexic 19-year-olds who could take their legs and wrap them twice around their heads. I felt like one of the elephants from *Fantasia*: clumsy, clunky, and fat. The only way I could keep going was to tell myself, "I have a Ph.D., so to hell with them!" Obviously, my Ph.D. had nothing whatsoever to do with exercise, but it gave me the confidence and courage to venture out into a new area and feel less intimidated by my unfamiliar surroundings. A safe place to stand gives us a place to regroup before we venture forth into the unknown.

That's the secret to making patterns work for you. When you feel lost, ask yourself, "Do I have areas of competence and *confidence* that I can steal patterns from to help me feel safe?" as illustrated in the following example.

❧ ❧ ❧

I lost everything I owned twice in the last six years through hurricanes and tornadoes. All of my possessions have been destroyed, including all the photos of my kids, who had died in a car accident. I'm sick with really bad arthritis, and it feels like this last disaster has wiped out my whole life. When I go and speak to people about trying to get past this, they don't give me anything to direct me. Everyone else thinks I'm so strong, but I need some direction.

— Althea, 67, Wilmington, NC

First of all, Althea, Mama Nature didn't wipe out your *life,* she wiped out your *stuff.* Of course it feels awful, but you're still alive, and that's a very important distinction.

It sounds to me as if you're focusing on your stuff because your real loss was not the *pictures* of your children, but your children themselves. Compared to that loss, these acts of nature seem petty, even if it does seem personal to you. On top of everything else, your arthritis is making you hurt, too. But rather than host your own personal (understandable but wasteful) pity party, try saying to yourself, "I don't know exactly what to do, but I've been in situations worse than this." This latest loss is likely reminding you of your previous losses, but there's no advantage to lumping all of your losses together. Instead, draw strength from what you've overcome in the past to remind yourself that although you feel lousy, you're making it through. That's how we as human beings take the next step forward—we look for patterns. "Have I been in this situation before?" and "What did I do to get through it?" are questions to ask yourself at this moment.

Losing one's children is one of the true tragedies of adult life. We all assume that we'll pre-decease our children, and when we survive them, it's truly catastrophic. Somehow you got through that, Althea, now you need to go back and figure out how you managed it, because that's the source of what you need to do now.

I think you're understandably pooped at this moment, Althea—you've gone through so much that you're probably thinking, *Dammit, I'm tired of this! I don't want to be resourceful; I want someone to take care of me!* which is a perfectly reasonable but useless way to feel. Fantasizing about somebody swooping in to make everything all right is unrealistic—it's simply not going to happen, kiddo. Since it sounds like there isn't anybody who can take care of you right now, you can remind yourself how valuable it is to be able to take care of ourselves in this life, even while we long for Mom.

Althea, you need to become an expert on *you*—not on your misery, but on your strength. You've gone through more than most have in this life, and somehow, cookie, tough little broad that you are, you've survived it. I know you don't want to do this anymore, but surrender isn't much of an option for any length of time. How about if you took the day off? Use that great head and heart of yours to say, "I've been through what other people have nightmares about, and I survived it. I need to figure out what I did." You may have utilized friends, prayer, writing, therapy, volunteer activity, or even denial. (Hopefully, your comfort wasn't found in drugs or food.) But whatever tool you used, it worked. Not only have you accomplished the nearly unthinkable by surviving the death of your children, but you've survived the death of your home—twice. Now, you need to take some time and sort through the resources that helped you in the past, because they're what will guide you in the present.

Use General Patterns to Your Advantage

Up until now, we've covered patterns that are unique, personal, and highly individual in nature. However, there are patterns that are general enough to be observable across the board. Some patterns are seen in male behavior, others through female actions, and some are consistent with birth order (being the oldest, the youngest, or the middle child). Since we're looking at patterns, being aware of the general as well as the individual is bracing.

Sexual patterns (differentiating between male and female behavior) are fascinating, and are some of the most basic of all. We learn them from the cradle from our parents, but these patterns have also been hardwired into our circuitry by millions of years of evolution (nature and nurture dovetail into our very own selves). Understanding these patterns can make life a lot less stressful and make conflict feel much less personal and hurtful.

For example, given a choice, most men would rather sit beside rather than across the table from a date. It's part of their programming, since males in the wild are always fighting for the Alpha position that gets them the best females and the best food. For male animals, eye contact is an aggressive statement, whereas side-by-side means they can count on one another, they're protecting the tribe—stout-hearted men (or gorillas) standing shoulder to shoulder. Women, meanwhile, want eye contact, for they see eyes as windows to the soul. They feel that by looking somebody in the eye, they can tell if someone's lying to them or if they love them.

Similarly, women like to talk about relationship issues, and men don't. When women think of talk, they think, *Tell me you love me,* or *There's something really going wrong in the relationship,* whereas men view "talking" as excuses. So upon hearing a woman say, "We have to talk," most men will hear: *Danger, Will Robinson! Run! Run!*

By understanding rather than resenting these patterns, a woman can opt for a male-friendly pattern when she wants to successfully communicate with her guy. She can start a conversation when they're both outside so he doesn't feel cornered physically. She can opt to walk side-by-side and hold his hand rather than talk face-to-face. She can also set up a pattern of listening to what's important to him— which may be baseball or work or that he's worried about their future—even if she's frightened by his fear or is less interested in baseball than in relationship issues. If she's willing to listen to him talk about what he's interested in, rather than exclusively what she wants to talk about, he'll feel more comfortable about talking in general and listening specifically to her concerns.

Let's say this hypothetical woman is annoyed that her man doesn't call her during the day. Saying things like "You're inconsiderate," and "You never think about me or my feelings" will make him feel like he did when his mother used to scold him. These feelings will, in turn, immediately trigger the emergency response pattern: "Yikes! Mom is trying to catch me. I have to withdraw and say nothing because anything I say can and will be used against me to send me to my room." So instead of telling him he's an unthinking, self-centered jerk who never calls her, the savvy woman might say instead, "It makes me so happy when you call me during the day. I love to think about what I'm going to do to you when we see each other tonight!" *Voilà!* She just changed the pattern. She's not his mom; she's rewarding his good behavior instead of hassling him about his bad behavior. And most important, she's giving him an option other than fight or flight—and that changes everything about the situation.

※ ※ ※

Just as sexual politics are usually learned in the family, birth order is another dominant pattern with the same familial origins. Jack feels that his situation is unique, but the patterns that underlie the behavior he describes are nearly universal.

> *My mom doesn't understand me. When I graduate from high school, I want to move to Los Angeles and promote nightclubs. I've already done it part time here, and I'm really good at it. But all she can do is cry because I don't want to go to college. She doesn't understand what I do and thinks that I'm going to wind up in prison or on the streets because I'm not going to Stanford like my brother did. What can I do to make her understand?*
>
> — Jack, 17, Atlanta, GA

Jack, I know you're the baby of the family and you're angry because your mother seems to favor your Stanford bro, but let's see what's really going on here. Instead of trying to make your mom understand what she has no desire to, what if you thought about changing *your* behavior? Mom isn't the only one who's being stubborn here. Try making a deal with her: You'll go to LA and pursue club promoting while attending college, maybe majoring in hotel management. If your career takes off, fantastic! If not, you'll always have a fallback, your mom won't be worried, and you can make valuable connections while you're in school.

To strike this bargain, you'll have to examine the reasons why you're so dead set against going to college. I'm not saying that college is right for everyone, but it sounds to me like you might have some issues with your brother being the overachiever in the family. Maybe you don't want to compete with your smarty-pants big brother, or maybe club promoting is your way of trying to outshine him, but it sounds like his academic performance is playing into your decision to avoid college. Is it possible you're afraid that if you don't succeed as your brother has, people will think he's better than you or Mom will love him more? Jack, instead of examining that fear and dealing with this ancient family pattern head on, you're letting it determine your behavior by staying away from college altogether.

Relationships with our siblings can define our life patterns. Oldest children are the overachieving caretakers, nurturers who watch out for the younger kids. Okay, I admit that as the oldest of six children, I do fit this mold. I've somehow translated my birth order into the perfect profession for me—taking care of others, listening to them and solving their problems. The pattern works great at work, but unless I'm very careful, it can be a disaster in my private life. The other side of the big sister role is: "You're not the boss of me; you can't tell me what to do!" Being bossy in relationships is deadly, and it really doesn't work very well with my family now that we're all grown. In fact, now I love to be taken care of by my sibs.

Youngest children, Jack, are notoriously charming and easy to get along with, which is why you excel in an interpersonal skills-oriented job like club promoting. The downside to being the baby of the family is the stereotype of the "prodigal son"—always hitting the parents up for money, help, and sympathy. Oftentimes, the youngest child is so used to getting whatever they want from their parents—be it love, money, or attention—that they refuse to grow up and take responsibility for themselves.

Jack, the time has come for you to examine the causes of your behavior. You want your parents to pay your way to LA, yet you don't want to do what they ask of you, which is to go to college. In fact, you don't even want to *entertain* the idea of going to college or negotiating with your parents. It's either your way or Mom's way . . . and it sounds to me like you're used to getting your way.

Find a middle ground that allows a compromise by dismantling the youngest-child scenario. Once you're aware of the way the family baby pattern plays out, you can change your behavior by keeping the stuff that works (the charm and sociability) and dumping the drawbacks (the sullenness, competitiveness, and petulance). You'll be in control . . . rather than being controlled by your birth order.

Playing Doctor

All right, folks, it's that time again . . . time to put what you've learned from this chapter to the test. Before you begin recognizing, interrupting, and using your own patterns, see if you can spot how patterns are affecting Rich.

> *I just finished school with a two-year degree. And it's not that I don't want to go to work, but I'm a little scared about getting a job because classroom life has come to be the only world I know. How do I deal with my new life?*

> — Rich, 21, Ventura, CA

1. Which of the following is the best question to ask Rich first:

    (a) What's your major?
    (b) Do you have any work experience?
    (c) Have you considered going on to get a four-year degree?
    (d) What is it that scares you about work?

The correct choice is "b." Choices "a" and "c" are completely irrelevant to the matter at hand. These questions do nothing to direct Rich to his safe place.

Since he's clearly lost, the way to plant Rich's feet back on solid ground is via option "b." If he's had some work experience, this is a safe place for him to return to. Getting him to think about his past experience with work (be it volunteering, work-study, an internship, or a part-time job) will remind him that he *does* have some competence in this area and that it isn't entirely unfamiliar terrain. After all, work is work. And although part-time work and internships aren't exactly the same as a full-time job, they *are* similar enough to give Rich confidence in his abilities.

(If Rich hasn't had any work experience, choice "d" is a reasonable place to start, since most of us have had chores or babysat or *something*.)

2. Assuming Rich says "yes" to your first question, what advice would you give him?

    (a) It's stuff you've already done before; you just get paid more for it now.
    (b) Talk to a therapist about antidepressants.
    (c) Come in early, leave late, and everyone will love you.
    (d) There's nothing to fear but fear itself.

The answer is "a." Choice "b" doesn't work because Rich isn't depressed; he's just a little nervous about doing something he thinks is new. Choice "c" is just plain poor advice. Sure, his employers might like Rich, but his co-workers are all but certain to find his overeager attitude off-putting. Furthermore, workaholism isn't a cure for first-job jitters—and neither are platitudes and clichés such as choice "d."

Choice "a" lays out the situation perfectly. Since we've established that Rich does have some sort of work history, he just needs to rethink the job situation. The same patterns he used to earn his degree and excel in new and unfamiliar classes can be implemented in a work environment. In short, there's no need to worry, because what he's about to do isn't all that new and different after all.

❧ ❧ ❧

Shrink Wrap

This is a great time to whip out a pen and paper. Patterns may be more evident over time if you can see them in black and white— writing focuses most of us far better than just thinking can. If something in your life isn't working, look for the pattern. Ask, "Have I been in this icky place before?" If the answer is yes, then you're probably doing something in a consistent but inappropriate way. And by understanding the consistency of it, you can change it. With some disruptive patterns, you only have to recognize them in order to interrupt them. Others take more work—so don't despair if you can't shake a pattern off so easily. But while some patterns can imprison us, others can serve as friends in times of need and be our lifelines when we feel lost. Following is a point-by-point breakdown of how that's done:

- **Take note of words such as "always," "never," "everyone," and "often"**—they may be trying to tell you that a pattern is at work.

- **Ask "Does this pattern work?"** or "Does this pattern make me feel miserable?"

- **If what you're doing isn't working for you, stop doing it.**

- **When you feel lost, look to patterns** that help you succeed in other parts of your life to see you through.

- **Use your understanding of general patterns,** such as male and female behavior and birth order, to analyze your behavior and meet your goals.

STEP 3:
❧ SELF-AWARENESS ❧

I've been crying all day, and I need your advice. I was called into my boss's office this morning, and the Powers That Be said that they were firing me because of my perfume. I don't believe this—I've been wearing the same scent for 20 years. It's my signature scent, and I only use one spritz in the morning. I've been working at this office for a year, and just six months ago, I had an evaluation that said I was a great worker. I don't know what to do. What do I say when I apply for another job?

— Marjorie, 42, Phoenix, AZ

Marjorie, the good news is that you're already planning ahead, focusing on your next job. To answer your immediate question, you can tell a new employer that there was a personality conflict, the commute got too long, they downsized, or it was time for a change—and leave it at that. You don't have to tell them that your boss said you smelled funny.

But the bad news here is that you're so immersed in this situation that you've started to doubt yourself. So let's solve your real problem—making sure that before you go into your next job interview, you're not worried about how you smell. I know that you're feeling sad and your feelings are hurt right now, but you didn't go running to the nearest cave to lick your wounds. You took charge of the situation by picking up the phone and asking me for help.

Basically, there are two possibilities here: Either what your boss told you is true or it isn't. By extracting yourself from your shame and self-pity at this moment, you can think about how hard it would be for *you* to tell somebody they smelled awful. It's reasonable to assume that it must have been equally difficult for your boss, so it's not very likely that he was lying to you or using your perfume as an excuse. But to be absolutely sure, I'd ask this of someone you trust in the office: "Look, I need the truth here. Do I wear too much perfume?" Or ask your closest friends to 'fess up if they feel that your cologne is overwhelming. And then listen carefully and objectively to what they tell you, because these people won't find it easy to respond to your question. However, if you do in fact wear too much perfume, then so be it—recognize and deal with the situation rather than ignore it. There's no need to anguish, obsess, or tattoo it on your forehead—remove the Krazy Glue and get unstuck.

Marjorie, you say you've worn the same perfume for 20 years, but maybe your body chemistry no longer reacts well with this particular scent. Perhaps you need to start shopping around for another perfume; or, if you really want to err on the side of caution, drop the fragrance habit altogether. But if it turns out that your cologne *isn't* the problem, then we need to figure out what it was that provoked your boss to fire you. Ask your same trusted advisors to help you figure out what's really going on.

One empowering thing that you can do right now is ask your boss for a letter of recommendation. If you're a hard worker and the real issue *is* your scent, then getting a letter stating that you're a great employee should be no problem (especially since your boss will probably still be feeling pretty guilty over the whole thing). A letter will be a valuable asset for your job search, and prospective employers will have no reason to suspect that you left this job under rather embarrassing circumstances.

If the perfume *was* just an excuse, then chances are your boss won't give you a letter of recommendation—but at least you'll know right away. Do this first thing tomorrow morning so you don't lose your nerve.

Asking about potential employers was your first step from panic to planning. Good for you, Marjorie. Once you can completely extricate yourself from panic, you can become objective and shift from your previous, full-tilt boogie, "What will become of me?" mode to the "What's really going on here and what can I do about it?" phase. If you do get that letter of recommendation, then you'll be one step ahead in your job search. You'll also have a reason to consult with those nice folks at the perfume counter who can help you select a scent better suited to your body chemistry. This way, you can feel calm about smelling sweet before you go on an interview. If your boss won't give you the letter, then you can assume that your job skills need a bit of an evaluation and some spiffing up . . . and I'd still think twice about using perfume on the job, so you have one less thing to worry about.

❧ ❧ ❧

Like Marjorie, it can be very difficult for most people to extricate themselves from their own lives in order to solve problems rationally. If you can see your life through the less biased eyes of an outside observer, your self-awareness will allow you to problem-solve rather than blame, which is the point of this chapter. I'll show you how to do this by:

- becoming objective by looking through someone else's eyes;

- reversing roles;

- playing the lottery (finding out what really makes you happy); and

- finding shelter from life's storms.

Becoming Objective

One day, I was striding through Harvard Square on my way to work. I was 19, had just graduated from Rice University, and was newly married to a Harvard graduate student. I remember very well having the incredibly powerful feeling of floating slightly over my own head. It was as if I were looking down at myself, thinking, *Look at that girl walking in Harvard Square.* I instantly told myself, "Whoa, don't do this to yourself. You clearly have the ability to abstract yourself from a situation, but if you do this all the time, you'll never be fully present in your life. Yech." I swear to you, I can still recreate the smells, sounds, and sights of that day—it's as vibrant to me now as it was then.

Of course, being a scientist, I was trained to observe—to coolly assess a situation without judgment. And while I realized that day that it wouldn't be any fun to spend my entire life being on the outside looking in, it also became clear to me what a useful tool objectivity could be. Yep, this could definitely lead to getting unstuck.

You can't be both a participant in and an observer of your own life—not at the same time, anyway. Since most of us are such eager participants, I'm asking you to at least try to learn and practice my Harvard Square skill of observation. Because while it won't help you live your life, it's an incredibly effective tool for solving your problems and going in a new and better direction. You can get your peculiarities, needs, and emotions out of the heat of the moment and into a position to be objective. Unstuck, baby, unstuck.

To analyze, you must be calm and unemotional. Avoiding panic means avoiding the overwhelming "What will become of me?!" feelings. In fact, instead of asking "What will become of me?" try "What's going on here?" Once you understand what's going on, you can begin to process *why* it's happening and *what* you can do about it. The point of this chapter is to teach you to make things better, not worse, by helping you understand *you.*

You see, in order to decide what to do in a productive way, you've got to achieve some sort of rationality, a degree of impartiality, objectivity, and balance—or at least something less than a completely self-serving or self-hating view of the situation—and that begins with a sense of what the situation is by understanding who *you* are, since you're the filter through which all experience passes.

Be Thy Neighbor, Be a Martian, or Be a Browne

I'm always running into people at parties who say, "I listen to your program, and I just don't understand how these people can't see that what they're doing makes no sense." All of us can be objective about someone else's life, but it's nearly impossible to be both objective and subjective about our own lives. We *can*, however, learn to take our emotional self out of the equation by asking, "What if this really wasn't about me? What if this was happening to my next-door neighbor instead? What advice would I offer *her*?" Let's try this technique on Stephanie.

> *I've been dating Sven for about a month. Last weekend, we went away together. When he dropped me off Sunday night, he kissed me tenderly, and it seemed as though everything had gone really great. Then on Wednesday, he comes over to tell me that he can't see me anymore because he's not attracted to me. I'm floored and don't know what to do. Is he just another user guy?*
>
> — Stephanie, 28, Schenectady, NY

Stephanie, I'm sure that a lot of our listeners have already figured this one out. They're sitting there thinking, *Like, duh! The guy finally got what he wanted, but the sex was so lousy that he's movin' on down the line.* Well, that's wrong! There's an entire realm of possibilities here. Stay tuned.

Okay, Stephanie, back to you. Take a deep breath and step back for a moment, because if you think about it instead of blindly reacting, you'll see that what you've told me makes no sense. Based on your story, we have to assume one of three things: (1) Sven is a crazy two-faced sociopath; (2) he's one hell of an actor; or (3) something else is going on here. The fact that you trusted Sven enough to go away with him for the weekend implies that he's not likely to be a psychopath. I also doubt that he's the next Olivier, so something else must be at work here.

Let's start with what we know for sure: When Sven told you he wasn't attracted to you, your feelings were understandably hurt. Since most of us take things very personally whenever anything goes wrong, your basic instinct was probably to blame yourself. I'll bet you said something along the lines of, "It's because I'm fat and ugly, or he discovered that I'm unlovable," right?

After the self-loathing subsides, the next step in this process is to go from blaming yourself to looking for a new target—somebody else. I'm sure you found yourself saying, "How could *Sven* have done that to me? *He* doesn't really love me. *He's* really a creep." In your case, all of this translates into: "He's just another monster!"

Stephanie, if I gave in to my impulse to be sympathetic, I'd tell you, "You're right. He's a loser and you're wonderful. Go forth and prosper." But that's not going to do you much good because you wouldn't be any wiser than you were before. And on top of everything else, you'd still be left feeling incredibly hurt and sad. So, instead of blaming either yourself or Sven, calm down and see if you can take your emotions completely out of the equation for the moment. Ask yourself, "If I don't assume that I'm ugly or that Sven is insane, is there some reasonable explanation for his behavior?"

When you extract yourself from your feelings, you begin the process of *awareness,* which can then be fine-tuned to self-awareness—being analytical about yourself and your behavior. You can ask yourself, "If someone else was describing this very same situation to me, what would I see?" Being aware of the *possibility* of more than one interpretation is a crucial and highly effective way to problem-solve. Without this ability to see alternatives, you're left seeing yourself as either victim or victimizer, which leaves you stuck in a miserable place. Believing that you're unlovable and something's wrong with you gives you Victim of the Month status. "He's a cruel jerk" gives you two negative feelings for the price of one—"I'm a loser for picking a loser!"—and still gets you nowhere.

1. Be Thy Neighbor

"Be Thy Neighbor" means understanding the situation without your own overwhelming passion. When you view the problem as happening to someone else, you're able to be outside of it. You can then be a resource, and use this technique to help, rather than indulge, yourself. If, for instance, someone says, "I'm not attracted to you," you could start pointing fingers or you could take a deep breath and objectively ask, "Could something else be going on here that didn't require fault or blame?" If you were playing friendly, objective, helpful, sympathetic neighbor, you might start by noticing the following:

- Sven and Stephanie had only been dating a month.

- They'd just gone away for the weekend.

- It seemed to have gone well.

- It was several days before Sven seemed turned off.

- He wanted to just end things, not talk or take a breather.

- He wasn't very tactful in explaining why he wanted out.

- His explanation wasn't consistent with his behavior.

Even if you don't feel like playing detective, you'd likely point out to the neighbor crying on your shoulder that even if Sven truly isn't attracted to Stephanie, it certainly doesn't mean that she's unattractive or that Sven is a wicked person. Using the objective approach is noticeably different from the "I'm too ugly to live" or "He's the biggest louse in the universe" technique that Stephanie's been employing.

So what reason could Sven possibly have had for not being attracted to Stephanie? Obviously, all of us go through times when we're not supermodel material. For example, if you're coming down with a cold, you're not going to be very attractive because you've got snot running down your face. Or someone might find you unappealing if they'd just eaten a bad batch of tuna salad and felt nauseated.

But then there are those chronic situations that cause people to lose interest in one another. Examples of this type of behavior include pushing someone away due to pent-up anger or lack of attention. Chronic situations, by definition, aren't one-shot deals. Just as Rome wasn't built in a day, most people don't go from generous and kind to stingy and nasty overnight. Change is a gradual process, something that occurs over an extended period of time. If you paid attention during the last chapter about patterns, then you'd be able to look back and realize that there were probably a lot of signs along the way to indicate that your partner was losing interest in you physically. So you'd be able stop and say, "Hey, what's really going on here?"

As a general rule, when someone tells their significant other, "I'm not attracted to you," it has very little to do with their partner's physical appearance. Even if somebody's looks have changed (perhaps due to age or weight), this change has been happening for a period of time. It wasn't that one day they were attractive and the next day they weren't— I mean, not many people go from hot babe to old bag overnight. Therefore, the lack of attraction invariably says more about the internal, emotional context of the relationship than it does about how somebody looks on the outside.

But let's get back to Stephanie. She and Sven had only known each other for a month when he dropped the bomb on her. Instead of following up her panic with the one-two punch of, "Oh my God, I'm not an attractive person!" and "What a shmuck, he lied to me," Stephanie can play Be Thy Neighbor. If Stephanie's neighbor came over to tell her what she told me, Stephanie might carefully consider the situation and ask, "Wait a minute, you saw him three days ago, you had sex, and you haven't seen him since. What might have happened in those three days that would make him suddenly feel this way?"

Sheer panic and extracting herself long enough to figure out what to do next are both options here—one just works better than the other. Panic doesn't allow thinking—just reacting. Now I'm not suggesting that Stephanie become an expert on Sven's psyche, but sorting through possible scenarios gives her some breathing space, as well as living room. It may be that Sven's old girlfriend called, or he felt he was getting too involved, or a friend teased him about his hickey. The idea is that while his behavior may have been brought about by any number of factors, none of them are going to be discovered unless Stephanie gets out of panic mode and stops feeling overwhelmed. She needs to chill out while taking some time to pretend that this nightmare is actually happening to someone else. Again, panic doesn't allow thinking, just reacting—extracting yourself gives you options.

2. Be a Martian

Be Thy Neighbor will work as long as you don't live on a desert island, hate your neighbors, or lack empathy. If this is indeed the case, you can, instead, "Be a Martian": Pretend that you're from Mars and you're hovering over Earth in your spacecraft. Look down at the situation, and describe what you see.

Being a Martian establishes objectivity by taking you out of the realm of human emotions so that you can observe the goings-on in your life with a fresh, logical perspective. Since Martians aren't human and therefore aren't subject to human emotions, conventions, or understanding, they'd see only *behavior* and be free to hypothesize content, motivation, and outcome. A foreign intelligence doesn't take for granted the customs and emotions that you and your neighbor are likely to share, and allows you to see your problem for what it is from the *outside* rather than what you built it up to be from the *inside*. Being thy neighbor takes *your* emotions out of the situation, but you're still part of a larger society that shares rules, assumptions, experiences, and institutions. By being a Martian and leaving all of those commonalities behind, you remove yourself one step further and enter another realm.

3. Be a Browne

If all else fails and you find that you can neither be a neighbor nor a Martian, try being a Browne—and by that, I mean me, Dr. Joy Browne. Now, while insisting "What's your question?" works beautifully on the air, if you go around saying "Get me to the point on this" to people in your life, you're going to wind up with an angry mob on your hands. So while this technique isn't one to use on others—it's a perfectly good way for you to deal with yourself. For instance, when I get into trouble, which I do from time to time, I say to myself, "Okay, if *I* called myself on the air and asked a question, what would the question be?" I force myself to be specific and to get to the point without whining. You can do the same thing. Be a Browne. Ask yourself, "Okay, what's my question? If I had to get myself to the point on this, what would it be?"

Distilling everything down to one good question is what Being a Browne is all about. When I was on the air in San Francisco, I told my callers that if they asked me a question in a sentence or less, I would answer in two words or less. The point was not to show off—although I must admit I *was* dazzling—but to help people understand the value of asking the right question. If you can get yourself to the right question, then how big a deal could my two-word answer be? The important thing is to find the right *question,* not the right *answer.*

❧ ❧ ❧

As you can see, by taking a deep breath, refusing to panic, and applying objective tactics to achieve objectivity, Stephanie can step back from this hurtful situation with Sven. She can see that it had nothing to do with her personally, let it go, and move on with her life—with her confidence in herself still intact.

Reverse Roles

Role reversal is a technique that comes in very handy in two specific situations: when you're trying to understand someone else's behavior, and when you're trying to elicit or avoid a particular response that you've already heard or said a gazillion times. To reverse roles, ask yourself these three questions:

1. "If someone told me what I'm about to say, what would I do, and how would I feel?"

2. "If somebody did to me what I'm about to do, what would I do, and how would I feel?"

3. "If I saw someone doing what I'm doing, what would I think?"

Once, during my brief but shining tenure as a news-program host in San Francisco, I interviewed a spokesperson for a nuclear facility and a representative of Greenpeace. The nuclear guy had said his piece so many times before that you could just press a button and off he'd go, saying that nuclear energy is cheap and that's how Americans want their energy. Press another button, and Mr. Greenpeace would say, "What about the environment?" Yawn . . . It was boring for them, it was boring for me, and I hate to think how the audience must have felt. So when it was time to go to break, I said, "Okay, when we come back, you guys are going to switch positions."

They were furious with me, but it was a really interesting experiment because both of them had to think through possible explanations for the other's behavior. It was good radio, good psychology, and good problem solving. If only for a minute, I had a nuclear energy proponent wearing Birkenstocks and somebody from Greenpeace in wing tips—talk about walking in someone else's shoes! Amazingly, I got away with it—not only because it was a public forum and the guys were polite, but because I believe that they were secretly mentally and emotionally engaged by the task.

Role reversal doesn't work 100 percent of the time, but it works more often than not. This is because all of us, even men and women, are more similar than dissimilar. Okay, so we don't express our feelings in the same way, but we do *have* the same feelings. So, if you're in a situation that you don't understand, ask yourself, "If the roles were reversed, what would I do, what would I say, and, most important, how would I feel?"

Next, ask yourself this: "If I were to hear what I'm about to say, what terms would make it acceptable or unacceptable?" Calling somebody a big phony obviously won't work, for when people are insulted or accused, they respond defensively . . . and it's off to World War III. Role reversal can serve as an incredibly powerful tool for getting at the heart of an issue, *if* you're willing to be sincere in trying to see another viewpoint—and no fair using sarcasm.

❦ ❦ ❦

This caller was stuck in her "I'm the Mom" authority figure/ warden role with her son. Let's see what happens when she tries role reversal on for size.

> *I'm concerned about Brad, my 16-year-old son. He told me that he's been smoking pot for a couple of years now. This obviously concerns me, and I'm worried about his physical well-being. We've discussed it and he says that he's researched marijuana and that there's no medical reason why he shouldn't do it. He also feels it should be legalized. Do you know if it's really addictive, or if there are any long-term effects that I should know about?*
>
> — Margaret, Boulder, CO

Margaret, I'm not sure you're asking the right question here. Certainly when you inhale marijuana, smoke enters your lungs and nobody's ever claimed that smoke is anything but bad for lungs. The consensus these days is that marijuana is more addictive psychologically than physically—it doesn't have the habit-forming ingredients that are found in morphine, heroin, or cocaine. Then again, people who try marijuana are much more likely to try the harder stuff than people who don't.

The real issue here is that people use drugs because they feel unhappy about something . . . their bodies or souls feel sick. And drugs do work for the short term—that's why people use them. The best way for you to deal with your son, or for any of us to deal with our kids, is to engage in the difficult and unpleasant task of remembering what it was like to be their age. Yeah, yeah, I know times change, and what's the matter with kids today, and all the rest of it—but still, this is the place to start. *Bingo!* It's time for role reversal.

Margaret, instead of being the parent, what if you became 16 again? (Don't panic—it's just for a brief moment, so no return to braces or acne.) What would *you* have done if *your* mom had started in with the lecture or punishment? That look would have come into your eyes, and you would have shut down, tuned out, and maybe even turned on. Not the outcome we're trying for here. For most of us, the hardest part about being your son's age was that we didn't feel that our parents knew anything very valuable, that they treated us like we were imbeciles, and our friends were as clueless as we were. So, when we really needed to think something through, we often had no idea where to go. You're lucky that your son views you as a resource. You yourself may also have been fortunate enough to be close with your parents and, if they treated you respectfully, you may have even listened to them. But I bet that when they ranted, raved, cried, or lectured, you very likely left the room—even if your body was still there.

So since it seems as if Brad is already something of an expert on marijuana, we don't need to focus on *what* to tell him about grass, but why he: (a) is having this discussion with you; and (b) is interested in doing this drug in the first place.

If you tell your son that you forbid him from using, that he's grounded for life, or that he's just bought himself a one-way ticket to rehab, what do you think will happen? What would *you* do if someone tried to order you around like that? Well, for starters, you'd probably stop discussing the subject with them, and that isn't your goal. You don't want your son to use drugs, but you do want him to talk to you. You don't have to read his mind . . . but you do need to assume that he has one.

Asking your son to explain why he's interested in using marijuana will initiate a discussion. He will most likely counter with one of five responses:

1. "It makes me feel good."

2. "It sharpens my perception."

3. "It expands my mind."

4. "I'm curious."

5. "Everyone uses it."

Margaret, that's your cue to tell your son that any drug will change his *perception* of reality, not reality itself. This only makes it that much harder to deal with real life. Trying to convince him that "marijuana is bad" is a waste—he's already refuting your arguments. Instead, try to help him understand *why* he wants to do it, and that should keep the communication ongoing. Ask your son to talk to you about how he *feels* when he's smoking pot; then ask him to do you a favor—to stay sober just once while the rest of his friends are getting high. What he'll probably find is that they sound and act like morons.

Finally, remind him that marijuana is illegal. If he tries to argue that the most deadly and popular drug is alcohol and it's legal, you can point out that alcohol *isn't* legal for people his age. It's worth emphasizing that if he gets arrested and convicted of so much as possession of marijuana (even at age 16), he'll be ineligible for any federal student aid whatsoever—that includes grants, scholarships, *and* loans—and a whole lot of professions later on in life. Furthermore, if he ever chooses to go to law school, he'll have to list the conviction on his school and state bar applications—even if he was a juvenile when it happened, and even if he'd had the conviction expunged. Remind him that you respect his good sense and realize that you can't police him 24/7, but if he plans to try an illegal substance, you'd just as soon he waits until he's 21 and old enough to pay his own bail, legal fees, and college tuition.

❦ ❦ ❦

Self-awareness is an ongoing process of gaining more and more knowledge of ourselves, our strengths, our weaknesses, where we can do more work, and where we can afford to relax. It's this process that puts us on the road to self-improvement, and it's the principle that was the basis for the advice I gave Wilma. Notice how well role reversal works here.

> *My 19-year-old granddaughter lives with me. She's very bright, but she didn't graduate from high school, and now all she does is work. The problem is that I caught her stealing makeup and hair-care products from the beauty salon where she works. I tried talking to her and even yelling at her, but she says that all the girls in the store take things. What can I do?*

— Wilma, 69, Baton Rouge, LA

Wilma, all three of us know that stealing is wrong, so allowing yourself to be manipulated into preaching to your granddaughter won't help anything. Instead, how about planting the notion in her head that it's an incredibly dangerous activity, regardless of whether everybody else does it or not. Simply tell her (without lecturing), "If you get caught, it will be on your record. If they catch you, saying 'everybody else does it' won't make a bit of difference—they'll still take you to jail."

It sounds to me like your granddaughter is a lost soul. Granted, most 19-year-olds aren't model citizens, but this one doesn't seem to possess the tools she needs for adulthood. Since she works, money is obviously important to her—my guess is that a relatively small amount of cash will make some impact on her life. What I would do is bribe her to get her GED, either with a few hundred dollars or with some family heirloom you know she likes. By motivating her to further her education, you'll ensure that she'll have an entrée into a higher-paying job or one with more opportunity.

I'd say, "You're a fantastic kid, hardworking and bright—but it disturbs me that you're stealing. I love you and I know you're better than that, so I'm willing to bribe you. Grandpa and I think you have so much potential that we're willing to put together $500 (or whatever you can afford) to reward you for finishing high school." Figure out what you know about this kid—what she's good at, what her skills are—and help her understand that she's not going to be 19 forever. You can be a beacon to her and help her see what's beyond the next obstacle. You can show her that there's a wonderful adult world out there, and she can do a lot of great things. But because all she sees is *now,* she has no diploma and no real life.

At first glance, you might be tempted to treat your granddaughter like Margaret's son Brad, the aspiring pothead, but actually we're taking the opposite approach here. Brad has to understand dire consequences, while your granddaughter must understand hidden potential, excitement, and golden promise! She knows that stealing is wrong and that she might get caught, but the danger seems remote, and the peer pressure, group acceptance, and adrenaline rush is pretty darn seductive.

If you focus exclusively on the dangers and immorality of stealing, you're going to lose her. She figures, *What the hell? I'm already in jail at home.* Your belief in her may allow her to view herself in a different light. Seeing her bright future through your eyes may help her transcend the grimness of being so young yet with so little to look forward to. Your job is to remind her that 19 isn't a life sentence . . . while also keeping in mind how it felt for *you* to be that age. Walking in your granddaughter's shoes for a while will give you the awareness you need for this situation.

Play the Lottery

As you already know, this chapter is about understanding yourself well enough so that you can separate yourself from your emotions in order to see your options. One assumption that's a real obstacle standing in the way of self-awareness is what I call an "if only." For instance, three of the most common of these presume that life would be incredibly different . . .

1.   . . . if only I had different (nicer) parents.

2.   . . . if only I had a different (sexier) spouse.

3.   . . . if only I had a different (larger) bank account.

Role reversal allows us to deal with anything relating to *another person* ("if only" numbers 1 and 2), but a different technique is necessary to clear away the ubiquitous and pervasive notion of "if only" number 3—that money makes us secure and happy, money makes the world go 'round, and money solves problems (well, it does . . . if the problem is an unpaid bill. *Gotcha!*). So ask yourself, "If I won the lottery, what would happen next?" Thinking this question through is a wonderful way to get to understand yourself. A classic example of this comes courtesy of a woman who called me up to whine about her husband.

"He runs around," she complained, "he beats me, and he has children with other women."

"Why are you with him?" I asked.

"Because I *looooove* him."

So I sneakily inquired: "If you won the lottery tomorrow, would you stay or would you go?"

All I heard in response was a long, pregnant silence.

That ain't love, that's dependency! So if you're angry about your relationship, your parents, or anything else in your life, ask yourself, "If I won the lottery, would I stay or would I go?" And if the answer is "I'd go," then get a job, sell your jewelry, learn to economize, take in laundry or baby-sit, but don't stay in a relationship that doesn't work.

Playing the "If I won the lottery . . ." game is a very useful tool precisely because money is *not* what makes people happy. I've done a lot of work with several groups over the years whose membership requirements involve making seven-figure incomes before the age of 40 (and this was long before dot coms)—talk about money defining self. These groups hire me to help their members define the "Now what?" phase of their lives, not just when they achieve membership into these exclusive clubs, but especially as they mature and realize that money isn't enough to serve as self-definition. These people find out that if they were unhappy when they didn't have money, they weren't subsequently overjoyed about the money they had sitting in their various bank accounts and investment portfolios. They may have felt good about their accomplishments, the recognition they received, the freedom, or the power—but it wasn't about the money. Money is just green, inert stuff that lies there.

The idea that we could satisfy our every need at will is a tempting one, to be sure, but I'd argue that it's more exciting as a *concept* than as a *reality*. Sure, going into a store and being able to buy whatever you want is really great fun . . . the first time you do it. But then what? I mean, think about it—how many items of clothing can you wear, how many pieces of jewelry can you own, how many bottles of wine can you drink?

Don't get me wrong, I'm not saying that being penniless is fun. But between poverty and being able to indulge your every whim lies a great deal of middle ground. For most of us, the idea that you actually have to save up for something you want, or that going out for a fancy dinner is something you do on a special occasion, is extremely appealing. Having the ability to do something whenever you want to isn't the same as actually doing it. It's great to know that if you choose, you can go out for a nice dinner; but gorging on a five-course feast every day of the week will probably just make you bloated, fat, and hungover—not happy. That's an important distinction.

Any discussion about money begs the questions I'd like you to ask yourself now: "What does money mean to me? What would I use it for? How would it change my life?" If you had a million smackeroos, what would you do differently? If you'd leave an abusive situation, then for heaven's sake, leave it—*now.* Why do you need the million dollars? If the reason is because you're afraid of starving to death, then figure out some way to eat. Get a job (or two), baby-sit, clean houses, cut lawns, bake cookies, sell your car and take the bus, cash in your IRA or 401(k)—do *something!*

What Does Happiness Mean to You?

To become truly self-aware, you need to learn what makes you happy. Now that you're no longer relying on money to answer this question, use the following two exercises to learn more about your needs, your dreams, and what lifts your spirits.

1. When Was the Last Time You Were Happy?

Close your eyes and think back to the last time you were happy. Some people might envision last night, when they had a great dinner with their spouse; others might remember last week, when they got a call from an old friend; still others might go back to their childhood. Your job is to think about what stopped that happiness—that's the obstacle that needs to be articulated into a problem and given a solution.

I often use this technique when people are having problems with their relationships. Asking, "When is the last time you remember being happy?" is an extremely useful tool because you can go back to a specific point in time and mentally retrace your steps until you see when you veered off of the happiness trail and why.

2. When Were You Happiest?

This exercise will help you fine-tune your vision of happiness and obtain a clearer view of your values. For instance, if you decide that you were the happiest when you landed your first job, you can begin to decipher whether it was the anticipation of an exciting career, the money, the social climate of the workplace, or the sense of having accomplished something for the first time that made you so happy. By extracting the details, you can come to an understanding of what's important to you.

Asking your partner this question also makes for a great parlor game. The discrepancy between when you and they were happiest can be very helpful, not only in pinpointing potential problems, but also in solving existing ones. I recall one couple in particular who had wildly disparate replies to this question—she was happiest when they'd gone on their honeymoon, while the best time in his life was when he was eight years old and on vacation with his mother. Not surprisingly, this marriage was on the rocks. Although it's clear that they both liked vacations, this couple was at odds because they were both looking for people to take care of them. We have to be aware of these hidden needs if we're ever to expose them to the cold light of reason and learn to deal with them as mature adults.

For those of us who think of childhood as our happiest time, the rest of our lives can seem rather anticlimactic. For instance, when I moved to San Francisco, I ran into an acquaintance with whom I'd been very close back in junior high school. She could remember everything about those days—right down to the nicknames of our teachers, the location of our lockers, and the names of our secret crushes. Although I remembered her with great fondness, most of her recollections were wasted on me. My life had gone on and become very complicated since then, while hers had clearly stopped at that time. For her, those were the best years of her life.

It's important to be aware of your happiest time and to understand what it implies in terms of what you're looking for, your mental state, and how you're going to behave. The point is that even if your happiest time is in the distant past, if you know what gives you joy, you can search for it in your ongoing life.

Shelter from the Storm

People call me on the air because something in their life isn't working and they want to change it. But wanting to change and actually doing it are two completely different things. You see, like all living organisms, human beings are creatures of habit and are resistant to change. In order to find the energy or courage to do something different, we all need to have a place within us that we can go to find courage, hope, and strength—a place that recharges our batteries and helps us to venture into the unknown.

Feeling strong enough to attempt the unknown and make a change means that you've got to remind yourself of your skills— to try something new, to know that you can recover if you don't succeed, and to remember that you've been in situations before where you either succeeded or failed, but didn't die trying. These skills can fall into two separate categories: (1) specific behavioral traits; and (2) emotional strength, which allows you to recover and move on when you try and fail.

By taking stock of ourselves and our skills, we remind ourselves that we don't need to be rescued, that we can be there for ourselves. We touched on this in the previous chapter on patterns, but the focus here is a more specific look at your individual talents, abilities, and styles. This will help you think of yourself as competent and confi- dent. You must find (or create) some part of you that feels calm and safe, a place of refuge from the storms of doubt and fear swirling all around you. Everybody has a place like this—all it has to be is a little piece of emotional real estate that gives you stability under your feet. Think of it as a place you can go for a mini-vacation, a tiny renewal.

Maybe your safe harbor is the spelling bee you won in the third grade. Or the day your aerobics instructor told you that you'd improved considerably. Or that moment you felt perfect love when your new puppy licked your face. For me, it's when I was on a boat that was pulling away from shore, feeling the gentle sway of the water and watching the lights in the distance. I was in a strange country at a less-than-happy time in my life, but I felt enormous calm, for no particular reason that I could ascertain—except that I love being on the water and I get very bored with my sad self. Now, whenever I find myself in a tough situation, can't sleep at night, feel melancholy, or get agitated about something, I can instantly remind myself of the particular moment that brought me so much tranquility.

Your place of serenity could be a skill that you have, an area you've visited, a relationship that worked, a smile from a stranger in the grocery store, or how you felt when your neighbor asked for your pork chop recipe. In short, it can be *anything*—and if you can't think of one single solitary thing, then you've really got your self-awareness work cut out for you.

You wouldn't believe how many times I've heard someone say, "There's *nothing* I like about myself. I can't do *anything* right. . . ." Whine, whine, whine. This type of "poor-me" individual is laboring under the misapprehension that if you bad-mouth yourself enough, someone will contradict you. Callers trying this approach out on me are in for a jolt. They're undoubtedly hoping that I'll reassure them they're great—which isn't my responsibility. Instead, they're likely to hear a somewhat impatient (but interested) "If I gave you a million dollars to tell me one thing that you like about yourself, what would it be?" For the bribe of a million dollars, folks do tend to come up with something positive about themselves—and if you look hard enough, you'll find it within yourself as well.

Finding your personal haven takes work, and in this society, we like getting things easily. Paradoxically, we tend to place more value upon what we've worked for rather than what comes too easily. Remember the movie *Rocky?* If Rocky Balboa had only needed to run up three steps to get to the Philadelphia Museum of Art, he wouldn't have raised his arms in elation—after all, any fool can run up three steps. But the Italian Stallion ran up *scores* of steps and felt fabulous about it!

This is really what self-esteem is all about. *Self* is "me," and *esteem* is "the act of valuing." And if you really feel that you don't have anything in your life that you can actually value, then get off your duff and *find something.* And it has to be something you discover in yourself. I mean, sure, our parents may have been responsible for giving us a sense of competence or confidence once upon a time, but past the age of five, we're on our own in the self-esteem department.

Others may provide a starting point by letting you know what they value about you, but it's what *you* value about yourself that matters. For example, some people have told me that they're impressed by my ability to think and speak quickly, but what *I* value about myself is my ability to keep my mouth shut when necessary. It's simple: For me, thinking quickly isn't very hard, but keeping my mouth shut is.

In the final analysis, *we* are the only ones who can define what's important and worthwhile for us. Of course, we're all going to be influenced by people applauding or booing, but we can't let that define our lives. There's a difference between safety and comfort: Comfort can be found in other people; safety has to come from ourselves.

Know Your Limitations

In large part, shelter can come from not just knowing what your skills and strengths are, but from understanding your weaknesses, too. Again, you've got to take stock in yourself.

There are a number of reasons to be aware of your weaknesses. For instance, our society places such an emphasis on winning that if we ever hope to have any empathy for those in need, we have to be conscious of the fact that none of us are perfect beings. Knowing your weaknesses will also help you understand where your defensiveness lies. If you're aware of an insecurity, then you're less likely to get defensive and overreact when someone touches on it.

Most important, you need to know your limitations so that you can work on overcoming them. For years, I never went to a party without a gift for the host. Although the behavior itself may have seemed very positive since I never showed up anywhere empty-handed, the fact that it was motivated by the assumption that I wouldn't be welcome *unless* I brought something turned it into a weakness. However, by experimenting, I converted that weakness into a strength. My great triumph was when I finally understood that I could arrive with nothing and still be welcome. But I had to be willing to try that out, to ask, "Hey, what's the unconscious assumption here?" After I faced this weakness, I started to bring gifts when I *chose* to, not because I *had* to—which was a much more genuine act of generosity on my part.

Even if you've decided that something is an integral part of your personality and can't be overcome, understand that there's nothing to be lost by trying. Let's say that you think you're shy. You define yourself as shy, you act shy, and people respond to you as shy. Unfortunately, this behavior becomes both a vicious cycle and a self-fulfilling prophecy. For me, once I figured out that if I went to a party and started handing out hors d'oeuvres, my shyness would disappear. I defined the problem, solved it, and felt better about myself, all in one fell swoop. Apparently, the problem wasn't so much shyness as feeling insecure when I walked into a room full of people. Knowing that my sense of competence is very strong, I started playing waiter/bartender to calm my initial anxiety (doing something positive rather than just feeling negative). It worked like a charm.

The same goes for those who can't seem to stop talking. We all know people who use words like lassos—if they're not always chattering and cracking jokes, they assume that others won't pay attention to them. If you find yourself fitting into this category, try not talking. Instead, see what happens with eye contact or when you relinquish the floor by admitting the problem up front: "I tend to talk a lot, but I'd love to hear about *your* life."

Once you have a sense of your strengths and weaknesses, there's always room to experiment. Our lives aren't scripts. Nothing is written in stone, and nowhere does it say that you have to play the "shy guy" or the "chatty Cathy" for the rest of your livelong days. We're our own masterpieces . . . but we're still works in progress, too.

Analyze Your Dreams

Dreams are one of my favorite ways to understand the part of ourselves that we keep hidden. When someone says, "I never dream," I remind them that 80 percent of people dream 80 percent of the time, so it's more likely that they just haven't learned how to *access* their dreams. By ignoring our dreams, we miss out on a valuable resource, the best bridge between our conscious and unconscious mind, which shows us our feelings, memories, wishes, and desires. Whether we're dreaming in black and white or in vivid color, dreams are our way of whispering in our own ears. That's why they provide such incredibly valuable perspectives on our own lives.

Dreams show us the uncensored part of ourselves—but they shouldn't be feared, because they're less about prophecy and more about reading our own minds. A dream about a plane crash doesn't *cause* a plane crash, nor does dreaming about killing your boss provoke a heart attack. But even though dreams aren't factual, that doesn't make them any less real or any fascinating, for they help us get to our unconscious selves, the essence of who we really are. Dreams are like discovering the foundation of our home—going down to the cellar and pulling back the plaster, the laths, and the insulation to get at the electrical circuitry. Our unconscious is who we *really* are . . . which isn't to say that we can't spend time picking out drapes for the living room, but the fundamentals of who we are is in the basement, and dreams are the way to visit that place.

The problem with dreams is that they have to be interpreted because we talk to ourselves in code. Since I do this for a living, I'll actually wake up in the middle of my dreams and find that I've been interpreting them as I'm dreaming. In one of my more memorable dreams, I was on my deck and I saw a sad little girl who looked just like me. As I watched her, she went over the side of the deck and started slipping away. I knew that the girl was me, and I was saying good-bye to her because she was leaving. It's hard to think of a more obvious symbol of letting go of some of my childhood sadness.

If you count yourself among the many people who don't remember their dreams, try keeping a pen and paper by your bed. Before you get up in the morning or so much as shut off the alarm, write down anything you can remember about your dreams. Soon, you, too, will be able to tap in to your unconscious and get a peek at the *real* you.

Playing Doctor

Now it's your turn to demonstrate how much you've learned about increasing your level of self-awareness.

> *I'm at my wits' end. My husband and I can't seem to agree at all. You see, I desperately want a baby, and he doesn't. I love him with all my heart, but he's completely unreasonable. What am I going to do?*

> — Abby, 34, Santa Fe, NM

1. Which of the following would you ask Abby first?

   (a) Why do you think your husband doesn't want a baby?
   (b) Are you sure you'd make a good mother?
   (c) Have you done everything possible to show him how much you want a baby?
   (d) Have you two tried agreeing to disagree?

The correct answer is "a." Choice "b" implies that somehow it's Abby's fault that her husband doesn't want a baby—the very finger-pointing that heightened self-awareness should help us to avoid.

While "c" might seem like a reasonable choice, Abby can only do so much to explain to her husband that she wants a child. The point is to come to some sort of a compromise, not to keep insisting that you're right. Choice "d" makes absolutely no sense. A baby isn't an opinion—two people are involved in the process, and they both need to feel the same way about it. There's no getting around that.

The first thing to do when there's a heated disagreement is to try to understand your opposition, which is what choice "a" entails. Asking Abby why she thinks her husband doesn't want to have a baby would allow us to find an explanation for his behavior (other than her claim that "he's completely unreasonable"), then we can try to do something about it.

2. What would you tell Abby to do to solve her problem?

   (a) Tell her husband again how much she wants a baby.
   (b) Talk to his mother and see if she could wield some influence.
   (c) Ask him to try arguing the case for having a baby, while she argues the case against having a one.
   (d) Divorce the sucker. With that attitude, what kind of a father could he be anyway?

The correct answer is "c." Choice "a" is bad advice, as it does nothing to extract Abby from her situation. In fact, this option seems to encourage deeper self-absorption. If Abby ever hopes to change her hubby's mind, she needs to stop focusing on herself and start trying to figure out what his issues are.

Choice "b" goes even further in the bad-advice department than its predecessor. Urging Abby to completely disregard her husband and appeal to her mother-in-law for help is likely to anger her husband and ensure his ultimate refusal of Abby's demands.

Option "d" is premature. Although divorce may be the unfortunate result for two people who can't seem to come to terms with their disparate values and life goals, there's no reason to assume that this is the case—at least not until they've attempted to reconcile each other's needs.

Choice "c" is the one that would work best in Abby's situation. As we learned in this chapter, role reversal is a highly effective means of conflict resolution. By allowing her husband to argue her case, Abby will give him the opportunity to gain insight into her desire for a baby. Meanwhile, she'll be able to understand and empathize with his reasons for wanting to forgo child rearing. In the end, hopefully, each partner will emerge with a better comprehension of the other's needs, and some sort of agreement can be reached by addressing each person's fears or objections.

❧ ❧ ❧

Shrink Wrap

Self-awareness is all about how you see and think about yourself. Oftentimes, we carry around completely false notions of who we are and how we project ourselves. Since we're the filter through which all experience must pass, a false sense of self can completely distort the way we perceive our lives. The movie *Fight Club,* starring Brad Pitt and Edward Norton (and based on the book by Chuck Palahniuk), is an extreme, dramatic, and stark depiction of a guy who creates a reasonable and rational alter ego for himself because he just can't face who he really is. But his anger allows him only to react without ever actually solving anything.

Knowing yourself is the only way to live a cohesive life, even though that knowledge is seldom easy to attain. Getting unstuck is about extracting your emotional self from a situation long enough to do the following:

- **Resist panic.** Ask "What's going on here and what can I do about it?" rather than "What will become of me?"

- **Resist the urge to lay all the blame on yourself or on someone else**—usually both reactions are equally misguided.

- **Be Thy Neighbor, Be a Martian, or Be a Browne** so you can be more objective about your own behavior.

- **Engage in role reversal** to understand the behavior of others and see how *you* would act under similar circumstances.

- **Play the lottery** to separate the fantasy of money from your self-appraisal.

- **Take an inventory of your skills, strengths, and weaknesses** so that you can take safe emotional vacations and find the courage to figure out what you need to change.

STEP 4:
❧ PERSPECTIVE ❧

I've been with my girlfriend for nine years, but now I'm not so sure that we're right for each other. Although we have a great relationship, it suddenly seems as if everybody we know is either getting married or doing a lot of casual dating. The problem is that I feel like I've been married since I was 20—but I've never really given the idea of a lifetime commitment the consideration it deserves. I think my girlfriend and I should take a break for a while, but what if I'm wrong? I don't want to lose her. What can I do?

— Benjamin, 29, Cedar Rapids, IA

Benjamin, you've got a tough decision to make. Seeing so many of your friends getting married is scaring you because you feel that if you follow their lead, your entire life will be plotted out for you. The decision to stay with one person for all your livelong days is a tough one to make, whether you've been with that person for nine months or nine years. Your assumption that your field-playing friends are only dating for fun and games may be accurate, but they could also just be trying like crazy to find the right person. Beware of "the grass is always greener" syndrome here.

I'm not suggesting that you don't have legitimate doubts about your relationship, ones that have nothing to do with how exciting you perceive your single friends' lives to be, but be careful. Being curious about what you might have missed is normal—especially since the two of you were so young when you paired up and you've been together for so long.

Obviously, I can't and won't make your decision for you—only *you* know what lies beneath the ambivalence you're feeling. But I can walk you through a couple of your options by asking you two questions: (1) What's the worst thing that can happen if you take a break? and (2) What's the best thing that can happen? You'll probably say that the worst thing would be if your girlfriend didn't want to take you back once you figure out that you really do love her; and the best thing would be finding a new, better-suited partner or returning to your girlfriend ready and able to make a lasting commitment to her and your relationship.

Now then, Benjamin, what's the worst that can happen if you *don't* take a break? You could spend the rest of your life miserable and wondering "what if," which would, in turn, make you a terrible mate. Or maybe you'll somehow come to terms with the idea of commitment without incurring the risk of losing your girlfriend (which, in my opinion, is highly unlikely).

Which of these possibilities sounds best? Based on what you feel, you can then decide to take a break for a specific length of time, or commit. But don't get stuck in the middle, Benjamin. Face the decision head on—don't wimp out and make both you and your girl-friend miserable.

❀ ❀ ❀

Perspective is derived from the Latin words for "seeing clearly," and gaining it is the fourth step in the process of becoming an effective problem solver.

To get some perspective on this chapter on perspective, let's consider what we've learned in the first three chapters and how they've led up to this point. Step one, time shifting, is a technique to escape the sticky grasp of our history. Step two is to look for patterns, which allows the past to be useful rather than entrapping. Step three is self-awareness, which roots and anchors us by giving us an understanding of who we are at this moment, the sieve through which all experience must pass. Perspective—standing in and being aware of the moment, using the past, understanding the present, and looking forward—offers a rational, thoughtful answer to life's eternal question: "What am I gonna do now?"

Perspective is both a fascinating concept and a practical tool. In this chapter, I'll show you how to:

- gain intellectual perspective by using time instead of letting it use you;

- obtain both emotional clarity and perspective by analyzing pros and cons as well as best- and worst-case scenarios;

- achieve behavioral perspective through change; and

- assess your perspective by becoming your own mirror and seeing yourself as others see you.

Time Perspective

Human beings possess the anatomic ability to see both near and far. When we're young, we're much more likely to be myopic, near-sighted, unable to see very far ahead. (I'm a psychologist, not an optometrist, so I see this phenomenon more as a social and psychological factor rather than an optical one—we lack the ability to see distance because we're so involved in our own lives.) But as we age, we find that we can see for great distances, but can't read the damn menu to save our lives! We lose sight of ourselves and the importance of the here-and-now. As we get older, we need bifocals because we have a harder time switching back and forth between the words in the book we're reading and the numbers on that clock across the room.

When we're kids, we don't see anything but the obvious—that is, only what's in front of us. With the march of time, however, we lose sight of the obvious but gain the ability to see far away. Unless you're clairvoyant, when I say "far away," I mean the past, not the future. When middle age hits, bifocals are our way of saying, "I need some transition." So we need to make the segue between seeing what's right in front of our faces and recognizing how past experiences relate to our lives today.

While it's hard on the eyes, that shift is very helpful to our brains. Being able to switch from seeing the immediate to seeing the distant, and vice versa, is what gives us a sense of our boundaries and parameters, our goals and values, and the direction in which we want to be moving. Since the ability to shift perspective on past, present, and future is such an amazingly valuable technique, I've developed three ways to help you learn it.

1. One Day to Live

A colleague of mine in San Francisco (whom I barely knew) called me one night while I was on the air and said, "I found out ten minutes ago that I have pancreatic cancer. Can you be my therapist?" Although I had a rule for myself that I would never see anybody in private practice who had heard me on the air, what could I say to someone who was dying?—"I'm sorry, I have this rule"?! So, of course, I went to see him in the hospital that evening. In addition to being a well-known public figure, he had a secret life as a closeted homosexual. His question for me was, "Should I come out?"

While he didn't have just one day to live, his life did have a clear end in sight. Working with someone in this situation was an extremely helpful experience for me, as it opened my eyes to the clarity that comes with a definite time limit and the therapeutic benefits that can be derived from asking, "If you had one day to live, how would you want to spend it?"

Because you wouldn't be alive to suffer any consequences, you might very well decide to put your credit card into meltdown, have sex with the entire Green Bay Packers backfield, or hunt down your ex and fling a javelin into his or her heart. But that's not the value of asking this question. The value lies in thinking, *How would I spend my precious time? What's most important to me?* Those of us who don't spend the greater part of our days immersed in fantasies of revenge or debauchery might decide to indulge in a fabulous gourmet feast, spend the day at the beach with our families, or get a full-body massage.

As for my closeted colleague, I asked him to focus on his private, rather than his public, life. I suggested that he spend more time with his significant other (even in public) rather than outing himself and spending his remaining days defending himself or fielding questions about his behavior. He decided that he was a lover, not a fighter, and that he wanted to spend his final days in peace, enjoying the time he had left. He chose what was right for him, but the important factor was not *what* he chose to do, but *that* he chose.

Once you ask yourself the "One Day to Live" question, time suddenly becomes something you cherish, instead of something you take for granted. With that new perspective, the superficial and trivial tend to fall away, and you end up emerging with a new-found understanding of your own values. So if you discover that gourmet meals are what matter, you could take a cooking class or go out to a fabulous restaurant once a week. If you find that being with your family is what's most important, you can begin clearing your social calendar and stay home more. The point is that once you become aware of what means the most to you, you're less likely to put off something that's really valuable for something that matters much less.

This lesson was forever emblazoned upon my memory by the story of a woman who was killed in a car accident. After the funeral, when her husband was packing up her things, he found a wonderful piece of lingerie in her drawer that he'd never seen before—she'd been saving it for a special occasion. Moral of the story: Our *lives* are special occasions. When there's only one day left to live, your idea of what really matters suddenly becomes very clear. And it's knowing the difference between what's important and what isn't that allows us to solve problems effectively.

2. Your Tombstone

The second way to get perspective by using time is the polar opposite of the one we just discussed. Thinking about what you'd do with one day left to live gives you insight into what you find *immediately* gratifying. Asking, "What do I want written on my tombstone?" offers the longest view of your legacy, and makes you think about how you can make the rest of your life worthwhile.

This is a policy that insures that if you want to be remembered as a great parent, you're not spending too much time at the office. When you think about it logically, "I made a million dollars" doesn't seem all that special when it's carved onto a headstone. Still, it's that lack of perspective that allows folks to fritter hours of their lives away on monetary rather than emotional goals. So, if you want to be remembered as a good parent, then spend more time with your kids. If you want to be remembered for finding a cure for cancer, then give more money to cancer research, or go back to school and become a biochemist. In the end, only after you've figured out what you want your tombstone to say can you begin to plan how you'll make that particular goal happen.

3. A.D. 2500

My mom is actually responsible for this one. When I'd get upset, she'd say, "Joy, 500 years from now, no one will know or care."

Since it's all too easy to get bogged down in the minutiae of our lives, lose perspective, and forget what's really important, this phrase provides us with a third way of using time perspective. The idea of A.D. 2500 drives home the point that while your life matters to you, it really doesn't matter much to anyone else. No one you know is going to be alive in 500 years, so when you think, *Omigod, I'm late!* or *I'm going to miss that plane!* or *I'm not going to meet my quota!* take a deep breath and say, "Hey, 500 years from now, no one will know and no one will care."

This isn't to say that nothing we do counts—of course our lives matter to *us,* but that doesn't mean that they make all that much of a difference in the larger scheme of things. This idea is sobering, calming, and exhilarating all at once: sobering because it acknowledges mortality; calming because it extracts the panic; and exhilarating because of the sense of freedom it offers. Panic makes us jam through a stoplight or elope at the first tick of our biological clock. Thinking about what really matters allows us to look both forward and back, learn from experience, and make educated guesses about our future.

❧ ❧ ❧

Donna called me because she was having a problem figuring out her future. Tombstone technique to the rescue!

All my life I wanted to grow up, get married, and have a family. But now that I'm 33, I'm starting to realize certain things about myself that make me wonder. For instance, I really enjoy going out to dinner and the theater. I like being spontaneous, having time to myself, sleeping late, things like that. I'm also not as energetic as I used to be. So I'm not sure that motherhood is a good idea for me anymore, even though I do love kids. But part of me still wants to have a child. My boyfriend and I have been together for two years, and he recently let me know that even though he loves me and is willing to marry me, he realized that he definitely doesn't want to have any more kids (he has children from a previous marriage). I'm not sure how much he's influencing my decision because I'd questioned my desire for children in the past, even before I met him. What do you think?

— Donna, 33, Hoboken, NJ

Donna, you said a mouthful when you told me that you're just not sure at this moment. While you were talking about how much you like your lifestyle, all I could think of was, *If I were you, I'd go buy a lottery ticket today.* Because if you win the lottery, then you could hire a staff—a nanny, chauffeur, butler, maid, and cook—so you could accomplish all that you want *and* still have a child!

You're really trying to see into a future that none of us can see clearly. But at least you can sort out your feelings. Donna, if you knew that you could *never* have a child, how would you feel? Ask yourself, "Will I be okay if I become everybody's favorite auntie, or if I volunteer to work with kids—or do I really want a child of my own? What do I want my legacy to be? What do I want written on my tombstone?"

In theory, you have the better part of a decade to decide. A lot of women who decide they don't want to have children at 30 all of a sudden decide that they do as they get closer to 40, even though the complications increase. But given the fact that you're seriously involved with a guy who doesn't want kids, my guess is that he's part of what's fueling today's doubts. He may be the critical mass tilting you in one particular direction at this moment. Presumably, the two of you are trying to make a decision about your future, and he's saying, "Definitely no more kids!" while you're unsure.

See if you can literally, figuratively, geographically, and emotionally walk away from your boyfriend for at least a couple of days. Take that time to ask yourself, "Okay, knowing what I know about myself, how would I feel about not having kids? Is this just about him, or is it about me?" But if you *do* decide to pair up with this guy, beware of trying to change his mind about this. Donna, if you figure out what you really want written on your tombstone, you'll know what to do now.

Emotional Perspective

Shifting your perspective on time allows you to see things differently. Shifting your *emotional* perspective takes you one step further, allowing you to actually try on a different feeling. Emotional perspective is a way of expediting your journey out of the tangle of your own emotions, which is exactly what Rebecca needs.

> *I've been married for two years and recently gave birth to my first child. I'm still on maternity leave from my high-powered career as a talent agent. I love my job, but my leave of absence is about to run out, and I'm torn. I'm afraid to quit my job, but I'm also scared of what might happen if I don't. My husband said that he'd support any decision I made. How do I decide what to do?*

> — Rebecca, 38, Los Angeles, CA

Rebecca, you're feeling understandably anxious because you're at an important crossroads in your life. You're faced with a decision that will impact your marriage, your child, your career, your sense of self, and how your mother talks to you. There's no obvious answer to your question, since only *you* can decide what makes the most sense for you.

Since none of us can see the future, the next best thing is perspective—about what's *been* important, what's *still* important, and what you think will *continue* to be important to you. For example, while I'm sure you're crazy about your child, and you've told me you really love your work, which place works best for *you?* What do you enjoy doing most? Do you like spending all of your time with the baby, or do you, in your heart of hearts, prefer the interpersonal and professional aspects of your career? And what about your husband? Is he really a Mr. Mom at heart?

Not only is there no obvious answer here, there's also no truly right or wrong option. But Rebecca, you've gotta be honest with yourself here. Your answers will give you insight into your own needs, wants, and goals. Pen and paper will help you focus. And don't let yourself be distracted by the realization that your husband has no such dilemma . . . he gets to be both working parent *and* loving dad, without worrying about a disrupted schedule or career path.

Make two lists: The first should enumerate all the pros and cons for staying at home; while the second should specify the pros and cons for hiring a nanny, job-sharing with hubby, working from home, or going back to work (either full or part time). To simplify: column one—work (pro); column two—work (con); column three—home (pro); column four—home (con).

These lists will enable you to face your fears and fantasies by putting them down in black and white. For instance, maybe you fear that if you resume your career, something terrible could happen to your child, but if you stay home, your child would be safe. Of course, once you put pen to paper, you'll realize that children can "fall down, go boom!" whether or not their mothers are home or at work, so you'll be able to rule out some of the irrational beliefs guiding your behavior. Armed with your four columns of pros and cons, you can now begin to figure out what makes the most sense to *you*. You may even be able to find a compromise that meets the majority of your needs.

Rebecca, making these lists is a way of shifting your emotional perspective. When we're faced with major decisions, we often allow ourselves to get carried away with possibilities that are rooted in emotions rather than rationality. By articulating our fears and fantasies, we can finally begin to think about them, see them for how irrational or reasonable they really are, and gain a much-needed emotional perspective.

On a day-to-day basis, figuring out what you like to do, where you're happier, and what allows you to be the best person the greatest percentage of the time, can help you decide to: (1) get a nanny; (2) work out of the house; (3) get a part-time job; (4) hire a replacement at work; (5) figure work out a time-sharing schedule with your husband; or (6) defer your career until your child (or children) are grown, in school, less needy, etc. Figuring out your priorities requires both an elongated and a shortened viewpoint—you've got to think about not only what you want now, but what you're likely to want tomorrow, next week, and next year . . . all of which will give you a bit more perspective (there's that word again) on what pleases you. Once you have some sense of how you'd like to spend your days, you can broaden your focus by asking how you see yourself in a year or two or ten. Would you rather think of yourself as Supermom or Hollywood Überagent?

The answers you unearth in your head and heart will give you a huge hunk of insight into what you really want to do.

By looking at your life from a variety of angles—time, space, focus, pleasure, and meaning—you're both defining and shifting perspectives, switching back and forth from how you think, feel, and behave now, to how you used to in the past, and how you might do so in the future. If it makes you feel any better, you're not alone in your dilemma. One evening, I happened to catch a rerun of the sitcom *Maude* (with Bea Arthur), in which she and a school chum got competitive about their lives. Maude extolled the pleasures of hearth and home, while her glamorous friend bragged about her beaux, wardrobe, salary, and contacts. By the end of the episode, they both admitted to feelings of jealousy, and Maude wisely (if sadly) said, "You can't have it both ways." End credits. Cut to mild-mannered psychologist at home, hollering at the TV set, "Why *can't* we have it all?! Men do!"

But I digress.

❦ ❦ ❦

Good decision making is improved by testing not only how things may look, but how they're going to feel. The following two exercises provide the best ways to help you gain emotional perspective on any given situation.

1. Best- and Worst-Case Scenarios

Let's go back to Rebecca, our ambivalent new mother and career woman. Here's an example of someone in dire need of emotional perspective. Trying to figure out if she should go back to work or stay home with her child, Rebecca is in danger of letting her worst fears get the better of her. Asking, "What's the worst that can happen?" can often settle some turmoil.

Rebecca might ask, "What if something happened to my child?"

"Like what?" I would ask.

"Well, she could get run over by a car."

"Could she get run over by a car when you're not at work?"

"Yeah."

Mission accomplished! Looking at our fears projects us into a vulnerable position, which may feel uncomfortable, but taking the emotional risk offers the same benefits as going to a scary movie . . . we're less afraid because we've seen what scares us and faced it (albeit while passively sitting in a movie theater). Projection is like having a nightmare and then turning on the light—the light doesn't change what's in the room; it just changes your *perception* of what's in the room.

Okay, so let's go through a couple of Rebecca's fears:

1. The child can be hurt by something—inside or outside the home.

2. The child can be hurt by someone—inside or outside the home.

So what's the real problem here? Not that something terrible may happen if she's not home, but that something terrible may happen if she doesn't get a trustworthy and reliable baby-sitter. The question, in this case, isn't "Should I go back to work?" but "How do I find someone who's suitable for taking care of my child?" and "How do I childproof my home?" Look at it like this: Catastrophes happen, both at home and at work, and there's only so much we can do about it.

Now that we've gotten the awful news out of the way, time for the best-case scenario of Rebecca returning to work: She could be making a lot of money and be really happy. Let's examine that . . . how much money are we talking about, and would that really make her happy?

As you can see, what we're doing is taking both the best- and worst-case scenarios and breaking them down, instead of indulging in them or swallowing them whole. That's the appropriate technique when you have a problem—make it as small as possible and break it down into its component parts, rather than allow it to loom larger and become a huge obstacle. When you make things small, you'll know what to do next; when you blow them out of proportion, you become immobilized.

Instead of turning problems into boulders, start crushing them into pebbles so they're as movable, understandable, and manageable as possible. Think of moving a truck—you could either pick it up and carry it all at once, or you could take it apart and carry it piece by piece. Which is easier? Yeah, all that assembly and disassembly might take longer, but that's the way to move a truck. (And don't talk to me about gears or towing—I'm making a point here.)

Back to Rebecca: Best-case scenario if she goes to work—she's rich and fulfilled by her work; worst-case scenario—something awful happens to her child. Best-case scenario if she stays home—she spends time with her child and loves every minute of it; worst-case scenario—she's bored, unhappy, and therefore not a very good mother.

In either case, there are steps and measures that Rebecca can take to ensure that the worst won't come to pass. For instance, if she decides to stay home, she can start thinking about ways to stay stimulated. The terrible secret that any mom will tell you is that cute as they are, toddlers can turn your brain to mush. With a limited vocabulary and short attention span, they can only do so much in terms of carrying on meaningful conversation. You can love your two-year-old, but they're just not particularly inspiring on an intellectual level. So is there a way for Rebecca to stay home with her child and be intellectually challenged? Good question—maybe she can run a business out of her home, take a correspondence course, or go to night school.

As you can see from Rebecca's example, once you start considering the best- and worst-case scenarios, you become aware of your values. If you cherish your child's safety *and* your own intellectual stimulation, there are steps you can take to ensure that both are covered—including hiring an outstanding child-care provider or running a home-based business.

2. Make a List of Pros and Cons

I once helped a client who had a big decision to make. I told her to make a list of all the reasons for and against her various choices, and she responded, "What if my list comes out wrong?" Translation: She'd already made her decision. Lists like these *can't* come out wrong because all items don't have to possess equal value. *You're* the judge, and you can weigh the reasons any way you want. Once you've listed the positives and negatives, you decide to do whatever you want, even if the choices outweigh each other. You've already made your decision—you know what you want to do. You may be uncomfortable or feel you're too emotional or not emotional enough. If that's the case, then run the list again; change whatever you like; and give yourself the time, space, or permission to accept your decision.

By writing out a list, you force an awareness. For example, Rebecca could say, "A reason to go to work is to make money; a reason to stay home is to be with my child." Now then, how do they stack up? Regarding going back to work, she might say:

- "I would have more money to do what I want."

- "I want to be able to afford massages."

- "Massages would make me a happier person."

- "Being a happier person would make me a better mother."

That's already four points on her list of reasons for returning to work. On the flip side, if she's afraid of being away from her child, she could write:

- "I would miss my child's first laugh."

- "I would miss my child's first step."

- "I would miss my child's first word."

- "I wouldn't be there to kiss the boo-boos."

And now Rebecca's got four reasons to stay home. The point is that the list will always come out the way you want it to come out. This technique doesn't change your reality, but it will help you discover that reality and to become *aware* of what you want and need as opposed to feeling victimized and locked into something.

Make a Change

The act of changing something about our lives—whether it means taking the train instead of riding the bus home from work, or eating dinner at the dining room table instead of on the coffee table—enables us to actually experience the shift as opposed to just viewing it (as we did with time perspective) or feeling it (as with emotional perspective). Changing what you're doing is a great way to alter your perspective through behavior. I'm a great fan of trying something different, of temporarily doing the polar opposite just to see what happens.

We human beings are naturally inherently resistant to change. Both prisoners and concentration-camp victims provide striking examples of exactly how hard it is for people to change. Prisoners, for instance, will often commit another crime just before they're paroled because as awful as prison may seem, at least it's familiar. These prisoners view familiarity as actually being better than freedom, because freedom is risky, strange, and very scary—especially if you're not feeling all that great about yourself. By the same token, many concentration-camp inmates were reluctant to leave after they were liberated at the end of WWII. It's unbelievable that *anything* could be worse than what they had to endure in those camps, but the ultimate horror of a dreadful situation is that it makes one feel incapable, incompetent, and unworthy of anything better. That's both the good news and the bad news about being human—if you've experienced something truly awful, your imagination will let you imagine even worse, while simultaneously convincing you that you're unworthy of anything better.

Prisons and concentration camps are extreme examples, so let's focus on situations that are more common: unpleasant working conditions (belligerent boss, gossipy co-workers, ambitious assistant) and toxic relationships (abusive spouse, jealous friends, nasty family members). As unhealthy as these situations are, people are frightened to upset the apple cart for fear of winding up with nothing in which to schlep their apples.

Once you understand that most people are reluctant to change, you can begin to peruse the really great reasons *to* make a change—including the fact that as the familiar becomes comfortable, we start to tolerate what should be intolerable. We get used to it, and even take it for granted. When you do something different, you'll in turn have a different perspective at that moment. You can then either prefer the new situation, which means you've figured out a better way to act; or you can decide that you liked the old way better, which means you value the familiar even more. Any way you slice it, trying something new is an extremely valuable experience, and it's amazing how little we do it voluntarily.

Ironically, just as making a change can make you feel powerful and in charge of your own destiny, it can also be incredibly humbling because by the time we're grown-ups, most of us know how to do *something* well. But doing something you've never before attempted will bring you in touch with how much of the world feels most of the time—shaky, unsure, and a bit overwhelmed.

For example, I've been exercising for a gazillion years. I'm strong, have a lot of endurance, and love to dance. However, I recently started taking yoga, precisely *because* it goes against my strengths. I'm not only the wrong shape, but I have little flexibility, a high center of gravity, and long legs. Still, I do it . . . partially because I know it's good for my body to do something different (bodies get into ruts just like heads), but also because it reminds me of how awful it feels—the embarrassment, the discomfort, the clumsiness—to do something you're lousy at for the first time. Yoga makes me a more sympathetic and empathetic psychologist and human being. It truly "opens" me up—which is what yoga is all about.

At the very least, change makes you grateful for what you have or shows you a better alternative. It's important to experiment, so if you're not used to change, start small. Change your breakfast cereal, or walk a different route to your neighborhood coffee shop. Don't necessarily sell your house, shave your head, or hand in your resignation today. Play with a pattern a bit—experimenting with small things that won't upset your life completely—and develop poise and confidence at the same time.

A great way to practice change is to ask yourself two questions:

1. If I could change one thing about myself, what would it be?

2. If I could change one thing about someone who's making me unhappy, what would it be?

Amazingly, most people are silenced by these questions. They either want to change "everything" or "nothing." Well, neither reply is useful or realistic. What we're in search of here is perspective. In relationships (with mates, co-workers, and ourselves), guerrilla warfare can become the norm if we're not careful and specific. Suddenly, we hate *everything* about that person or ourselves, which is both inaccurate and pointless. Think about changing *one thing* about yourself. What would it be? If a million characteristics spring to mind, you're not being concise—upon careful consideration, you'll likely discover that most concerns are traceable to a limited source. Once you've identified this core issue, you can decide to focus on it, thereby allowing all of the other minor, petty disturbances to evaporate.

Changing a characteristic that we hold near and dear, no matter how counterproductive, is challenging. Yes, it's uncomfortable, but it's not impossible. It doesn't cost much (okay, maybe some anxiety and a couple of bucks for antacids) to at least *entertain* the possibility of something new.

❦ ❦ ❦

My wife complains that I don't talk enough. But I'm just not a very talkative person. What should I do?

— Juan, 39, Miami, FL

Juan, listen up, buddy—start talking. Your taciturn ways are clearly a sore point, and it's a good thing that your wife can be so specific about what she'd like you to modify. If you value her happiness—and your own—think about and then practice talking more. I understand that you see yourself as the strong, silent type, but maybe you can take a 24-hour break from that concept. For the next day, challenge yourself to do the talking, maybe even *all* the talking.

First, tell your wife what it is you're trying to accomplish. That way, your sudden loquacity won't catch her off guard, and you'll have built some accountability into your exercise . . . meaning that if you don't follow through, your wife will let you know. Tell her, "Okay, for the next 24 hours, I'm going to start our conversations and tell you all about my day, my favorite team, what I had for lunch, and my ingrown toenail."

By changing *your* behavior, you'll find that she'll change *hers.* Maybe now that you're talking so much, your wife will decide that she liked the old you better and will stop complaining about your nonverbal communication style. Or, maybe she'll be happy to take a break from working so hard to make conversation. She might be calmer and more content to see that she doesn't have to expend so much energy to bring you out of your shell. And you might even decide that it's kind of fun and liberating to be able to open up. For all you know, the idea that you don't just have to turn off and that there's a positive energy to speaking may actually appeal to you. By changing, you'll see possibilities that are closed to you now. After all, seeing possibilities is really what perspective is all about.

Look in the Mirror

Oscar Wilde once said, "I put all my genius into my life; I put only my talent into my works." You go, Oscar! As I mentioned before, we're our own masterpieces and our own works in progress. As such, we can look in the mirror and assess our own lives to gain perspective. Be willing to look honestly and specifically at what you want, who you are, and your strengths and weaknesses—that old paper and pen will come in quite handy here.

1. Examine Relationships

One of the best ways to look in the mirror is to examine your relationships and ask yourself what you like best about your friends. In terms of perspective, understanding what you like about *somebody else* will help you begin to understand *yourself* better. For instance, if you notice that you like the fact that your friend does all the talking, then you'll realize that you like to listen.

The flip side to this is to ask what you dislike most about your friends. You may dislike someone for being overbearing—again, this relates directly back to you. If you don't like your friend's overbearing qualities, then you probably dislike your own passive qualities.

2. Examine Yourself

Thinking about your friends should bring you one step closer to making an inventory of your own positives and negatives. After all, looking in the mirror is about looking at yourself, not at the guy standing next to you. Take the time right now to list three things that you like about yourself and three things that you don't.

Sometimes your ideas about yourself have been inherited from your family. Maybe your mother said, "Stop being so stuck-up!" and now you think your modesty is an admirable quality. But once you take a closer look, you may realize, *I'm not modest, I just dampen my own sense of exuberance and pride in myself. I ask other people to praise me because my mother made me feel that I was conceited if I praised myself. Now the problem is that I'm always asking someone else to do it for me, and that's a burden on my relationships.*

By looking at your list and analyzing it, you'll get a different perspective on your personal inventory.

❦ ❦ ❦

Looking in the mirror to assess and analyze our perspective allows us to evaluate ourselves and others. This is the challenge for Jessie.

I'm having a hard time with my 15-year-old daughter. She's been doing a lot of storytelling lately. For instance, she recently wrote an e-mail to someone saying that she's having an affair with one of her teachers. I know that's a lie. I also got a call from her dad saying that she told her stepbrother she was having oral sex, and I know she isn't. On top of all of this, last week she found two adult videos in her stepfather's closet. We've been married two years, but my husband has lived with us since she was ten. I confronted her and she immediately tried to turn the situation around on me, demanding to know why the videos were even there to be found. I told her that my husband is 45 years old, and while she might not understand, he definitely has a right to have the tapes in his drawer. What's most disturbing to me is that she knew he had the videos and that she watched them. She's so young and just developing her views on sex, and this is what she sees.

— Jessie, 43, Lakewood, OH

Jessie, first things first: Why are you so convinced that your daughter is making up these stories? After all, you probably didn't tell your mother when you first had sex, so why would you expect your daughter to tell you? Few kids make an announcement to Mom when they decide to become sexual. It's not clear whether she actually is having sex or not, but your refusal to admit the possibility is going to blind you to reality either way. You're saying that 15 is a little young, and while I might agree with you, she may not. She certainly wouldn't be the *only* 15-year-old in her class to be having sex, so let's not lose sight of the forest for the trees here. On average, it's likely that you had sex two years before your mother did, as she did before her mom— that's what happens with succeeding generations. If your daughter *has* had sex, we might think it's a little early, but statistically, it's really not remarkably so.

Should she have rummaged in her stepfather's closet and watched the videos she found? No. Privacy is privacy. And hopefully, you don't go into *her* closet, because you need to strongly make the case that, "In this house, we respect each other's privacy." Jessie, you also say that she knew the videos were there. That means that she's aware her stepfather is looking at porn, which could be an opportunity for you to discuss your views on pornography and the compromises that are made in marriage.

Your daughter has been prematurely sexualized because you and your husband lived together in the house before she was old enough to understand and deal with it. Rather than go off the deep end because you're feeling guilty, sit her down and say, "I want to discuss a few things with you. Number one, if I had to do it over again, I wouldn't have lived with your stepfather before we got married because I think that made you aware of sex before you were ready to deal with it. Number two, you might not want to talk to me about having sex, but here are some ways to make sure you're protected physically as well as emotionally [then give her information about birth control]. Number three, boys tend to talk about girls who have sex—whether that's right or wrong, that's just the way it is. Number four, stay out of your stepfather's closet."

From a Distance

We talked a lot about the concept of *extraction*—that is, looking at your situation from a distance and seeing it in context, not moving forward or back, but instead zooming in and zooming out—in Step 3. Distance, as we discussed in the last chapter, is an attempt to cleanse your perspective of emotion so that you can clearly and intellectually see and review alternatives. For instance, I knew a lot of people who were in the World Trade Center area when the two hijacked planes crashed into the Twin Towers. Believe it or not, many of them had no idea that what they'd witnessed firsthand was the worst case of terrorism on American soil to date until they came home and turned on their TV sets. There's something about being in the eye of the storm and in the heat of the moment that keeps us from seeing clearly. We really have to move away from the center of activity to see and understand the full scope, scale, and implications of any situation.

We're so involved in our own lives that perspective allows us a way out of the moment. I know we talk a lot about "seizing the day" and "staying in the moment," but when you're trying to problem-solve, you want to do exactly the opposite. You have to get out of Dodge and figure your options—see the road into town, the crossroads, *and* the road out of town.

Playing Doctor

Time to test your perspective IQ by using the skills and practical tips in this section to solve Mitch's problem.

> *I have a 17-year-old stepdaughter. We live in a small town, and she works at the local McDonald's. She'd been bugging me to get her a car so that she can get a better job, so I got her a $200 special, worked on it all summer, and got it going. Now she thinks it's fine to take it to school. On the last day of her junior year, she drove it without asking my permission, and took off with her friends. Am I being unrealistic in my expectations of her?*
>
> — Mitch, 44, Streator, IL

1. What would be your first piece of advice for Mitch?

   (a) Ground her for the summer.
   (b) It's her car, so let her do with it as she pleases.
   (c) Remember back to when you were 17 for a second and consider yourself lucky that she didn't take that car to Vegas.
   (d) Put the car up for sale. That way, you won't have to worry about your teen behind the wheel, she'll learn that there are consequences to her actions, and you might even make a tidy profit in the process.

The correct answer is "c." Choices "a," "b," and "d" aren't relevant because Mitch's question is (rather wisely) not how or if he should punish his stepdaughter, but whether or not his expectations of her are realistic. To kids, a car is the very embodiment of freedom. You can't very well give them the keys to liberty and then expect them not to use them.

Mitch is doing the adult amnesia thing—sounding as if he's from another galaxy where no teenager drives a car. If he'd close his eyes and remember the last day of his junior year in high school, he'd have the answer to his question. I mean, think about it—you're 17; you've got a driver's license; you've got your own car (a clunker, but you love it), a full tank of gas, and a few bucks; it's a lovely spring day; you've got your impressionable, awestruck, jealous friends . . . . You know that what you're doing isn't strictly kosher, but your friends are saying "Why not?" and you're thinking, *If I could get it back in time and fill it up with gas, I could probably get away with it. Worst comes to worst, they'll ground me. But hey—it's worth it!* That's how 17-year-olds think—they're creatures of impulse, not of consequence, which is why they're assigned parents. Hopefully, Mitch's stepdaughter didn't smash up the car, but expecting her to only drive this car to work is forgetting what it was to be 17.

We're working for clarity, not charity, here, so try this perspective puzzler.

> *My fiancé's sister-in-law, Samantha, has made it very clear that she doesn't want me to be a part of their family. Although we got along all right at first, now she won't speak to me at family occasions, gives me dirty looks, turns her back to me, and completely ignores me. Rick, my fiancé, has picked up on this, but he refuses to confront her. The problem is that they have two little girls, and we want them to be involved in our wedding. How do I handle this woman?*
>
> — Wendy, 25, Spokane, WA

1. How would you guide Wendy?

   (a) Speak to Rick's brother about asking the nieces to participate in the wedding.
   (b) Invite Samantha to participate in the wedding along with her daughters.
   (c) Forget about involving her would-be nieces in the wedding plans.
   (d) Insist that Rick intervene and confront Samantha.

Choice "b" is the correct answer. Choice "a" is wrong because it will only serve to heighten the hostility, isolation, and exclusion that Samantha already feels. Since she's acting out mainly because she feels that she's somehow been slighted by Wendy, adding insult to injury might really derail Wendy and Rick's wedding plans. Angry as Wendy may be, making Samantha her enemy is a lose-lose situation. It just doesn't make any sense. And choice "c" will only serve to help Wendy pile up still more reasons why Samantha is her enemy. In the end, Wendy will be the loser.

Choice "d" is wrong because there's probably not much Rick would be able to do about it, and Wendy doesn't want to start a war here. Wendy wouldn't be wise to involve her fiancé in this, because it's a situation that he can't win. If he takes on his sister-in-law, he'll then have his brother and mother mad at him, and in the end they'll all blame Wendy, not him.

What Wendy *can* do is just ignore Samantha's rudeness, and win her over by charm—keep in mind that it's easier to trap flies with honey than vinegar—so choice "a" is the correct way to handle the situation. If Wendy is far enough advanced to think about having Samantha's kids in her wedding, then she's far enough advanced to have Samantha involved. Think about it for a moment. If you had a couple of kids, and someone came to you and said, "I'd like to have your kids in my wedding but not you," you'd probably be pretty hurt. If Wendy wants to be smart as well as nice—looking to the future as well as what will work *now*—she'd get Samantha involved and on board. Samantha's probably hurt because Wendy likes her kids, her husband, her mother-in-law . . . but Wendy not only leaves Samantha out but treats her like scum.

Wendy needs to lighten up, open up, and see the world through Samantha's hurt eyes for a moment. It's possible that Wendy may even have helped create this mess. After all, most of us really aren't very sweet to people who we think don't like us. Even if Samantha started the war, Wendy can end it by being the bigger person here. She should go up to her future sister-in-law and say, "I'd really love for you to be involved in the wedding. If you'd like to be a bridesmaid, I'd like to have you. But if you feel as if that's an expense you don't want to go through, let's figure out something you'd like to do because it would mean a lot to me. After all, we're going to be family." This approach will make life much easier for Wendy in the long run—unless she secretly is reveling in the cold shoulder she's already been experiencing courtesy of Samantha, or she wants to start an outright family feud . . . when she's not even actually in this family yet.

Shrink Wrap

Perspective is a practical tool as well as an interesting abstraction. We have to see, feel, act, assess, and extract ourselves to gain true perspective in any situation. It's simple but not easy, challenging but incredibly useful. Achieving the perspective necessary for valid judgment and good decisions requires the following:

- **Using time to achieve perspective by asking yourself three questions** to help figure out what your priorities are and what really matters to you: (1) What if I only had one day to live? (2) What do I want written on my tombstone? and (3) Will any of this matter in A.D. 2500?

- **Finding the emotional perspective required to problem-solve** by evaluating best- and worst-case scenarios and by writing out lists of pros and cons.

- **Learning to use change instead of fearing it** by getting in the habit of occasional change and voluntarily modifying things in your life, one at a time.

- **Examining yourself, your relationships, and your dreams** so that you can become your own mirror, seeing and assessing yourself as others do.

- **Getting the perspective that comes with distance.**

STEP 5:
❧ BUILDING BLOCKS ☙

A woman I dated about five years ago contacted me last week, and we've since exchanged some very friendly, super-ficial e-mails. I'm still single, but I heard that she got married, so I figured that maybe she wrote me because she's single again. But in yesterday's e-mail, she told me that she's still married. Why would somebody do that? Should I write back and say, "Are you nuts?!" or should I just not write her back at all?

— Robert, 35, Tacoma, WA

Okay, Robert, slow down. You're getting way ahead of yourself here. E-mailing you to see what you're up to doesn't really qualify as a romantic overture—it's not like she proposed or even proposi-tioned you. This could be more about your interpretation than her behavior. It may just have been a benign, innocent "Hi, how are you?" on her end, not an attempt to tease you or start something torrid. Maybe she was cleaning out a drawer, found a picture of you, and thought, *Hmmm . . . I wonder how Robert's doing.* Sure, she might have been more honest with you from the get-go by saying, "I was just cleaning out my husband's junk drawer while the baby was sleeping, and I came across a picture of us. What's up with you?" But married people often get in touch with old friends or ex-lovers because they're curious, nostalgic, or even a tiny bit lonesome—it doesn't necessarily mean that they're looking for an affair.

Now then, if you're asking me, could there be an "I'm feeling a little fat today, and it would be nice to talk to someone who once thought I was really gorgeous" subtext to her messages? Sure. But if you're going to assume—which I'd *really* rather you didn't—why not assume something that makes you cheerful instead of panicky?

I think writing back "Are you nuts?!" is perhaps a little extreme— even though it does have a rather dramatic flair to it. Ignoring her is also a little harsh. Instead, you could say something along the lines of, "I have a rule to not flirt with married women. I wish you well, but I'm really looking for a life mate and don't have time for this." You can also decide to be very honest and say, "I wasn't clear about what your motives were." Then again, you may decide that it would be kind of fun to have her as a friend, but I think it should be a very platonic, asexual, occasional kind of friendship, because you still don't want to mislead either her or yourself.

❦ ❦ ❦

Assumptions are the ultimate way of being stuck—in the past, in your own worldview—and they just plain stink. They say everything about you and nothing about the other person. Worse still, they're unspoken, and trying to be a mind reader isn't even being stuck in the past—it's being stuck in Neverland. The first four chapters of this book covered the general tools needed to get moving and unstuck; this chapter gets down to the nitty-gritty, which is why it's titled "Building Blocks." In this chapter, I'll teach you how to:

- become aware of your assumptions;

- understand that the only mind you can ever read is
  your own, so if you must make an assumption, assume
  something that makes you happy;

- realize that feeling good about feeling bad keeps you good
  and stuck;

- establish independence;

- buttress freedom with interdependence;

- stop yourself from blaming so that you can escape the past;

- recognize and avoid lose-lose games;

- practice niceness; and

- value hard work.

Beware of Your Assumptions

Humans have always made assumptions, from "the earth is flat" to "the sun and stars revolve around the earth" to "solar eclipses are the gods showing their wrath." Assumptions are often popular or convenient, but they're not always accurate or even helpful.

When our assumptions become personal, they're seldom positive—"I'm unlovable," "I just know that I'm going to get fired," and "It's always my fault" are examples of this kind of negativity, which is the natural by-product of believing that no matter what we do, we'll never be quite right. In this country, all of us grew up in a society that sells us things we don't need. If you're in advertising, the way to make people want your product is to convince them that they need it because of a flaw they have—they smell wrong, look wrong, and act wrong, which is why they're unhappy and no one will ever love them. But, miraculously, if these same losers use a particular mouthwash, buy a certain car, wear this brand of jeans, apply that hair color, or drink that kind of carbonated beverage, then *voilà!*—all of their problems will magically disappear and they'll become lovable.

So it's not surprising that we grow up feeling that we're not good enough. Fortunately, that's why adulthood was invented . . . so that if something isn't working, we can examine the assumptions inherent in these messages that have been handed down to us. If you're thinking, *Gee, does this have anything to do with self-awareness?* then good for you. You're paying attention. All of us make assumptions, but we're seldom aware of them. In fact, it usually isn't until somebody calls us on them that we even become aware of these flaws in our reasoning.

I'm not suggesting that we can live a completely assumption-free life. *Some* assumptions are necessary to function, for if every action had to be thought through, we wouldn't be able to do things like breathe. Assuming that gravity will keep our feet attached to the earth, for example, even though none of us have ever actually seen gravity, is a useful assumption. We just need to question the assumptions that get us in trouble.

Dangerous assumptions are based on a little bit of data leading to a giant leap, followed by a completely unreasonable conclusion. For instance, a third-grader might think, *I got the best grade in the class. That must mean I'm the smartest kid in the world.* Okay, this kid's made a major-league assumption based on some minor-league data. And as ridiculous as these assumptions sound once we articulate them, we have a whole bunch of them rattling around in our heads.

Not only do we make assumptions about our own behavior, but we do it about everyone else's behavior as well. For example, I once was on a plane headed for some exotic destination, and since I've never been crazy about flying, I was feeling a little tense. When I'm nervous, I talk, so my seatmate and I were involved in this great conversation for about 45 minutes . . . when I realized that he didn't speak any English. What I had done was ask a bunch of yes or no questions, and while this person didn't understand a word I was saying, he knew to say yes or no whenever I paused. True story.

The need to clear the air of any unwarranted assumptions holds especially true when we're talking about something as complicated as emotions. In such cases, clarity is crucial. For example, if you say to your husband, "Call if you're going to be late," you may think, *I'm being clear—what's not to understand?* Well, plenty. He may think you mean that he should call only if he's going to be really late, or that he should call by some specific time, or that he should just call at some point and apologize. In other words, when you tell him to call if he's going to be late, you assume that: (1) someone is paying attention to your timetable; (2) that the words "call" and "late" mean the same thing to both of you; and (3) that the request has the same weight for both of you. These assumptions can be costly.

Better communication with fewer assumptions is accomplished by saying: "If you're going to be more than 15 minutes late, please let me know, either in person, or by leaving a message on my cell phone. I know it might be an imposition for you to feel like you have to call me, but it would really help me out. This way, if I hear that you're going to be late, then maybe I'll take some more time to finish up what I'm doing." Now that's a very different kind of statement from "Call if you're going to be late," for it clearly makes your point in a few concise sentences.

❧ ❧ ❧

The more intimate the situation, the more dangerous assumptions can be. For example, Gillian's assumptions are crippling her relationship.

> *I've been seeing someone I adore for a few months now. We're great friends and have a good time, but we come from opposite poles. I have a child and am on good terms with my ex-husband; I've also lived with someone since I got divorced. This man I'm dating lived with his mother until he was 33 (he's 46 now). We have a lot in common, but he's only had a few relationships and none of them were very committed. He's very special—he calls me every night and we spend every weekend together—but I'm still meeting and dating other people because I never thought that I'd go out with someone in his 40s who hasn't been married. Is that silly? I'm worried that he can't sustain a relationship, so is it okay to go out with other people for this reason?*

> — Gillian, 43, Nashville, TN

Gillian, if your rule is "I won't date someone in his 40s who's never been married or had kids," then I have to wonder why you're wasting your time on this guy. Rules are either ironclad or they're not. It's like people who say, "I'll only marry someone who's Catholic like me, but I'm gonna go out with this Jewish guy." Why would you do that to either of you? If your rule is absolutely set in stone, then don't continue to date this man; if it's not, then enjoy going out with him and see what develops.

All of us have these little rules, Gillian. Remember when we were in high school? We had these impossibly long lists of attributes our dream guy absolutely had to possess—he had to be tall, dark, and handsome; be of a certain religion; make a certain amount of money; live in a certain part of the country; and look like a certain actor or rock star. Back then, we were young and stupid enough to think that dating was like going to a car dealership and ordering a new vehicle. Reality check: That's not what life's about.

Gillian, you can make whatever rules you want, but be sure that they make some sense. Is the rule "I won't date anyone in their 40s who's never been married" viable? There are lots of reasons why people don't get married—maybe they're late bloomers, took vows of chastity, never met the right person, got caught up in their careers, or were taking care of a sick parent. Who knows? But don't automatically assume that these people are all just emotional midgets.

It sounds like you enjoy being with this guy, but you've only been dating a couple of months. It's too soon to think about whether he's marriage material. It usually takes six to nine months to decide if the person you're dating is someone with whom you want to sustain a relationship. So instead of seeing other people, why don't you see this guy a little more and figure out if this is a relationship worth pursuing? See where you get in *this* relationship. Stop trying to be so far ahead. Stay in the moment. If you like being with this guy, be with him; if you don't, then break it off with him. But be true to yourself . . . and don't make assumptions that are encumbering both you *and* him.

Don't Worry, Be Happy

Recently, a distraught woman called me to complain that her husband gave her a dishwasher for her birthday. "If he loved me, he would have known that I didn't want that!" she cried.

"Well," I responded, "what if he had said that you should know that the dishwasher demonstrated his love by making your work easier?"

"What am I," she said, "a mind reader?"

This woman, like most of us, wanted it both ways. We tend to feel that if someone really loved us, they'd be able to read our minds. However, we're completely unwilling to return the favor, and we impatiently insist of them, "Just tell me what you want!"

As such, the signs of true love include, but aren't limited to, our partner's ability to know such things as:

- the exact dinner we want;

- the exact movie we want to see;

- the exact itinerary we have in mind for the evening;

- the exact sequence of sexual positions we'll find most satisfying; and so on.

These are pointless and dangerous games. The secret to good communication is knowing what you want *specifically,* and finding the words and the courage to ask for it. Asking doesn't guarantee that you'll get what you want, but it certainly increases the probability. Being wary of mind reading is part of understanding the dangers of assumptions.

I'm also of the opinion that if you're going to make assumptions, make ones that make you happy because making an assumption means that you're going out on a limb all by yourself. Now, if you're going to be out there all by yourself, why not at least make yourself happy? For example, if you're going to make assumptions about why so-and-so didn't call, why not assume that they're out there buying you some lavish gift, instead of inferring that they met somebody else and don't want to be with you anymore? This way, you'll at least be happy until you find out what actually happened. Sure, you might end up being disappointed, but why not at least enjoy a period of time when you're happy?

This reminds me of one of the very first clients I ever had. This woman had recently been widowed, and she was unhappy that I was young, female, and her therapist. In truth, I was probably too green to take her on because she was one of the angriest people I'd ever seen. I swear, every time she wiped her nose, I was absolutely sure that it was going to come off in the tissue.

I finally got her to the point where she was actually *talking* to me, instead of just crying and being furious. She excitedly told me that her grown son had just come home to spend Thanksgiving with her and her teenage daughter, and it was the first time I'd ever seen her anywhere near happy. Her eyes glowed as she told me how much she'd looked forward to her son's arrival, how much fun the dinner had been, how her daughter hadn't argued with her for days in anticipation, how the stuffing was perfect and the turkey was moist, and how everyone had a wonderful time.

But then she told me that in the middle of the meal she began to realize that the holiday would be over in a few days, her daughter would start acting up, her son would leave, and she'd be alone again. I could actually see the transformation unfolding before my very eyes—this woman had snatched defeat from the jaws of victory by making all of these assumptions that had no particular validity. Finally, she finished her story by saying, "So who cares, the holiday was ruined." Of course the holiday hadn't actually been ruined until she spoiled it herself—by focusing on a made-up, bleak future that made her miserable.

Clearly, the last thing my client wanted was to be disappointed. However, in her desperate and irrational attempts to head off the big letdown, she wound up creating just that. If she'd been able to either make no assumptions and just stay in the moment, or assume that this was the first of many wonderful Thanksgivings her family was going to share, then her holiday could have had a chance to unfold pleasantly.

Regina is a perfect example of someone who needs a good dose of positive thinking.

> *I've been married for 13 months now, and my husband and I have a four-month-old baby. We stopped having sex while I was pregnant—and we still haven't made love. I can't even bring myself to talk to my husband about it because I don't want him to think that he's obligated to do it. We dated for a year and half before we got married, and we certainly never had this problem before. I know he loves me, but I'm going out of my mind here.*
>
> — Regina, 26, St. Louis, MO

Assumptions say a lot about us and nothing about reality, but because we believe our assumptions, they end up *becoming* our reality—a reality that is often completely at odds with what another person is thinking or feeling. Regina, if you're going to assume *anything* here, assume the best-case scenario—that, like you, your husband really is interested in resuming your sex life, but he's just afraid to approach you about it.

The two of you got pregnant so soon that you didn't have a lot of time to settle into being a couple. If you didn't live together before marriage, then there were three huge adjustments to make right away: cohabiting, marriage, and pregnancy. At this moment, your husband could very well be waiting for *you* to give him some signal that you're ready to be sexual again. And if he's like many men, he may also feel that he has a rival in the house. A part of him is thinking, *This kid's got Regina's body. Hey, those are my breasts!* (I know, I know, this is an assumption on my part, but at least it's one that has been statistically borne out.)

In this society, we women grew up with the message that ladies should wait for men to make the first move, especially sexually. Now it's time to stop playing the blushing virgin, Regina—just pounce. I know it might feel uncomfortable, but I want you to call your husband at work and tell him that you're going to jump his bones tonight. You need to assume that everything is okay and proceed as if he's just waiting for you to come to him.

Victimology

Victimology is feeling good about feeling bad. I can hear you saying, "Why on earth would anyone ever do something so stupid?!" Well, some people feel that they have a lot to gain by this behavior, such as a ton of attention, a great deal of coddling, and the sense that by expecting the worst, they're somehow fully prepared for whatever may happen in life.

In fact, I'm convinced that 99 percent of my callers want me to say, "Oh, you poor thing! Here's a way to stomp on whoever is making you miserable and get away scot-free." When somebody's making us unhappy, we want them to stop—and if they won't cut it out, we want them to die . . . painfully and slowly. Okay, so this isn't our nicest characteristic, but it proves that deep down inside, we're all a teensy bit vindictive and a whole lot human.

The problem with the "poor me" mentality is that it gives away your power. Once you assume the role of victim, and someone's doing something terrible to you, there's that chance that they may stop and let you get on with your life. But if they do, it will have been for reasons that have nothing to do with you. It could be because they've decided to be nice, got bored bothering you, or suddenly felt guilty. There's also the chance that they won't stop—or if they do, they'll start up again whenever they feel like it. The point is that by laying all of the responsibility for your misery on someone else's shoulders, you give away all of your power to change the situation. It's much more difficult, but a lot safer, to ask, "Okay, what can *I* do?"

One of the very first on-air questions I ever had to deal with concerned schoolyard bullying, which is a classic example of victimology. I instructed the parent who'd called that they should tell their kid to befriend the bully. Right after that, somebody else called in and said, "That's the worst advice I've ever heard. What the kid should do is deck that bully!" The caller had a point—if a bully's realm is physical intimidation, don't be intimidated. Instead, try asking, "What are my options?" You could change schools, but the problem with viewing yourself as a victim is that you'll be victimized at any school you go to. Or you can decide to stand up for yourself. So now, my advice to kids who are being bullied is to try charm first. If that doesn't work, go take a few karate or boxing lessons, or get your dad or older sibling to show you how to fight. Sometimes just knowing that you won't be intimidated anymore is enough of a message. (Hey, countries have used this theory for centuries.)

Worst-case scenario is that you may have to challenge the bully and you might get punched. But you know what? In the world of living creatures, wounds occur, *but they heal.* Sure, getting hit is uncomfortable, but it's often less painful than the *fear* of getting hit.

Speaking of wounds, we humans tend to not only *be* victims but to *remain* victims by picking at old hurts and keeping them open. For instance, when relationships end, it usually feels terrible. If we go on and lead our lives, however, the wound will eventually heal, and the pain will go away. But no . . . we insist on going back to it, explaining why the other person is terrible, how we really loved them, and how they rewarded our devotion with treachery. We'll pick at that damned wound so that it never gets a chance to heal, when what we need to do is accept the fact that bruises, scrapes, cuts, scratches, and even scars are just badges of being alive. We have to learn from them and move on! In large part, that's what being a victim is about—never getting over our wounds, but keeping them fresh and raw.

❦ ❦ ❦

Al has kept himself a victim for years, while also shirking responsibility for his behavior. Nothing has improved, and he's stuck in a time warp of misery, self-flagellation, blame, and self-righteousness.

Ten years ago, I was engaged to a woman for two years.
She wanted a child, so I had my vasectomy reversed. The day

*of the wedding, she looked me in the eye and said, "I'm preg-
nant with your child, but I'm not going to marry you." Six
months later, I went to court, and I've been paying $1,200 a
month in child support ever since. Now I'm trying to
straighten my life out, going back and making amends. I
haven't seen this little boy because I was a father to three
kids from a previous marriage, and I knew how tough it is to
be a weekend dad. I didn't want to do it to that kid. But this
is really bothering me. I don't know what to do or where to
go from here.*

— Al, 58, Stamford, CT

I'm glad you're upset about this, Al. That's why the conscience
was invented—to make you itch when something needs to be
scratched. You can't undo what you've done, but you can come up with
a strategy, figure out what you want to do, and decide on the next step.

You want to relieve your painful conscience; *I* care about your
doing right by your kid. Interestingly enough, my concern about your
son and your concern about yourself can be served by the same function, which is why I want you to figure out what you want to do.
You've got to stop your narcissistic, self-centered self from hosting
this pity party for one. You have a responsibility.

Now, the kid's mom may have used you as a sperm donor, but
that's irrelevant at this point. You have a *child* here. If you didn't, if
this was just some woman who had taken you to the cleaners, that
would be one thing—you could lick your wounds, wallow in self-pity,
or even walk away. But you can't walk away from a child whom you
helped bring into existence. And giving yourself all sorts of reasonable-
sounding claptrap about being a weekend dad isn't going to change
anything—a weekend father is better than no father at all. You know
that, and I know that.

Try to make up for lost time with this kid. I don't know what kind
of reception you're going to get, but you have to do the right thing
here. Instead of feeling sorry for yourself and making up some non-
sensical background story that allows you to remain uninvolved, go

see your son. Apologize to him for being irresponsible, explain that you were hurt because you'd really wanted a wife, and that you weren't rejecting him because you'd never gotten in touch before. Then ask him what you need to do to be allowed into his life.

Don't try to be a father yet, since you haven't quite earned that right. But be a presence in the kid's life—perhaps as a friend or mentor—and maybe someday, with his permission, you can be his dad. But *get going on it.* Don't put it off—do it this weekend. This is the right thing to do. Start giving and see where it gets you. And Al, you're right . . . it *will* make you feel better.

❦ ❦ ❦

Dora provides another case of someone who has "Victim" practically tattooed on her forehead.

> *I have a 30-year-old stepson who fathered a child for a lesbian couple. Once in a while, he, the two women, and their 11-year-old son all come over to our house for the weekend. My problem is that when they come over, I feel uncomfortable because of the things these women say—it's almost as if they're trying to provoke me with their shocking statements— and also because I often don't agree with how my stepson acts around his son. What should I do?*
>
> — Dora, 52, Milwaukee, WI

Dora, maybe it's time to start asserting yourself. If the way these women talk is making you uneasy, try saying something like, "I really enjoy spending time with you, but I'm a bit old-fashioned and would appreciate it if you didn't use that particular phrase," or "This subject makes me uncomfortable." They may roll their eyes, but so what? Remind yourself that it's your home and you're entitled to set the ground rules and request a certain standard of behavior from people visiting you.

Okay, one issue down, one to go. Regarding your stepson and his parenting, we're talking about something completely different here. Just know that most folks are really touchy about being criticized on their parenting, so if you really wish to comment on something, be specific, offer an alternative, and make sure that this isn't just a stylistic difference between the two of you. Ask yourself if there's harm being done here; if you're convinced that your stepson is doing something truly wrong, explain your concern gently and specifically, picking your time and your words wisely so that your advice doesn't come off sounding like an attack.

Dora, make sure that you're aware of the danger of your passivity. If you're going to sit back and allow people to assault your sensibilities without saying something (I'm not suggesting you take up hollering—just be civil, specific, and calm), then it isn't okay to complain to your hairstylist, your friends, and random individuals in the grocery store about the rude folks you have to suffer gladly just to be allowed some time with your step-grandson. Communicate your feelings to the appropriate people rather than garnering sympathy from your friends.

Instead of complaining *about* those people who have done you wrong, Dora, complain *to* them. Tackle the problem by directing a few, well-chosen words to the right people with some hope of resolution, rather than continuing to play the victim by rehashing the situation to anyone who will listen. By staying silent and choosing the path of least resistance, you're ruining your own day. No one can make you feel uncomfortable without your permission. And just remember that not saying no is often just the same as saying yes. If you're going to be passive, you'd better choose people who want exactly what you want. Expecting someone to read our minds is a fast shortcut to misery.

Independence

Our lives are lived in the confusion between wanting to feel like we're like everybody else and hoping that we're not. Presumably, what makes us like everybody else is our desire for companionship;

our wish to love and be loved; and our need for food, sleep, relaxation, fun, giggles, and chocolate. Then again, we also have to understand what makes us unique, and most of us are amazingly unaware of where the distinctions lie.

For instance, shame is what makes us like everybody else. It's an unproductive emotion that isolates us—we don't talk about it, but all of us feel it. We all have something we don't like about ourselves, something we try to hide from other people. Once we begin to talk about it, however, the shame dissipates, and we understand that in those respects where we felt most isolated, we *are* just like everybody else.

On the other hand, what makes us unique is what we know. Now we're usually not even aware of this because we assume that everybody knows what we do—and what we don't know, we assume no one knows either. Both assumptions are equally false, but that's part of being an adult. As kids, we feel that we don't know jack and that adults bully us; as adolescents, we feel that we know everything. Adulthood is really about trying to figure out what about us is like everybody else and what makes us different.

I'm convinced that my radio program should be called "What's Normal and What's Not." It's extraordinary how many people don't know the difference. For instance, many people don't know that at some point, it's perfectly normal to dislike your kids and want to throttle them. Then again, actually smacking your kids is *not* normal. Once people understand normal *feelings*, they can work on controlling their *behavior*.

So part of our job as adults is to do an inventory of what separates us from others and what unites us. In addition, we have to find a way to stand on our own, which can certainly feel lonely and scary. Often it's much more comfortable to blame someone else for our dependence than to assert ourselves. "I can't be independent because [fill in the blank] won't let me." *Pshaw!* Independence isn't a gift—it's a choice. For everybody who says they have a controlling boyfriend or mother, my question is, "Why do *you* have to be so passive?"

For example, 19-year-old Tara called to complain, "Dr. Joy, I have this really nosy co-worker."

"Okay," I said. "You be the co-worker, and I'll be you."

"'How much money do you make, and how many hours do you work?'" she asked me.

"'My paycheck always comes on paper, and I work all day long,'" I replied.

"What are you talking about?" Tara asked, back in her own voice.

"That's my point, Tara. Just because someone asks a question doesn't mean you have to answer it."

"Well, then she'll be snotty to me," Tara complained.

"Look," I said, "you need to choose—either you're going to be dependent on her response to you, which means making her happy and you unhappy, or you're going to be independent of her, which means that you can make yourself happy, whether she's happy or not.

"Now," I continued, "if you want to find a middle ground, you can decide that you'll moderate her unhappiness *and* your happiness. You can say to her, for example, 'I really like you and would like to be your friend, but I'm a little shy about sharing personal information.'"

"But I *don't* like her," she said.

"Fine. But you still have to choose," I said. "Either you're going to be independent of her and her emotions toward you, or you're going to be dependent."

Again, this young lady was grappling with the same issues the rest of us face, such as "Where does someone else stop, and where do I begin?" That's the quintessential issue of adult life—what am I willing to do to get my own way, and how much am I willing to accommodate somebody else?

❦ ❦ ❦

Angie, another caller, brings up a point about the importance of independence as it relates to romantic relationships.

I just started dating this guy, and he's absolutely wonderful. But he told me he broke up with his girlfriend of two-and-a-half years about three months ago. It wasn't working out, and they decided to just be friends. Should I give this some time, or should I keep dating him and see how things go? We've had about five dates in the past week.

— Angie, 20, Berkeley, CA

Angie, if I said to you, "Why not let this guy go for a while; we all know it's much too soon," it's unlikely that you'd listen. So, realistically, I'd at least encourage you to slow it down. Five dates in one week is moving awfully fast, especially given his recent breakup. The main reason to let somebody recover from a long-term relationship is to give them time to evaluate the relationship and let go of baggage. You don't want to be unfairly compared to someone who isn't even in the picture anymore. For instance, if he loved the fact that his ex-girlfriend was a great cook, he may try to get *you* to start cooking for him, even if you're not a great cook and you don't want to prepare his meals for him. If she was sexually uninhibited, he might want the same (or the opposite) from you. Angie, you want this guy to see who *you are,* not be shadowed by who *she was.*

You want to allow for recovery, a period of time during which this guy gets over the bad stuff, integrates the good stuff, and becomes more stable in terms of what he wants a relationship with you to be. You both get a vote here, but a degree of stability is a lot more likely if he's *over* rather than *getting over* her. Try telling him something like, "I think you're great and this has been a fantastic week, but I'm a little nervous because you just got out of a relationship, so let's slow down and go on one date a week for a while." You don't have to dump him, but let both of you catch your breath.

Angie, people seldom call me when they're having a great time in a whirlwind romance—they call me when things start to go wrong. Right now, you're probably wondering, *What am I doing? This doesn't feel right.* Hence, your call. Trust your gut, and either tell him to slow down, or even better, promise to call him in a month after both of you have had some time to think.

❦ ❦ ❦

When we enter into a relationship, we "cathect," or invest emotional energy in another person. We become entwined with them. Different degrees of intimacy involve different degrees of involvement. For example, if you walk down the street and smile at someone, it's as if a little tendril comes from you to them. The third time you see them, you might approach them and say, "Hi, how are you?" And now there are more tendrils between the two of you, and some may be intertwining and thickening. When you shake their hand, hug, or have some sort of physical contact, that connection grows thicker still. By the time you meet for your first cup of coffee, tendrils start sprouting like crazy. So when we've been in a relationship with someone for a while, there's serious intertwining going on.

When that relationship ends (because of a breakup, a betrayal, a death), we're not like vacuum cleaners—we don't come equipped with a button that can make the tendrils come whipping back to us like a cord into a slot. Nope, instead we have to go through the lengthy and painful process of "decathexis,"pulling back our tendrils one by one, as we simultaneously deal with the holes left by our lover's tendrils. To feel intact and fit enough to enter into a new relationship, you need to have all those holes healed over so that you're your best self, neither guilty nor overly defensive, but intact and healthy.

Let's say your last love was always late, which drove you crazy, and you finally decided that it was so disrespectful that you had to dump him. Now you're in a brand-new relationship, and the "newie" is five minutes late. You're all over him like white on rice because you're still locked back in the relationship and the problem with your "oldie."

It might help to observe what I call the "One Year Rule." You see, as human beings, we're really very symbolic, so going through a Christmas, a New Year's Eve, a birthday, and a Labor Day on our own allows us to find who we are again. Take this time to be alone, to fill in and spackle those little holes in yourself and become whole. Also, keep in mind that you *choose* to have a person in your life—you don't *need* to have a person in your life.

Interdependence

If you're in a relationship, you're going to be affected by it, for better or worse. So how do we maintain our independence while in a relationship? The answer is *interdependence*—not dependence or independence, but a mixture of the two.

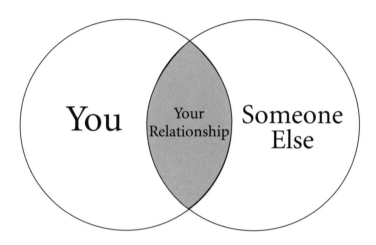

If you think of your life as a circle and your significant other's life as one, too, your relationship is that portion where the spheres overlap. That's where our lives intersect. For example, the intersection between employer and employee is from 9 to 5. So anything that happens between those hours affects both of you, but anything that happens outside that period of time is yours and yours alone. This means that your boss may never know your brother's name, you may not know the name of her mother, and the two of you may never have seen each other's homes. On the other hand, you may know way more about your boss's business than her husband does, and she may know more about your talent with numbers than your children do.

Now then, let's take this concept into a love relationship. I once got a call from Daniel, who said that his girlfriend of six months had been in a business relationship with a guy, and Daniel was afraid that what they were doing wasn't quite on the up-and-up. Daniel told her that she should stop, but she still continued to do business with this other man. He asked me, "What should I do about it?"

I told him that I didn't think any of it had much to do with him. After all, it's not as if she was asking him for money. He could certainly tell her, "I don't want to know about any of this," or "I'm not going to bail you out of jail if the business is shady," but her professional life fell outside of their intersection. It's possible that Daniel was jealous of her relationship with this other man, and that colored his perception, since if he really felt that his girlfriend was capable of immoral or illegal behavior, why was he willing to stay with her? If she had told *him*, "I think your boss is taking advantage of you, and I'm going to go talk to that SOB first thing in the morning," Daniel probably would have gone ballistic, and would have had every right to say to her, "This isn't your business—it has nothing to do with you, so stay out of it."

Part of Daniel's problem was that women tend to talk about their problems as a way of solving them, while men tend to feel that *If she's talking to me about a problem, she wants me to fix it.* So sometimes we women can give our men the idea that we're expanding that intersection of our two worlds, when all we're doing is venting. So I told Daniel to make a deal with his girlfriend: He wouldn't try to tell her what her business dealings should be, and she wouldn't confide in him about them anymore.

It's crucial to be very clear about the intersection of your lives and interests, so that you can focus on what's relevant to the relationship, not what isn't.

❀ ❀ ❀

Jenny needs to narrow the intersection between herself and her best friend if she is to maintain their relationship.

> *I've had a close friend for several years who is in the process of trying to have a second baby with her husband. Her first child is healthy but was born three months premature.*

I recently had a baby, and I had a wonderful pregnancy. Thinking of everything she went through made me thankful for having had such an easy time. But just a few weeks ago, my friend came to me to say that she was jealous of my pregnancy and my healthy baby. She automatically feels bad whenever I tell her about my baby, even though she knows I'm not doing it on purpose. I don't know what to do. This is a girl I've talked to every day since we met, and now I'm always the one calling—she never calls anymore. And when I do talk to her, she doesn't really have anything to say back. Is there anything I can do to keep her as a friend?

— Jenny, 30, Grand Rapids, MI

Jenny, this is a golden opportunity for you to expand your circle of friends and pick a new *baby* friend. It could be somebody from your Lamaze class or your play group, or that neighbor who pushes her stroller down the block at the same time of day as you. Go to the person you like best and ask her, "Can we have coffee on Thursday mornings and talk about our babies?" For now, you can share all that energy, enthusiasm, and wonder with someone who's just as excited about her baby as you are with yours.

You and your longtime friend can certainly continue your friendship . . . with an *adult* relationship that isn't based on babies, husbands, or formula. She's not going to be the least bit interested in *your* baby's earache because *her* baby was in an incubator that entire time, but the two of you do have pre-baby things and interests in common, and you can rediscover those together now. Call her and say, "I just got my first baby-sitter. Come with me to an art gallery—I need to stop feeling like a human milk bottle."

It's difficult, because while friendship is really resilient, and we want to be able to talk about everything that's most important to us, there are always imbalances that require us to divert our concerns somewhere else temporarily. Our friends don't have to be our mirror images, they just have to share some overlap in our lives.

Turn that Finger Around

Sitting out the blame game is the cornerstone of the getting unstuck process. The first way to stop blaming and start moving is to understand that none of us are perfect creatures. Most of us have been brainwashed—through Norman Rockwell prints, McDonald's commercials, and *Brady Bunch* reruns—to believe that perfection is an actual state of being. Wrong. Once you understand that nobody's perfect, you can stop beating up on yourself and everybody else when you come face-to-face with imperfect lives.

There's no such thing as perfection, only problems and solutions. So we need to problem-solve instead of blame, because assigning blame keeps us stuck in the past while making someone else angry or defensive *now*. Recognizing and solving problems, however, frees us to move forward without hurting or infuriating other people (or at least not as much).

In order to quit blaming and start getting unstuck, we need to recognize and overcome a basic human need—the desire to point a finger and punish instead of finding a remedy. Our entire legal system is based on finding crooks and punishing them for their behavior. And while that's a great way to keep social order, playing the role of detective, prosecutor, *and* judge in your own life won't bring you kudos or a guest spot on *20/20*. It will, however, bring you a lot more trouble than you ever bargained for.

※ ※ ※

Bill's blinding desire to point the finger is derailing him. Time to retire his blame game and get unstuck.

> *I own a contracting business, and the other day I came to the site to find $300 worth of equipment missing. There's no way that anyone other than one of my three employees could have taken it. I called one of them in, and he said that he'd never do such a thing. The second one said that he thought he*

saw an open window that somebody could have used to get on to the site and steal the equipment. And the third said that he'd have to be crazy to steal anything, since he has a wife and child to look after. Which one do you think did it?

— Bill, 49, Boise, ID

If I *had* to pick one, I'd guess that the employee with the ready-made excuse about an open window is the culprit, but would that really amount to anything resembling conclusive evidence? Nope. Not only would our guesswork not stand up in any court of law, but you wouldn't sleep any easier knowing that you'd based your decision upon such a sketchy premise.

As much fun as it is to play Sherlock Holmes to your Watson, Bill, given our limited knowledge of the circumstances, let's admit that we can't be sure about what happened here. Without the aid of a lie-detector test, uncovering the truth is iffy—any one of the three could have done it.

Instead of racking either of our brains for a definite answer, let's focus on your main motive for asking the question—to find a solution and get on with your life. You not only want to know the truth, but you want to act on it, too. The question isn't so much "Who did it?" as "What should I do about it?" Most likely, you want to blame the guilty party, fire the thief, and punish the criminal element, all in one fell swoop. And you have two perfectly good reasons for wanting to do so: (1) to avoid looking like a chump; and (2) to make sure that justice is done. Yup, probably even in that order.

Although it might seem like fuzzy logic to you, admitting that you don't know "whodunit" is the first step to achieving your primary objective. Saying "I don't know" is hard for all of us, but just consider the alternative: firing a perfectly innocent employee and letting a guilty one off. Bill, that's a one-way ticket to Chumpsville—not to mention the sleepless nights, bad reputation, and possible lawsuit this decision would engender.

That brings us to your second objective—making sure that justice is done. Seems noble, yes? Well, maybe, but justice is sometimes little more than gift-wrapped revenge, pure and simple. In your angry state, it's likely that you're looking for someone to blame, someone whom you can force to pay for your current problems, someone whose distress will make you feel better—in other words a "bad guy"—rather than justice per se. Bill, give it up. You don't know who's to blame and, at this rate, you never will. You've got to change your focus. Instead of trying to right past wrongs, concentrate on improving your current situation by: (1) asserting your authority; and (2) making sure that the employee doesn't steal from you again.

You see, a subtle shift in concentration—from dwelling on the past to working toward the future, from blaming to moving on—can give you the tools to make your problem disappear. Showing your employees who's boss and ensuring that the stealing doesn't happen again are the two positive outcomes that can result from what's obviously a very negative situation.

To achieve these worthwhile ends, you'll have to do some serious thinking. Impulse won't do here. The trick is to establish accountability. It's likely that the innocent employees know who's guilty and aren't coming forward for the simple reason that they have nothing to gain and don't want to be viewed as snitches. Trying to instill fear with empty threats and blind accusations will neither make you look good nor bring your equipment back, Bill. Instead, talk with all three employees, and then dock each one a third of the cost of the stolen equipment. I bet that this action will cause one of them to come forward with the information you need. If not, you'll at least be reimbursed for the costs and ensure that your equipment is safe in the future, since the innocent will now police the guilty.

Your question, however, does shed light on a basic human need—our desire to point a finger and punish others instead of finding a way to remedy the situation. It's much easier to look for a bad guy than to figure out a way to make the person, the situation, or ourselves better. When we lay blame and say, "You're wrong," we establish that "We're right"—that we didn't leave the window open, that we are good managers, that we were clear about job responsibilities, and so forth. Pointing the finger and playing the blame game will keep you stuck, Bill . . . you have the option now to *move.*

Don't Play Lose-Lose Games

It's amazing how often we get into situations where no matter what, everybody loses. This is what's known as a "lose-lose situation." Obviously, the best games to play are win-win games, situations where everybody walks away a happy camper. For instance, a woman once called me up to ask, "Do I have to go to my son's wedding?" I didn't even have to think about it. I said, "Absolutely. Why wouldn't you?" And she said, "Hell, it's expensive." So I told her, "This is your *son.* And if you don't go to the wedding, you're going to feel terrible that day, and so is he—everybody loses. Why would you do that? On the other hand, if you go to his wedding, you'll feel good and he will, too."

There's also something called a "zero-sum game," where somebody has to win and somebody has to lose. The idea at the root of this game is that if we win, someone else has to lose or vice versa. Somehow we don't mind losing so much if everybody loses (which is a ridiculous philosophy), but we're damned if we're gonna stand by and watch someone else win. If we're gonna lose, we're taking everybody down with us. That's the definition of a lose-lose game, and it gets us nowhere.

❦ ❦ ❦

Maggie demonstrates a classic example of a lose-lose game—pursuing unwinnable arguments to prove a point.

I'm calling on behalf of my mother, who's 81 but can't hear very well on the phone. My younger brother is coming to spend some time with her. He's had two marriages and one long-term relationship, all of which he ended because he believed they were cheating on him. Finally, he had a nervous breakdown, which led him to seek treatment. He was ultimately diagnosed as being pathologically jealous. My mother and I don't know how to support him because we really feel that he needs more help. What should we do when he tries to convince us that he's been right all along?

— Maggie, 57, Billings, MT

Let's just assume for a moment that you and your brother have radically different views on politics. What would you do if he tried to engage you in a debate? You'd probably say something like, "Let's agree not to talk about this. I'll talk to you about anything you want, with the exception of politics." Your mother can do the same thing with this issue. She can say, "Okay, I just won't talk to you about your marriages. We disagree, let's leave it at that."

I can hear you saying that this is easier said than done. Isn't everything? Yes, your brother may keep trying to bring this issue up, and when he does, you and your mom can keep changing the subject. You don't even have to be sly about it—you could simply say that you'd rather talk about something else.

Maggie, this is one of those situations that can't be won, so get off the playing field. To do that, you and your mother have to give up the notion that you're right and that you have to convince your brother. But if you guys *can* overcome your desire to prove him wrong, your mom can tell him, "I'm really looking forward to your visit. Let's agree ahead of time that we're not going to talk about your marriages, because I know it makes both of us unhappy." Problem solved.

Smile, Be Nice

Somewhere along the line, we've made irony and sarcasm the central characteristics of our national character. We got the notion that ugly is best—that the bigger, meaner, and more violent we are, the cooler we must be; that being nice and turning the other cheek are signs of weakness; that rudeness is a valuable tool, and being nice is strictly for wimps and fools.

Wrong! Lashing out is the easiest thing in the world to do because it's what we're naturally inclined to do. When someone says something that hurts us, what we instantly want to do is hurt them back. Anyone can allow their anger to get the best of them because that doesn't require any particular intelligence, sophistication, or self-control. What's much more difficult is to turn the other cheek and be pleasant in the face of hostility. Wars are easy to start. But if you hit me, hitting you back makes it very likely that you're gonna hit me again. To think before acting on impulse, and to figure out why that person hit in the first place and what made them so angry that they were willing to lash out is the ultimate test of strength, self-discipline, and general good-guyness.

Mahatma Gandhi spent his life stressing the importance of peace and nonviolence. Centuries earlier, Buddha taught how to counter anger with passivity, action with stillness, agitation with calm. The fact that negativity can be diffused by kindness, sweetness, or, at the very least, serenity, is surprisingly effective in social interaction. Saying, "He started it!" is a legitimate rationalization when you're five years old—although it always got me sent to my room—but it's not a particularly mature or effective technique. This isn't an invitation to go to the land of the victim. You can be assertive without being aggressive and calm without being a coward. Taking the high road is much more difficult, sophisticated, and complicated—it's also much cooler than being ugly in return.

❧ ❧ ❧

Ashley has every reason to act out. Faced with her situation, many people would opt for negativity, anger, and resentment. Fortunately, Ashley doesn't simply react; instead she's thoughtful and reflective enough to focus on solving the problem.

My father left my mom about five years ago for another woman, and he's still seeing her. Lately, he's been asking me to go out with the two of them. I really don't like her, and I can't see myself being around her because of what's happened. But he's pushing the issue. He doesn't have a lot of time, and he's been doing things with her rather than with me—it almost seems like he's choosing her over me. I was wondering what I can say so that he understands that my feelings have really been hurt. He says that he's not serious about her, so what should I do?

— Ashley, 16, St. Paul, MN

I know you that don't want to hear this, kiddo, but your dad's girlfriend isn't the "bad guy." The person to be mad at isn't her; it's your dad. Presumably, if it hadn't been her, it would have been someone else. Your dad just didn't behave very responsibly. Now, I'm not dumping on your dad; I'm just saying that being mad at the girlfriend is kind of a waste of energy, and you're displacing what is rightfully your dad's responsibility onto her.

If your dad left your mom for this woman five years ago and he's still with her, he's making her a part of his life. I agree that his telling you he's not serious about her is confusing, so let's temporarily ignore that mixed message and focus on the real issue here. If you don't want to spend time with your dad's girlfriend, that's okay. But, rather than focusing on the negative, which is "I don't want to be with that witch," you can say, "Dad, I'll bet that you probably wouldn't want to spend time with me and my boyfriend—not because you don't like him, but because it's nice to have some one-on-one time just with me. I can understand that. So let's see if we can't find some time for just the two of us to go to the movies, have a pizza, or take a walk and talk."

Keep focusing on the positive. Don't whine, "You're always picking her over me." After all, given a choice between having dinner with your dad or with your boyfriend, you'd probably choose your boyfriend. It doesn't mean that you don't love your dad; it's just that hormones are serious stuff, even when you're a grown-up. Focus on the positive without griping and without commenting about her. And if your dad should show up with her, then you're old enough to be charming and polite rather than a stinker about it. If nothing else, it will surprise everyone and be a lot more fun for you.

Ashley, your dad might not win any "Father of the Year" awards, and you may feel that he's acting more like an adolescent than you are, but he is who he is. Your goal is to spend time with him because your life will work better if your dad is part of it, even if it's a dad who tends to be a bit goofy sometimes.

Hard Work

On some unconscious level, we believe that good people have it easy, that they don't have to work so hard, and that their goodness will be rewarded. If, on the other hand, you're going through a rough patch, it's difficult not to believe that it's because you're not smart enough or because you don't deserve to succeed. To further complicate matters, our society has a stubborn and longstanding belief in luck. So we tend to believe that good people have good luck, and bad people have bad luck. This is a contradiction—because even as we assume the existence of luck, we maintain that we make our own luck by being good or bad people.

Debunking this myth is as straightforward as pointing out that success and luck are not one and the same. What most of us think of as "luck" is actually the fruit of hard labor. Haven't you noticed that the luckiest people tend to be the hardest working? That's what we need to remember, because it's not luck but hard work that makes us feel good about and value ourselves.

We need to figure out what's difficult for us, because something that comes easy to someone else may be difficult for us, and vice versa. This goes back to our understanding of how we're like everybody else and unlike everybody else. When something doesn't come easily to us, we must embrace it, not beat ourselves up about it. In the end, it's hard work that takes us beyond the boundaries we thought we had, defines us by changing our perception of ourselves, and enhances our lives by showing us our true potential.

❧ ❧ ❧

Barbara finds herself in a difficult position. She wants to protect her grandson by taking the easy way out, but what she needs to realize is that the easy way is quite often not the best way.

> *I need some advice. I'm the guardian of my eight-year-old grandson who has cerebral palsy. The court wouldn't let my daughter keep him because of her alcohol and drug abuse. At first, I had joint custody with my brother who lived in Georgia, so my grandson lived with him and his wife from the time he was eight months old until my brother passed away four years ago. At that time, my sister-in-law called and said that she couldn't take care of my grandson anymore, so he came to live with me full time. Now she's in town and would like to see him, but I've been vacillating back and forth. Can you give me any advice as to what to do if he says, "I wanna go back home to Georgia"?*

— Barbara, 53, Raleigh, NC

Barbara, she gets to see him—not so much for her sake but for his. It's not going to be easy on you, and it's not going to be easy on your grandson, but he needs to have the sense that people don't just disappear from his life. After all, his birth mother and father did, and his acting mother and father did, so yes, he has to see your sister-in-law. I'm not guaranteeing that it won't be somewhat upsetting to him, but I think that the short-term upset will be worth the long-term sense that people don't just stop loving him and they all won't just suddenly disappear from his life.

If your grandson says that he wants to go back to Georgia, you can explain that sometimes we want things that don't make much sense or work very well. For instance, he may really want a gerbil, even though he really can't take care of one. Through this analogy you can help him understand, in his vernacular, that your sister-in-law really loves him but she just can't take care of him. You can understand that he would miss her and that she would miss him, but it's kind of like his trying to take care of a gerbil—it's not that he wouldn't love it, it's just that the gerbil would suffer because he can't take proper care of it.

Your sister-in-law is the woman he knows as his mom. You have to make him understand the truth, which is that she loves him but she just can't take care of him. And that's why it's really important, Barbara, that he be able to see her so he has the sense that she still loves him, and that she hasn't just disappeared from his life. Because this kid, in his eight little years, has had two moms disappear on him, and that's a lot of sadness for such a little soul.

Playing Doctor

This chapter covered nine important life skills that can dramatically improve functioning. In this section, you'll get a chance to use the skills you've learned to solve other people's problems. Before you do that, however, you might want to give yourself a quick pop quiz: What were the nine building blocks discussed in this chapter? Once you've got a solid grasp on these, you can try your hand at helping the following callers.

> *My ex owes me $15,000 in back child support, and with my 19-year-old about to go to college, I'm feeling the crunch financially. The problem is that my ex is homeless—he's an alcoholic who lives out of his car or stays with friends. I'm worried about the message that this is sending to my son about responsibility. Should I try to take his father to court for the child support?*
>
> — Susan, 49, Iron Mountain, MI

1. What advice would you give Susan?

   (a) Forget the whole thing.
   (b) Take the deadbeat to court and get a lien against him.
   (c) Wait until her ex gets his act together before approaching him about child support.
   (d) Keep her son away from his father until she gets the money she's owed.

The correct answer is "c." Susan's taking her ex to court and putting a lien against him (choice "b") isn't going to incite him to shape up; it's only going to make him feel more frustrated and powerless. I mean, this guy is drowning, so taking him to court really won't accomplish much.

Choice "a" is wrong because Susan really is due some money, and to forget the whole thing would mean to let her ex off the hook—*if* he's ever capable of repaying her. And choice "d" is also an example of a lose-lose game. There's no way that Susan should make both her son and his father suffer because she's not getting her due financially.

Choice "c" is the option that works best here. Susan needs to wait until her ex is on solid ground before approaching him about the money. And the message that he's sending to their son by not paying child support is irrelevant here—the guy is homeless! The only message her son needs to learn is the one about the dangers of alcohol when you're genetically prone to it. What's relevant is that there's nothing to get. Susan's ex may or may not be a bad guy, but he's certainly on a downward slide, so to go out, pay a lawyer, insult her ex, and still wind up empty-handed is the very definition of a lose-lose game.

❦ ❦ ❦

Recently, I found someone with whom I'm very compatible, but she's mourning her love of 15 years (who died almost three years ago) and doesn't want to be in a committed relationship. I'm 84 and she's 77, so I'm running out of time. Should I break up with her?

— Sal, 84, Newport, RI

2. How would you answer Sal's question?

   (a) Make a quick and clean break so that you don't run out
       of time with nothing to show for it.
   (b) Try to get closer to her. Persistence pays off, so if you push
       her, she may decide to commit to you.
   (c) Break up with her, and then try to make her jealous by flirting
       with her friends.
   (d) Don't worry about running out of time. Just respect her wishes,
       give her the space she needs, and date around for now.

The correct response is "d." For now, Sal should view this
woman as a friend with potential and check out his other options.
Sal is making two questionable assumptions: first of all, that his
hourglass is about to run out of sand; and second, that looking for
someone else doesn't mean that he'll find anyone he likes. These
are the two key reasons that choice "a" is wrong. Choice "b" is also
wrong because Sal can't move this woman closer, but he can certainly
back off a little bit and date around while she's in mourning and trying to figure out her feelings for him. Choice "c" is patently wrong
because it's a lose-lose game. Trying to make this woman jealous
would only result in upsetting her and making her less likely to trust
Sal in the future.

Shrink Wrap

Faulty assumptions, lose-lose game players, and issues of independence are a normal, if uncomfortable, part of everyday life—but
by recognizing these obstacles, learning life skills, and seeing options,
we can minimize their wear and tear on our hearts, heads, stomachs,
and relationships. We can do this by recognizing the following:

- **Assumptions are dangerous,** so pay attention when
  someone challenges yours—it may be a sign that you
  need to reevaluate, even if it feels crummy.

- **If you have to make an assumption, assume something that makes you happy.**

- **Stop complaining and do something** to make yourself feel better in the long run, rather than settling for the role of victim when you notice yourself feeling good about feeling bad and trying to win sympathy from people.

- **Think about who you are,** and how that makes you similar to and different from everybody else.

- **Figure out what aspects of your relationships are vital** to the maintenance of those relationships, then focus on improving them instead of worrying about things that are irrelevant.

- **Get out of the past** by learning to stop blaming and start problem solving.

- **Avoid playing lose-lose and zero-sum games.** Everybody *can* be a winner.

- **Redefine the term *cool* so that it means being nice—** because what we often think of as cool (aloof, snotty, uncaring) gets us nowhere.

- **For every bit of good luck, there's a bit of bad.** In the end, it's not luck that's responsible for success, but hard work.

STEP 6:
❧ GOALS ❧

I've been with my boyfriend for about six months now. When we started dating, we agreed to talk about living together after seven months. Although I have several piercings and a couple of tattoos, I'm actually a very traditional kind of girl at heart. I know it's too early for us to be talking marriage, but I want him to know that, after we've lived together for a couple of years, I will want to marry him. How do I express my intent for marriage without having it sound like an ultimatum?

— Antoinette, 25, Charleston, WV

Antoinette, how about telling him what you just told me, but after *he* brings the issue up? If he doesn't do it soon (say, within the next month or so), you can get more information by asking, "Should I assume that since you haven't brought up the idea of moving in together, you've changed your mind or your timetable?"

If, however, he *does* bring up living together, this would clearly indicate that you're both on the same wavelength. Plus, you'll be able to avoid the Ultimatum Ursula role, or the girl-does-all-the-work thing. He'll be saying, "This is something *I* want to do." Yeah!

At that point, you can say, "I'd really love to move in with you, but I want us to make sure that this means the same thing to both of us. I need you to know that as far as I'm concerned, this will be sort of a marriage with training wheels. It's an opportunity for us to sort out whether we can be happy with each other forever. I think we should sit down at the end of our first year of cohabitation, have a conversation similar to this one, and decide to get married, go our separate ways, or put off the marriage decision for another year. What do you think?" And you can sweetly and sincerely add, "The last six months have been the happiest of my life. I would love to move in with you, but just understand that, in spite of all my piercings and tattoos, I'm an old-fashioned girl. I don't want to be living with you when I'm 90; by then, I want to have been married to you for a gazillion years."

As women, we often do too much (if not all) of the work in a relationship, which results in our feeling ripped off and men feeling pushed around, incompetent, and irrelevant—since we seem to be perfectly capable of doing the whole relationship thang on our own. But Antoinette, you can and should be honest with your guy. You're talking about sharing your rent, your bed, your body, and your nose ring with him . . . so share what's going on in your *head*—along with some of the responsibility for this relationship.

❧ ❧ ❧

Antoinette's goal is pretty straightforward—she wants to get married. Her boyfriend, on the other hand, may want to live with her strictly for her companionship, culinary expertise, beautiful singing voice, or so his mom will finally stop asking if he's gay. Or, he may also be looking to settle down and start raising a brood of tiny tattooed tykes. In any case, each person involved in this relationship must be able to articulate their goals to see if they match or clash.

Before two people can have a relationship, both need to understand what "behavior" means to both. To accomplish this, each person has to be honest and forthright about their goals, hopes, dreams, expectations, and even fears.

Since we're already six chapters into this book, you may be wondering why we haven't tackled something as basic as goals before. That's because before we can look ahead, we've got to: shift our focus from the past; extricate ourselves from patterns; become aware of who we are; gain perspective; and acquire some basic life skills. Whew! And this is just the preliminary stuff!

Now's the time to check out our metaphorical boat to ensure that it's seaworthy, that navigational aids are on board, that we know how to read the charts, and that we're truly ready to cast off the lines and pull away from the pier. Now the question is, "Where are we going?" That's what this chapter is all about . . . *direction.*

We'll talk about understanding your goals so that you're neither so far from land (and the here-and- now) that you don't know what to do next, nor so oblivious to any future port that your actions wind up causing you foreseeable problems down the line. Here's where we discuss what to do *next*—the next act, the next day, and the next rela-tionship—so that you're not just reacting, but actually formulating what you want and going after it. To be goal oriented, it's crucial to do the following:

- understand the difference between tactics and strategies;

- be more specific in your plans;

- incorporate the Serenity Prayer into your life;

- set both short- and long-term goals; and

- revisit old goals and figure out if they're still what you want.

Strategies vs. Tactics

All of us need to be both tacticians *and* strategists in our lives. Tacticians decide what to do next; strategists decide what to do when there's nothing you *can* do. For example, if your kid has just called you from jail to plead, "Can you come and bail me out?" you're in need of a tactic, *pronto.* Do you: (1) bail him out; (2) bail him out with conditions; or (3) call your spouse, a bail bonds person, or a lawyer? These are all *tactics.* A *strategy,* on the other hand, is, "How do I help my child grow into a better person, one who doesn't call me to bail him out of jail in the middle of the night, or even better, someone who isn't in jail in the first place?!"

The answer to the second set of questions is a lot more time-consuming, thought-provoking, and just plain difficult than figuring out a tactic. A strategy is often a long, sustained campaign planned with military precision. It's a long-term perspective on what you're trying to accomplish (your objective), and tactics are the steps you take to move closer to that objective.

The reason we need both strategies and tactics is because, in times of crisis, most of us tend to be less than analytical. An event that demands immediate action—such as your kid calling from a holding cell or your girlfriend telling you she's leaving you for someone else—seldom offers the luxury of sorting through alternatives, talking to somebody like me, or even calling on the most rational part of yourself. Quite often, you just have to decide what to do next. And it's your strategy that guides your tactics, telling you where to put your armies and your resources. It reminds you of your long-term goal, and it's what will help to make your tactics more focused and effective.

Perhaps the best way to describe the difference between strategy and tactics is to say that strategy is more of a mind-set, while tactics are a set of behaviors. One of the pitfalls of strategizing is the seduction of abstractions: "I want to have a good life" might seem like a strategy, but it's actually a waste of breath. A statement such as, "To me, a good *life* means good *health,* so I'm going to stay fit, lower my cholesterol, and lower my blood pressure" has an objective, a strategy, and tactics to boot!

Generals, politicians, and publicists are all engaged in the art of strategies and tactics. They break down their campaigns around objectives (a.k.a. goals), strategies, and tactics. Here's how it works. First, you must decide your objective. In this case, it's "To be very healthy." You might write down a list that looks something like this:

Objective: To Be Very Healthy

Strategy	**Strategy**	**Strategy**
• Stay fit	• Lower cholesterol	• Lower blood pressure
Tactics	**Tactics**	**Tactics**
• Exercise	• Decrease fatty food intake	• Reduce salt intake
• Eat healthier	• Take cholesterol-lowering drugs	• Reduce stress
• Reduce calories		• Meditate daily

Tactics may not be obvious, but with a strategy (which often reduces the anxiety and randomness of choosing tactics), they often emerge organically as you go along. A tactic is more than just reacting—it includes planning, understanding, direction, feasibility, efficiency, and, *voilà!*—the very real possibility of success.

Be More Specific

The more precise you can be about your goals, the clearer you're going to be, both to yourself and others. I'm a great fan of specificity and an absolute foe of abstraction. I ended up learning this lesson firsthand soon after I became a psychologist. The Commonwealth of Massachusetts enacted Chapter 766 of the Public Education Law, which mandated mainstreaming special-needs children and adults to be productive citizens within society as a whole. The state asked licensed psychologists to draw up plans for each individual, which could then be implemented by nonprofessionals. At the time, I had no money—but I *did* have student loans and a brand-new Ph.D., marriage, and baby, so I thought, *Wowee! This has got my name written all over it! I think logically, I'm a problem-solver, and I'm a licensed psychologist. Quick, easy money, and I get to do a good deed at the same time. What a way cool thing for me to do!*

My first client was Darryl, a charming 18-year-old man with Down's syndrome. After interviewing him, I thought, *Well, all he really needs to do is become more self-sufficient.* So I wrote up this wonderful report that essentially said, "Darryl needs to become more self-sufficient." Done! A week later, while serenely awaiting my first check, the report bounced back to me, with "Be more specific" written across it in huge red letters. Mind you, I didn't get paid a cent until my *entire* report was accepted, so I didn't waste any time writing about the extent of Darryl's verbal skills, his level of functioning, and his IQ-test results. It was returned again: "Be more specific." I rolled my eyes and proceeded to delve into Darryl's hand-eye coordination as well as what I'd observed about his personality. Busted: "Be more specific."

I'll spare you the reams of paperwork that went back and forth between the Commonwealth of Massachusetts and myself, all of which was based on their telling me to "Be more specific," and my trying to satisfy this demand. Suffice it to say that by the time my report finally was accepted, I could describe exactly how Darryl needed to put on a sock. Saying, "Put on a sock" was not good enough for them. Oh no, *I* had to explain that in order to put on a sock, a person would sit on a chair with their knees bent and both feet flat on the floor, that they would then proceed to shift their weight onto their right haunch, move their right hand from the shoulder down their leg, move their left hand over . . . I could go on and on, but I think you get the idea. To make a long story short, this description of how to put a sock on one foot took something like four pages, with 25 lines per page.

Even though I was irritated beyond measure, and I'm sure all of you reading this are thinking, *What a bunch of bureaucratic idiots!* the good people of the Commonwealth of Massachusetts did have a point. When I said, "This person has to become more self-sufficient by learning to dress himself appropriately," what did that mean?! The statement begged a few questions: (1) What does "appropriately" mean? (2) what does "dress" mean? and (3) how do you help someone who doesn't know how to dress himself to do just that?

The entire exercise helped me grasp exactly how much we take for granted in this world, as well as how large most of our concepts are and how useful it is to be able to break them down. By the end of my experience with this, I became so precise about Darryl that I could specifically describe the upper left quadrant of his left nostril. When *you* can become this precise, you'll know exactly what your next tactic is. Now the only way to get to the point where you can turn strategy into tactic is to make your strategy as specific as possible. For instance, "Helping somebody become more self-sufficient" becomes "Helping somebody become more self-sufficient by teaching him to dress himself." Refined even further, the strategy becomes, "Helping someone become more self-sufficient by teaching them to dress themselves for a workplace environment in underwear, socks, button-down shirt, pull-on pants . . . "

The moral of the story is that when you're thinking about strategy and tactics, write "Be More Specific" at the top of your mental list, for specificity is the key to problem solving. We human beings tend to take molehills and make them into the Himalayas, when it makes much more sense to knock those suckers down to gravel. Whining "My boss has always hated me" is taking a problem and turning it into an insurmountable obstacle—now we're stuck and we can't problem-solve. On the other hand, "My boss came into my office and said that he didn't like it that I was coming in late every day" is a manageable problem that you can get around, for now you know exactly what to do next.

Taking a huge challenge and making it small is the secret to effective problem solving, and the only way to do that is to be as specific as possible. I went from saying, "Make Darryl more self-sufficient" to detailing how he puts on a sock. This means that a good-hearted soul could actually be taught how to instruct somebody to put on a sock because I'd thought it through enough to be useful to both teacher and student. All in all, that's how I went from being an expensive extravagance to helping people figure out both strategy and tactic.

❦ ❦ ❦

At first glance, it might appear that Yvette has quite a dilemma on her hands. So it's time to break this behemoth of a problem down into manageable, bite-sized strategies and tactics.

>*My brother Isaiah is 12 years old, and I have to decide if I want to take him from my mother. She's 41, works two jobs, and lets him run the streets. She's apparently too busy to take him to the doctor, even though he's developed a benign tumor on the side of his face. He's already been held back twice in school, and my mother hasn't gone to a single one of his parent-teacher conferences. But I know he would listen to me because he respects me. He also looks up to my husband and minds him really well. But my husband will only agree to take him in if my mother gives us legal guardianship, and I don't think she wants to do that. If we don't take him, I'm afraid I'm going to lose him to the streets, which is what happened with my other brother. How can I make sure this doesn't happen to Isaiah?*

>— Yvette, 23, Hawthorne, CA

Let's just play this out a little bit, Yvette. First of all, your brother is old enough to be given some degree of choice in his living arrangements by most courts. If you think that he'll come to you voluntarily, pursue the course that creates the least upheaval in the family. Presumably, Isaiah loves his mom and loves you—therefore, if you can work it out so that everybody agrees, it would be easier than having to go to court. Here's what I suggest you do:

- Make sure Isaiah is willing to live with you.

- Be certain that your husband agrees that you don't necessarily need permanent guardianship right now.

- Talk to your mother about it.

If Isaiah *does* want to live with you, and your husband agrees to take him with temporary rights, then you can approach your mother about signing an informal document granting you those rights. This will probably be the hardest part, but be as sensitive and tactful as you can. Try to say something like, "Ma, I know that you're working really hard, but we'd really love to have Isaiah live with us for a while. He gets along so well with my husband, and there's a special program at school that we think he'll do great in."

In other words, the point isn't, "You're an incompetent idiot of a mother!" but "This might be good for us all—how about if we try it for a semester?" If you tell your mother that she's a mess, then she's naturally going to lash out and fight you; if you present your case in an orderly, nonjudgmental, nonthreatening way, then you'll leave the door open to an amicable resolution where everyone agrees. Don't base your strategy on forcing your mom to admit that she's not a good parent. Admitting our errors isn't one of those things we humans do best, especially when it comes to parenting.

Your mother may feel that it's okay for Isaiah to live with you if he won't wind up hating her. Fortunately, you don't have to make her the villain to make this a good situation for him. In fact, you can set up weekend visitations with Mom to assure her that she's still loved and important. Spend the next couple of weeks being very diplomatic, Yvette. You have to convince three people—your brother, your husband, and your mom. If you tackle this systematically, everyone can walk away happy.

The Serenity Prayer

Teaching people to change their lives by appropriate action is the goal of psychology, religion, the penal system, self-help groups, your grandmother, this book, and Alcoholics Anonymous (AA). AA has distilled their credo down to its essence in the Serenity Prayer: "God grant me the serenity to accept the things I cannot change, courage to change the things I can, and wisdom to know the difference."

It's extraordinary how often we confuse what we can change with what we can't. Clearly, it's the *wisdom to know the difference* that's the trickiest. When you're confronted with a problem, instead of taking all your energy and essentially dumping it down the Black Hole of Calcutta, ask yourself, "Is there something *I* can do here?" The emphasis is on the "I," so if you find yourself wondering, *Can I change someone else's behavior?* or *Is there something they can do?* you're way off track.

If there *is* something you can do, then find the courage to do it— discover that resolve within yourself (this is why we spent so much time on self-awareness and your safe place earlier in the book). Recently, a woman called my radio program and said, "My husband makes me responsible for his four-year-old daughter, and we've only been married for two years." It turns out that he'd started dating her when the child was only a few months old and he was still living with the mother. Now we already know he's a creep, but making him a better dad seemed worth the effort. My response to the caller was: "Why don't you point out to him that while you're flattered to be a positive influence in his child's life, the really important person in her life is Daddy, not Daddy's wife. Explain that you're willing to facilitate the father-daughter relationship by being generous about his time with her, cooking for both of them, or going to the movies with them if he wants, but that you're not the one she cares about."

"Well, I've talked to him about it," she said. "I told him that this child really needs to be with him. And he said, 'I pay you money, so do as I tell you.'"

Yikes! This woman had never focused on the real issue, which wasn't her stepdaughter, but her marriage.

"The problem isn't how he treats you as a baby-sitter, but how he treats you in general. I'm afraid you've married a thuggish bully, and you need to decide what you're going to do about it," I firmly told her. "His little girl isn't the problem. In misdiagnosing the problem, you'll miss the difference between the things you can and can't change. You can't change his behavior toward his four-year-old, but by looking at how he treats *you*, you can decide if you're willing to tolerate it or stand up to your husband."

Talk about not knowing the difference between what you can change and what you can't! Could this woman ever change her husband's behavior? Probably not. But can she change her tolerance for his behavior? She damned well better.

❧ ❧ ❧

Expecting people to do what we want is unrealistic. Once you accept that you can't change someone else's behavior, you can start looking for the courage to change your own. Debbie is a perfect example of this.

> *My 18-year-old son got a 15-year-old girl pregnant. The entire time, she was saying it was his, and he was saying it wasn't. They went to court, and the baby did turn out to be my son's. I told him all along that if it was his child, it's my grandchild and I want to be involved. Now the mother has a new boyfriend, and they're after my son. They tried to run him off the road the other night, and she goes around saying that she's going to "get him" because she's mad at him for not seeing the baby, even though he does pay child support. Meanwhile, I've taken the baby in with open arms, baby-sitting and just really loving that baby, but I don't know how I can keep helping the mother while she's going around badmouthing my son and lying to my face.*
>
> — Debbie, 40, Omaha, NE

Debbie, if you can let go of all of those judgments you have, you can come out of this with a grandbaby that you adore. The baby may have lunatic parents, but that's partly because they're so young. Your job isn't really to judge either of them—even if one of them is your son. As a grandparent, it's your choice to baby-sit or not, but if the mother badmouths your son to you, instead of arguing, defending, pouting, or storming out, just say, "He's not perfect, but he's my son and I love him, even if I don't always approve of his behavior. You're a mom now, so you'll understand this one of these days, too."

Remember, you're dealing with a teenager. At this moment, you're awfully easy on your son and pretty hard on the baby that he got pregnant. *She was 15 years old!* Calling her an irresponsible, crazy kid, when your son not only impregnated her but walked away, makes it easy to judge someone else's kid rather than your own Mr. Less-Than-Perfect, Debbie. He had unprotected sex with a minor, lied about being the baby's father in the first place, and is now happily shirking his responsibilities rather than stepping up to the plate to be a male presence in his child's life. If you want to lecture a child, lecture your own.

You can't control this girl any more than you can control your son. They created this mess, and they're the ones who are going to have to work it out. *You* have no place in this equation. What you have to do is to decide whether or not you're going to be a grandparent to your grandchild. You could decide to punish the mother by neglecting the child, but that won't help anyone. Instead, realize that while you can't do anything to make the mother nicer to your son or your son nicer to his baby's mother, you can change your attitude toward the mother and open your mind to the facts, which are:

- Your son isn't an innocent party in all of this.

- There are two sides to this story.

- Your best bet is to keep your opinions to yourself.

- The people who will suffer the most from your decision not to help your grandbaby's mom are you and your grandchild.

- You can win a grandbaby—and likely the undying appreciation (and maybe even affection) of a very young, confused, frightened 16-year-old mother—by being a charming, nonjudgmental, loving, *mute* granny.

Long-Term vs. Short-Term Goals

Paradoxically, the difference between long- and short-term goals is often the difference between success and failure. How do you *carpe diem* and live every day as if it were your last when you're thinking about how much you have to do to meet your next deadline? The truth is that you have to coordinate, consider, and compromise.

The Cuban Missile Crisis happened just before my first big junior high school math test. I lived in Denver at the time, and we all passionately believed that the Denver mint was a primary target for nuclear attack. So, as a skinny 12-year-old math nerd, my dilemma was, "Okay, if this is, like, my last night on Earth, do I really want to spend it studying for a math test? *No way!*" But then it occurred to me: "What if this *isn't* my last night on Earth? Tomorrow I'll wish it was if I don't study and I subsequently flunk the stupid math test!"

Negotiating between the demands of short- and long term-goals can help you become both a math whiz and a sentient, sane human being. This technique turned out to be particularly useful when I got to college. It only took one invitation to the Houston Astrodome the night before a big exam to convince me to study well enough in advance so that I could go the next time. (I also decided that psychology left more room for dates than being a math major.)

All of us need to learn to balance what we want *now* with our expectations about the immediate and near future. If you're one of those people who tends to plan very far in advance, yet is hopeless about what to do today, then you need to shift your focus more to the short-term. On the other hand, if you've stashed a to-do list in every nook and cranny of your house but haven't the faintest idea where you want to be in five years, then you obviously need to think more about the long-term.

I'm a great fan of New Year's resolutions because they allow us to look both forward and backward, to formulate both strategy and tactic, and most important, to consider both our long- and short-term goals. When I talk with people about making New Year's resolutions, I try to convince them to not look at the coming year as a whole.

Saying, "In 365 days, I want to lose weight, stop smoking, or spend more time with my family" is simply too overwhelming for most of us to handle.

Instead, I urge people to be more specific and incorporate short-term goals into their long-term plans. "I want to lose weight" is at the top of almost everybody's resolution list, but few actually accomplish any long-term success in this area. Instead, if you say, "I want to lose 20 pounds this year—I will start by losing two pounds by the end of January" and plan your month accordingly, this helps you break down your goal into manageable pieces. Using both short- and long-term goals is much more effective than using either separately. If you only think of the short term, then you're gonna be off that diet and feeling deprived by February. But if you only concern yourself with the long term, then you'll find yourself ending every evening with a pint of Ben and Jerry's Cherry Garcia, wondering why you haven't lost any weight by the end of the year.

❦ ❦ ❦

For Mary Ann, understanding the difference between short- and long-term goals is vital. Her short-term goal makes good sense, but formulating a few key long-term goals as well will make her plan more effective overall.

> *Our two grandsons, ages 12 and 14, visited with us during the month of July. On the next month's phone bill, I discovered that we'd been charged over $200 by a sex line. The children had unlimited access to our computer and, as naïve as it sounds, we had no clue that they would do something like that. Nevertheless, the charges got removed when I spoke to the phone company and told them the ages of the children, so that's not at issue here. My question is: Should I talk to their father and let him deal with it the way he wants to?*
>
> — Mary Ann, 67, Highland Park, TX

Mary Ann, this isn't the end of the world—you're not even out the money. But there are three separate issues that concern me here. Number one is your grandkids' attitude, which appears to run something along the lines of, "We can behave like little creeps at Grandma's house and get away with it!" Holding them responsible is crucial to avoiding a repeat offense. Number two: Getting the money from them reinforces the harsh reality that we all have to pay our debts in this world. Number three is the morality of this escapade, which involves pornography, cheating Grandma, and running up bills that young boys can't pay.

Write each of the little snots a nice note saying, "I love you dearly, but you each owe me $100, which I will take in payments of $5 a week. As long as the money is forthcoming, this stays between us. If, however, I have to go to the credit company (your father), then that's what I'll do." I think it's perfectly okay to keep this between the three of you because you're saying, "Don't mess with Grandma," thereby establishing yourself as a serious person to be dealt with; it tells them that if they run up a debt, they owe a debt; and if you go directly to their father, of course he'll punish them, but then it's one step removed from you.

Don't give in to the temptation to let Dad straighten them out— Dad has enough stuff to punish them for on a day-to-day basis. You can do a great job yourself in a way very different from Dad's. I'm a big fan of the grandparent relationship, which allows for a little less discipline and a little more love; a little more rocking chair and a little less prison warden. The primary issue isn't punishment, but *responsibility.* By saying, "Don't mess with Grandma—I'm no fool," you're strengthening your relationship with the kids for the short term. In addition, they owe you some money. (Don't even think about telling them that the phone company wrote it off.) You can either send the money to the phone company in a year or donate it to charity, but in the long term, this will help the kids grow into responsible, respectful adults. If they happened to have heard your call to me, you can explain that while the phone company may be generous, Granny wants to make sure the lesson is learned and learned well!

Is It Real, or Is It Memorex?

In this chapter, we're concerned with knowing *what* you want, not necessarily how to get it. Being clear in your goals requires constantly asking yourself: "What do I want *now?*" All too often, we lose sight of the fact that what we wanted for ourselves at the age of 20 isn't necessarily what we want at 30. This is what I call the "Memorex theory of life"—unless we play back the tape and remember who we were *then,* we can't be clear on what we want *now.*

Did you ever wonder why, for instance, so many law or medical school graduates drop out of the field, never practice, or "forget" to take their licensing exams? Students decide to go into law or medicine at a young age, for reasons that have very little to do with the actual profession and a great deal to do with how the career is portrayed on TV, how much money it promises, or because that's what their parents wanted them to do. Oftentimes, it isn't until that person is in their last year of school that they're jolted into realizing that the career for which they've studied and sacrificed for so long really doesn't match up with their current goals.

So, part of getting what you want is making sure that you actually still want it. Every once in a while, you have to stop to redefine your goals so that you're not blindly striving for something that may have been meaningful to you in the past, but has long since ceased to matter. The flip side of this is reevaluating what you *don't* want. For instance, just because you hated brussels sprouts as a six-year-old doesn't mean that you still hate them now that you're 40. Making certain that what you used to find intolerable is still just that is an integral part of attaining your goals. After all, many of us believed that we'd *never* marry someone who was balding or who had children from a previous marriage—these were the givens that we simply never thought to question. This is why we have to reevaluate the things we think we want and the things we think we *don't.* Because what you once thought was gross or unacceptable may actually be okay once you've given it a second chance.

Things change—our taste buds, our sense of smell, our perspective, our ideas. . . . For example, when I was an engineer, I worked with a man who only dated gorgeous, leggy, fake-breasted blondes. He'd always ask me and my husband to double date with him. One evening, he brought along this short, flat-chested brunette who wasn't even particularly pretty. I remember thinking, *It must be love.* At some point, perhaps even without being conscious of it, this guy reexamined his priorities and concluded that what he once thought of as absolute necessities clearly weren't. This is something we *all* need to do. Now I'm not saying that we should live our lives accepting things we truly don't want, but we do need to be certain that the rules by which we run our lives continue to make sense. A long-term goal doesn't mean that it's a goal forever. This is what we have to remember about goals—they're dynamic and fluid.

❦ ❦ ❦

Elaine is a good example of someone who's so intent on maintaining her marriage that she's willing to overlook the fact that her husband has long since ceased to be what she wanted, or that perhaps he never really was the person she wanted to share her life with.

I've only been married for about seven months, and my husband is still obsessed with his ex-girlfriend, with whom he has four kids. When we got married, she was out of the picture, but soon after, she came crying to him when she got into some major legal problems. She was indicted for federal bank fraud, and the next thing I know, she's living with us to keep from being arrested. He can't get over her, and while I'm at work supporting him, the two of them are having sex every day. When I found out, I had her tossed in jail because she was ruining my marriage. My husband is really mad because she's the love of his life and they have kids. But he told me that he still loves me. How do I survive this?

— Elaine, 33, Pittsburgh, PA

Elaine, take a deep breath, sit down, and call your lawyer. Your husband is never going to be able to give you his heart, so divorce him and move on. You might even be able to get an annulment if that's what you want. Your husband's behavior is unprincipled—to invite someone into your house because she's in trouble is one thing, but to have sex with her under your roof is disrespectful to you and a complete affront to your marriage vows. Tell him, "You're going to have to choose. This is unacceptable." But I think he already *has* chosen.

My guess is that if you'd known him longer, it would have occurred to you that he was never going to be emotionally free of this woman. Elaine, they have four children in common, a bond that he's going to have with her no matter what happens. Now if he was just being kind and bringing her in because she's the mother of his children and has nowhere else to go, that would be understandable, but having sex with her is beyond the pale. This guy is a piece of work, and I'm willing to bet that if you knew then what you know now, you would never have married him.

However, if after careful evaluation, you still think that there's something here that's worth fighting for, then separate from him for at least several months and give him some time to decide *who* he wants. It sounds like she's in the slammer right now, but you don't want to be the runner-up, Miss Congeniality. This is a brand-new marriage, and he's not committed to you at all. He hasn't forsaken all others, that's for sure. If you honestly feel that you love him, give him some time to sort this out, but living with him right now is going to break your heart and weaken your spirit.

Playing Doctor

The purpose of this chapter is to illustrate the ways you can use goals to direct and focus your actions so that they'll take you where you want to go. Play doctor and see if you understand strategies, tactics, and long- and short-term goals.

My husband and I have been married for 17 years. He's a great father to our three children, but for the past year, he's had no sex drive. He tells me that a lot of marriages don't involve sex, and he won't even say that he loves me. I'm hurt and confused. What should I do?

— Kay, 42, Stowe, VT

1. What advice would you give Kay?

   (a) Call him every name in the book and then kick him to the curb.
   (b) Say nothing. This, too, shall pass.
   (c) Make him his favorite meal or rent his favorite movie, and then tell him how you feel.
   (d) Decide that your husband is right: Sex *is* an overrated part of marriage.

We need to understand Kay's goals if our advice is to be effective. Although many people would find her husband's behavior intolerable and demand a divorce on the grounds of sexual abandonment, that's not Kay's objective. Even if it were, I still wouldn't suggest choice "a." Indulging your feelings and acting on impulse isn't going to solve the problem and get Kay what she wants. Answers "b" and "d" are incorrect because if Kay's objective is to have a better relationship with her husband, and her strategy is to improve their sex life, then these are inappropriate tactics.

Answer "c" is the only one that offers Kay a possibility of achieving her goal and getting what she wants. She should try doing something fun with her husband, and then saying, "This is a *marriage*. Yes, you're a great father and companion, but I want *you*. I'm not going to be passive or nag you about this, but I do want us to rejuvenate our sex life." Of course Kay may get rejected, but then again, she may not. In any case, she's not going to wind up feeling any more rejected than she feels already. And given a choice between going along with Kay or hurting her feelings, my guess is that Kay's husband will probably want to at least try to make her happy.

❧ ❧ ❧

I'm getting married for the second time. My fiancée and I both have kids from previous marriages: I have two sons, ages 16 and 12; and she has a 10-year-old daughter. My fiancée and her family live in another state, and neither one of us wants to uproot our families. My 16-year-old son has a friend he can move in with, but the two youngest are a problem, since one or the other will have to switch schools. How do we decide who should move, me or my fiancée?

— Arnold, 45, South Bend, IN

1. How would you handle Arnold's question?

   (a) Watch out for your 16-year-old. He's the oldest child, and he should get the deciding vote.
   (b) Tell her it's simple mathematics: You've got two kids, she has one. You win—she moves.
   (c) It's a toss-up. Flipping a coin is the only fair solution.
   (d) Whoever has the best school district gets to stay put.

The correct answer to this question also depends on strategies and tactics. If raising their kids right is the goal, then allowing the 16-year-old to move in with a friend isn't good parenting. It will send a clear message that "Dad's choosing his new family over you." The correct answer is "a." As the oldest of the children, the 16-year-old has the most connections to his school—and if he's willing to move away from his family to stay at his school, it's obviously very important to him.

Answer "b" is incorrect simply because it's bullying behavior—there's no rhyme or reason behind it. The same goes for "c"—tossing a coin is the very definition of random action. As for "d," which may seem reasonable to some, this is also incorrect. Although school districts are important, that's a very subjective matter. Many people are fond of the schools in their area, so you don't want to start a completely irrelevant war over whose is better.

Shrink Wrap

I'm going to ask you to do something a little different here. Now that you've finished this chapter, I'd like you to put down this book for a day or two and spend some time really thinking about your goals and how you hope to achieve them. While you're at it, try to identify and reevaluate the goals that have been with you for years, just to see if they still apply. Before you start, remind yourself of the following things:

- A **strategy** is a mind-set or an idea about how you'll accomplish your objective.

- **Tactics** are behaviors that stem from your strategies.

- **Being as specific as possible is the key to effective problem solving** because it allows you to break down your problem into easy-to-handle steps.

- **You have to understand what you can and can't change.**

- **Long- and short-term goals must be negotiated.**

- **As we change, so do our tastes, wants, needs, and goals.**

STEP 7:
❧ A DOZEN TOOLS ❧

Right before I graduated from high school, I fell in love with a girl a year younger than me. She was my first girl-friend, my first love, and my first sexual experience. I always thought that no matter what happened, at least we'd remain friends. She broke up with me to see other people, and a few weeks later, she ran away from home. I haven't talked to her or heard from her since she ran off three months ago, but I'm still having a rough time with the breakup. I've been on a couple of dates that haven't worked out, and I get sad . . . because I always end up thinking about her. What's wrong with me?

— Joe, 18, Little Rock, AR

Joe, there's a message here if you're willing to see it. Recurring thoughts about your ex are a signal that you're not ready to date yet. When we're young, our attention spans are pretty short and our feelings pretty intense, so we can get involved too quickly and burn out too fast; then we just rush into the next relationship (and the next heartbreak). As we get a little older, we realize that running our lives in this way can be very expensive: We expend gobs of energy and wind up with nothing to show for it. After a while, we learn to get to know people a little more slowly and carefully, as friends first. It's not quite as exciting as getting swept off our feet, but it's not quite as terrifying either.

Given the fact that this girl was your first and that your life changed dramatically right around the time you got involved with her, your fond memories are to be expected and may even be a bit exaggerated. But instead of just jumping into a new relationship, take this time to investigate what went wrong with this one so that you can figure out how to fix it next time. Analyze both the good and the bad, what you've learned, and what you want to make sure happens or doesn't happen in your next relationship.

Finally, Joe, ask yourself, "What reason could there have been for this girl to have come into my life?" Formulating an answer that makes sense may take some time, but once you find it, letting go of your feelings for her will be possible and you can use what you've learned in your next relationship.

❦ ❦ ❦

Most of what we've discussed in the past six chapters has been very practical and instructive. This chapter, however, is a bit more philosophical in nature. The advice is as useful as any in the book, but we're talking about general tools that will work in more than one situation. So, the chapter is about how to think about *solutions*. Think of it as a toolbox that contains screwdrivers, hammers, nails, and drills—all numbered, categorized, designated, and ready to be put to work. The tools we'll be working with are the following:

- Listen to the Universe's voice.

- Accept that doors open and close.

- Blur your perspective.

- Do good.

- Don't confess.

- Tolerate differences.

- Watch your words.

- Communicate, don't expect.

- Adjust your attitude.

- Bribe when all else fails.

- Beware of all-or-nothing situations.

- Prepare for change—it's inevitable.

Tool #1: Listen to the Universe's Voice

At some point in our lives, most of us have come across something that we desperately wanted. We used intelligence, tenacity, intensity, and energy to get it—and it just didn't work! At the time, the disappointment was overwhelming, acute, and painful, but often we can look back and see that what we wanted really wouldn't have worked out for us. In retrospect, it's clear that *things happen for a reason.* The trick is to accept it at the time.

When we go through a breakup, lose a job, flunk a class, or even miss a train, we often feel devastated, miserable, and hopeless. Somehow (and with a mysterious regularity), the failures that seemed the most important and regrettable magically become blessings in disguise. We end up breathing sighs of relief and saying, "Yeah! If that wretched thing hadn't happened, I would have never had the chance to experience this wonderful thing."

If we accept that our perspective might be flawed and that we don't always know what's right for us, then we can begin to understand that our lives always end up working out for the best. Believing that people and situations appear in our paths for a reason—and that those encounters, though often painful, are often incredibly valuable—can be enormously comforting. For instance, anybody over the age of 12 can look back and remember a breakup that marked an all-time low; in time, we realize that without that heartbreaker, we would never have met the next person, who, whether permanent or not, turned out to be a definite improvement.

Rationalization, God's will, karma, destiny, predetermination, a master plan . . . call it what you will: My way of describing it is "the Universe's voice." When something awful happens, you can either shake your fist at the heavens and cry out, "Why me, God? *Why me?!*" or take a deep breath, step back, and say, "I assume that things happen for a reason—which may not be logical but is a sane assumption because it makes me feel better—so maybe I'll look for the reason."

I'm not suggesting that we have to adopt Pollyanna as our new role model, demand that our shrink adjust our dosage, or subscribe to the wide-eyed optimist's philosophy of, "All's for the best in the best of all possible worlds." However, if we can believe that things happen for a reason (no matter how obscure that reason may be at the time), then we can gain a wider, more reasoned, more *seasoned* perspective on our lives. And it feels a lot better than moaning, whining, and decrying our lousy luck.

Even with something as devastating as the terrorist attacks on the United States, we've already reached the point where we can say, "For the first time in decades, America came together," or "The world united as a community against pointless, horrifying violence," or "People began to understand what was important in their lives," or "Hollywood looked at how often the message they manufactured was one of violence." None of this is to say that any of us would ever wish for horrible, God-awful things to happen. In fact, if I owned a spectacularly powerful magic wand, I'd certainly eradicate all pain and suffering from the face of the planet. But regardless of what *I* want, bad stuff does happen, so instead of taking it personally or allowing it to destroy your spirit, ask what the reason for it might be.

Now let me add a word of caution: Saying this to someone else might send them lunging for your jugular vein. When somebody loses a girlfriend to their best friend, a job to downsizing, or half their life savings to the fluctuating stock market, your saying, "Well, it probably happened for a reason" isn't going to make you very popular.

Listening for the Universe's voice is a strictly personal philosophy, a quiet internal voice that reminds us that there's something more than the immediate.

❦ ❦ ❦

Howard is a good example of someone who needs to stop and listen to the Universe's voice so that he can relax and go with flow.

> *The woman I'm dating is 44, has never been married, and we've known each other for about nine years through work. We've been seeing each other once or twice a week for most of our three months together, and I still haven't been introduced to anyone in her life. When would you expect to meet the other person's friends?*
>
> — Howard, 54, Paramus, NJ

Howard, there's no rule of thumb. The timetable for meeting friends depends a lot on the circumstances. *You're* ready to meet her friends, but *she* hasn't suggested it yet, for which there could be a number of reasons. First of all, if you think about it, you've only had about a dozen dates. It's possible that you're used to going a little faster than she is.

If the two of you had been seeing each other three to four times a week for six months, I'd say, "It's time already!" But you haven't even had 20 dates! Cool your heels and wait a couple of months. She probably *is* talking about the relationship with some of her friends, but she wants to make sure that it's solid before she puts you (and herself) under their microscopic scrutiny. I wouldn't push for the introductions now, but if you still haven't met her friends two months down the line, suggest a barbecue where you *both* invite your friends.

Don't take offense—maybe she doesn't feel sure of your relationship yet, and perhaps that's a good thing. Her wariness and your abandon could be creating a sort of equilibrium. It may be that you're used to being shown off as a "catch," and her caution may make you work a bit harder here. Trust that there's a reason for your not having met her friends yet. Let time take its course—if you're meant to meet your girlfriend's circle of friends, you will.

Tool #2: Doors Open, Doors Close

Our lives contain certain built-in concepts: (1) Going in one direction necessarily precludes going in another; (2) most of us are at least subtly aware of the road not taken; (3) there are things that happen to us in spite of our planning, no matter how organized we are; and (4) there are times to give up control.

I'm not proposing that we lay back, cease being involved in our own lives, and just enjoy the ride. Far from it. But since we just spent a whole chapter talking about heading off in a specific direction, it's important that you understand that you may be knocked off course from time to time, and it's unlikely to be disastrous. As meaningful as your goals may be, side trips are learning experiences, and you'll be a lot more relaxed as you undergo what the Universe has in store for you.

Admittedly, detours can be uncomfortable, scary, and distracting because the new wrinkle isn't under your control. But remember: Doors open, doors close. You can't get the next job until you've lost this one, you can't find the next relationship until you've ended the one you're already in, and you can't go on to the next step of enlightenment until you've suffered through whatever lesson you have to learn in this one. Granted, it's a lot more fun when you get to choose where and when to go, but that's not always up to you. At these times, it's crucial to remember that the sound of a door closing is really an example of the universe going, "Yoo-hoo, darlin'—listen up!"

※　※　※

Grace's future stepdaughter is having trouble accepting the closing of a door, and that's causing problems for the entire family.

I recently got engaged to an 81-year-old widower. He's been widowed for 6 years, and I've been a widow for 16. We each have two children and four grandchildren, and everyone is happy for us except his daughter, Jane. Although she has her own family, she's been on call in a sense for the past six years because of my fiancé's physical problems, and now she's having a hard time with our news. How do we help her accept this engagement and move on with our wedding plans?

— Grace, 74, Bar Harbor, ME

Well, the odds are certainly in your favor—you've got most of the family behind your plans. But, just as you pointed out, Jane has felt very important to her dad. So she's feeling as if now that he's healthy again, he doesn't need her, and she's being discarded like an old shoe. You might think that your taking over should be a relief for her, but she obviously doesn't feel that way. We all need to feel important—even if we complain sometimes, we're also patting ourselves on the back for being needed. Step into her shoes for a moment and understand from her point of view that, yeah, it may have been a pain in the neck to be on call and take care of Dad, but it made her feel really important.

Grace, you may think that you've taken the burden from her shoulders, but Jane feels that you've taken the spotlight from her, thereby making her less significant. In most families, sibling rivalry is a fact of life, and for a while she probably felt that she was the most beloved of the children because she was the one her dad called on. And now she's feeling that her specialness has not only fallen away, it's been transferred to you. So she feels—in a slightly silly way, but our emotions aren't always as advanced as our years—that you're her rival and that you've beaten her at the game of "Daddy love."

You and her father need to make Jane feel that she's still important, reassure her that she'll still get the advantages of having a healthy dad who loves her, and let her know that she's still special so that she doesn't have the sense that she was there for him in times of trouble and now he's just discarding her. Do something for Jane apart from the other children and grandchildren: Maybe you can ask her to do something special at the wedding, take her out for a lavish meal, or get her a personalized token of your love and appreciation. You need to communicate the idea that she'll continue to be special, but now she won't have to work as hard to get the attention.

This isn't to say that you have to wait for Jane to come around before you get married. You don't have to put off your wedding any more than she had to put off *her* wedding when she decided she wanted to get married. Grace, you and your fiancé are grown-ups—you can do whatever you want. So, if you tell Jane, "We're not going to get married until we get your approval," then the longer she withholds, the more important she becomes, and you don't want that. If you decide to go ahead and wait for her blessing, you'll be waiting a *long* time. Move on with your plans, and she'll hopefully come around in time—especially if she understands that even though she's still special, her veto power has expired.

Tool #3: Blur Your Perspective

We've already devoted an entire chapter to the practical aspects of perspective. Here, however, we're going to take a more philosophical view of it, shifting from discussing what to *do* to attain perspective to exploring a way of *thinking* about your perspective. Perspective means seeing the *parallax,* that point where things begin and end, separate and converge. In this section, we're going to temporarily set aside the perspective-achieving tips we covered in Step Four, and accept that sometimes what we need to do isn't sharpen our point of view, but blur it. Blurring distinctions and boundaries allows you to ignore your absolute certainty that the horizon ends.

Human beings hate uncertainty, so we spend a large part of our lives trying to superimpose a perspective on ambiguity, to pretend that we know things that we don't. Most of us want to have a clear idea about what's going to happen next. This is why psychics and astrologers are so popular—they offer us the sense that there's order to our universe, and while that very well may be, that order is often quite difficult to sort out.

You need to accept *not* knowing, and emotionally squint enough to "see" beyond what you can physically view with your eyes. Therefore, instead of striving to see exactly where your past, present, and future connect, you can put things in a softer focus by asking: (1) "Could there be a lesson here that I'm ignoring?" and (2) "Is there another point of view here? Can I see the trees rather than the forest, or vice versa?"

❧ ❧ ❧

Sometimes we may feel like we know a situation inside out, like Peggy does, but we have to blur our perspective to understand that there may be certain forces at work of which we're unaware.

> *My youngest sister is 36 and recently divorced, due to an affair she had with her female next-door neighbor. The problem is that her children, ages 7 and 10, have begun to act out. They've gained a tremendous amount of weight and don't understand what's going on. The ties between my sister and the rest of our family have been cut, and the children are kept at a distance. It's heartbreaking. My family loves my sister regardless of her sexual preference, but we're worried about these kids. What do I do?*
>
> — Peggy, 47, Great Neck, NY

Divorce is always painful, but this one's a twofer, not only between your sister and her husband, but between your sister and your family. Somehow, your sister got the idea that your family is a threat to both her children and herself. Since many of us go to family members when life gets difficult, somebody must have said something to make her think that her family won't be such a safe haven after all.

It's time to talk to your sister face-to-face (because you need as much information as you can get here) and mend your relationship. You can even say to her, "I was concerned enough about this that I actually called Dr. Joy Browne, who said that if you're not coming to your family in a time of trouble, it's because you view us as less than supportive. I can't speak for the entire family, but I can tell you that *I* support you and your decisions, and if there's anything I can do to demonstrate that to you, I'd be delighted to do it. I miss you and the kids."

Peggy, it's really important that you don't make your sister feel as if the family's only concern is her children, because that will make her feel used and abandoned at a time when she's already frightened and unhappy. Make sure that she doesn't assume that her kids are the only reason any of you want to be with her, or she'll think, *No one cares about me, I'm just the path to the kids,* which would hurt anybody's feelings.

"I want you to know I'm here for you in every way" is a very different statement from "We miss the kids." Focusing on the children is just going to make her feel like, "I can drop off the face of the earth and no one would even miss me, or they'd be grateful I was gone because the only thing I'm good for is driving the kids back and forth." Blur your perspective enough to entertain your sister's, and the two of you may end up seeing eye-to-eye.

Tool #4: Do Good

At the risk of sounding like the ultimate goody-two-shoes, or Mother Teresa, Santa Claus, your Sunday School teacher, and your granny all wrapped up into one, I'd like to go on record to say: *Do good.*

Our society teaches us that it's hip to be cool, sullen, competitive, aloof, blasé, edgy, and always looking out for "Number One." *Hello?!* Folks, winning at any cost doesn't make us feel nearly as good about ourselves as human beings as losing a fair and tough fight does. I'm not saying that we should strive to lose, just to do good. And when I say, "Do good," I mean across the board. Even something as minor as ignoring that piece of trash that missed the wastepaper basket can harm us, whether anyone's there to see it or not. Human beings have consciences, so even if nobody knows, *you* do.

As a society, we've overlooked the importance of conscience for way too long. We've made getting away with something a virtue, and committing the perfect crime admirable. There's no such thing as a perfect crime, because no one ever really gets away with anything. Think about it—even if we're never caught, we've caught ourselves, and the weight of feeling that we're not a good person is hard to schlep around. Knowing that you littered on the street, cheated on your income tax, lied to your mother, or betrayed your boyfriend are all heavy burdens to bear. Each of us knows our personal truth. Even if no one catches us, *we* know.

The problem with knowing our own misdeeds is that a guilty conscience is the ultimate barrier between ourselves and the person we want to be, the person we really like being. To understand the power of goodness, you have only to look at the glow on the faces of children when they've done something good. We all have that ability to beam with pride in our own actions; we just have to remember that doing good is not only a moral imperative, but a truly pleasurable, *feel*-good route to spiritual, emotional, and mental well-being.

Let's face it, life is a relatively impersonal experience. There are five billion people walking the planet, but few of us will know more than a couple of hundred in the course of our lifetimes. So why squander any opportunity to positively impact another human being? If you can make a difference in someone's life, do it! Not for *their* sake, but for *yours*! Doing good makes you feel connected, like you matter, that the little dash between your birth year and your death that is your life hasn't been wasted.

❧ ❧ ❧

Although Harriet is distressed and rightfully confused about what course to take, the idea of proceeding by doing good clarifies, while also offering her the peace of mind she seeks.

About two weeks ago, my neighbor Maria rang my door-
bell. I invited her in—even though I'm embarrassed to say
that all I really knew about her was that six years ago, her
21-year-old son died in a car accident. Anyway, Maria
begged me to help her find her son's old girlfriend, who had
been a friend of my daughter's. Apparently, Maria has kept
her son's frozen sperm and she wanted to see if the former
girlfriend would have his child. I almost fell off my chair. I
know how distraught any parent is when a child dies, but
I didn't know what to do. I'm certainly not going to go look
for this girl—she has a family and children now, which I
pointed out to Maria, but she didn't care. She has this in her
mind and she's desperate for me to help her. Is it okay to just
tell her that I can't find her son's old girlfriend?

— Harriet, 48, Millsboro, DE

Harriet, grief hits everyone differently and often has a very long
half-life. Maria's quest indicates a longing for what might have been,
and I'm not sure that technology is our friend in this particular situation. Luckily, you don't know where this girl is, and you certainly
don't have to help Maria search for her. However, if you want to
appear helpful *and* remove yourself from the situation, you could
direct her to the various people-locating websites on the Internet.

But before you suggest finding the girl, you can do an even better deed by gently explaining that she's probably moved on with her
life. Maria has constructed an entire fantasy around her dead son's
sperm, a fantasy in which the girl he left behind still carries a torch
for him. Maria sees herself helping the young woman raise the
child, hoping the baby will be a boy so she can have a part of her
son back. The idea has a cockamamie but understandable emotional
resonance to it.

While stranger things have happened, I agree that it's highly
unlikely that the young woman will agree to take part in this plan,
since to do so means that both of these women would be dedicating
their lives to a ghost. I would worry about this hypothetical child, as

he would come into the world with expectations heaped upon him that no one could fulfill. How could someone even try to be the embodiment of a dead father whom he never knew?

You can certainly tell Maria that you weren't able to locate the girl. But if you want to, you can look at the wider context of this issue, which is that Maria is a very lonely woman who is fixated on bringing her son back to life because she has little else going on. Without dealing with the specifics of Maria's request, you can still be a friend to her by responding to her unexpressed need, which centers on her lonely, meaningless life. Maybe you can suggest that she get involved with children, either working in a homeless shelter or with AIDS babies at a local hospital. Since she clearly continues to haunt you, you could even say, "Maria, I've been thinking about you a lot. What do you think about the two of us going to work with children together? That way, you can keep your son's spirit alive by seeing some of his behavior in other people."

You don't have to comment on the limitations of her scheme, the questionable viability of the frozen sperm, the feasibility of fertilization, or the uncertain future of a child who's going to grow up with a ghost for a father. But you *can* do good by focusing on a lost soul who could use a little bit of guidance and friendship.

Tool #5: Don't Confess

This tool is a companion to Tool #4. While that one was about doing good, this one is about not doing anything you need to confess. If you behave yourself, then you'll have nothing to confess. I can hear some of you scratching your heads and wondering, *What in the world is so wrong with confession? It cleanses the soul!* Well, in reality, confession is one of those things that sounds great in theory but is disastrous in reality. Confession feels good only from the giving end—it's rotten to receive.

The two most common and socially acceptable modes of confessing underscore these difficulties, since they take place in a church confessional or a psychotherapist's office, and include confidentiality and secrecy. These safeguards exist for excellent reasons. Confessing to civilians, on the other hand, alleviates the guilt of the confessor while burdening the person receiving the confession. The "confessee" is left with one of two options: (1) forgiving the trespasser, thereby letting that person off the hook; or (2) punishing the sinner, who usually responds with something like, "Hey, I was only being honest." Either way, if you're confessing to a nonprofessional, you're just manipulating someone who trusted you because you screwed up. There are only two ways to avoid falling into the confession pit, thereby qualifying for the title of "Biggest Jerk on the Planet": Don't confess and don't screw up.

Nobody's perfect, but if you think about your actions and their consequences, you'll find that you *do* have a conscience, as well as an innate sense of right and wrong. This is a bit more complicated than just doing good. Now we're saying, "Think about what you're doing, be aware of your motives, and don't be mean." To avoid evil-doing, you must understand that doing bad stuff is really self-indulgent, for you're giving in to the childish, selfish, lesser part of yourself. It's as if you're saying, "I matter more than anybody else. My feelings are more important, what I want is more important, and *I'm* more important." That's the kind of self-aggrandizing, bully mentality that lets us hurt another human being and then rationalize it after the fact.

We're most likely to behave badly when we're feeling lousy about ourselves. We act the ugliest when we're hurting, and the most generous when we're feeling great. It's hard to share when the cupboard is bare and there's nothing to spare. When we feel ripped off, we're much more likely to hurt someone else. Then as we do wretched things, we feel bankrupt, and as we continue to feel poor, we're going to demand things of other people. If they don't going to give in to our demands, we're just going to take what we want, and wind up feeling even more bereft and justified in doing so. It's a vicious cycle. By the same token, if we're generous, giving, and loving to people, they'll respond in kind. And even if they don't, we at least have the insulation of knowing that what we're doing is right and good, and that it *feels* good to *do* good. I'm not saying that we should just "turn the other cheek," but as long as we can protect ourselves, maybe we won't have to hurt anybody else.

That said, if you *do* make a mistake, you need to live with that knowledge rather than confess and shift the burden of responsibility to some innocent party. This is *not* to say that you should never admit you're wrong—when you make a mistake, apologize. But a confession is *not* an apology, it's asking something of someone that you've wronged, and that's not okay.

🌿 🌿 🌿

Michelle has a strong yearning to purge her soul.

> *I was trying to have some fun with my husband by sending him anonymous e-mails. He thought I was his old girlfriend, and he started saying some very sexual things—bringing up things from the past that they did together, and so on. This went on for three to four days and when it got too risqué, I sent him an e-mail that said, "Ha ha . . . my husband and I had a bet to see how fast I could ensnare an old flame. Watch out that your wife doesn't find out." Well, that night he confessed everything to me. I feel terrible. Should I tell him the truth? My heart tells me I should.*

> — Michelle, 27, Provo, UT

If I were you, Michelle, I'd keep my mouth shut and never do something like this again. If you tell your husband, you've both humiliated him and caught him in the act, and that's going to start a war. I would go to my grave with this one—which means don't tell *anyone,* because you certainly don't want him to hear this from someone else.

Since you've both learned your lessons, I don't think there's anything to be gained by confessing except relieving your guilt. So, shoulder the burden of knowledge and don't play any more games. Remind yourself that if he had confessed and you *hadn't* been involved, you'd be furious and hurt right now, not gloating. Michelle, go nuzzle him and be the sweetest wife possible for the next couple of months—that will confuse the daylights out of him—but keep it to yourself. His confession didn't do *you* any good, and all your confession will do is make him furious with you. Forgive yourself, learn your lesson, and move on.

Tool #6: Tolerate Differences

Living in a competitive society, many of us have embraced "My way or the highway!" as a personal philosophy. We're either actively aggressive about getting our own way or we're passive-aggressive about it (as in, "Well, of course, do what you think is right. Don't worry about me."). For lots of folks, each passing decade means that we become less and less willing to accept the possibility that we're not the smartest guy in the room, that someone else might have a better idea, or that nice, honest, sincere people can have legitimate differences of opinion.

Tolerating differences is about the value of letting someone else have their way *and* of learning different ways of thinking and doing that might never have occurred otherwise. By being clear, as well as reasonable, we can state an opinion, listen to alternatives, and find compromises: "This is what *I* like; what would *you* like?" *Ta-da!* It's *amazing* how pleasant people can be when they feel they're being listened to and appreciated . . . and how unpleasant they can be when they're feeling ripped off and all they hear is "Do it my way!"

This isn't even altruism (which is a misnomer, since we always do what we choose to do)—but good, old-fashioned self-interest. Try experimenting with and practicing the theory that doing something nice for someone else feels terrific, not so much for them but for us. If nothing else, it could be a good learning experience. The "I'm sane, you're all nuts" school of life has never produced a

Nobel Laureate or a popular saint, so finding out why someone else behaves the way they do can be a tremendously enriching and eye-opening experience.

🌿 🌿 🌿

In Sarah's case, the difference of opinion she has with her boyfriend is of life-altering proportions. This is all the more reason to try to understand his point of view.

> *I've been dating a guy for two years, and we've been living together for a year and a half. We were talking about getting engaged when, about a week ago, he dropped the bomb on me. He said, "I'm overwhelmed, I'm freaked out. I don't know if I love you anymore. I need to be on my own, and I'm moving out." And he did that within two days. He said, "It's not anybody else. It's not you, you're kind and wonderful. I'm not sure if I love you, but I care for you. I need to be on my own while I figure this out." Should I move on or wait for him, especially since he doesn't know how long it's going to take?*
>
> — Sarah, 36, Austin, TX

Sarah, this just happened. You're not going to move on in the next couple of hours. I mean, you're still in love with him—after all, you were planning to marry him. The first thing to do here is don't take this so personally. I know it feels like rejection, but what if you instead assumed that he truly is anguished? For the next couple of months (at least), I would keep yourself out of harm's way: I wouldn't focus on him, but I wouldn't tell your friends that you're back on the market either—because you really won't be available while you're still emotionally entangled with him.

Sarah, if you assume that he's being sincere, that he thought about this for a long time, that he cares about you, and that he's not a bad guy, then you'll buy yourself some breathing room. And thank goodness he had sense enough to do this before the wedding invitations were sent out. He has to decide what he wants to do about this.

So for right now, your real question is, "What do *I* do in the meantime?" Answer: Keep yourself busy. This is a time to throw yourself into work, spend a lot of time with your friends, take up folk dancing, learn to macramé, become a great gardener, study yoga, whatever—it's just not a time to date. By the end of the year, you'll know what's going on—not only with your boyfriend, but with *yourself* and your own feelings, goals, and wishes. You don't have to sit around and wait, but you also don't need to involve yourself in a relationship right now. Assume that he does love you, that he's sincerely trying to work out how to calm his fears and anxieties, and try not to punish him to protect your hurt feelings. If you can handle your emotions differently, you can take things less personally and give both of you some space.

Tool #7: By Describing It, We Bring It into Being

A couple of years ago, I was asked to give a speech about "Dealing with Difficult People." My first thought was that the title had to go. Think about it: Once you've called someone "difficult," you're going to *act* as if they're difficult, and *voilà!*—they'll *become* difficult!

Once, during a temporary lapse of sanity, I asked my then six-year-old daughter how she felt about being an only child. Her reply? "Lonely." *Whoa! Stab through the heart! I'm a rotten parent!* Fortunately, there was a guardian angel sitting on my shoulder, and I asked her to clarify: "Honey, what does 'lonely' mean?" She said, "Oh, you know, fun, get all the stuff." *Whew! Sweet relief!* Clearly someone had said to her, "You must be lonely because you're an only child." She had no idea what "lonely" meant!

We need to be careful about our words because by describing something, we bring it into being. By "careful," I mean that if we're going to describe things, we should aim to describe them as positive. For example, when I was helping out with the relief efforts at the World Trade Center, I saw Bertha, a woman who was as sloppy, clumsy, and clueless as she was well-meaning. It's likely that she shouldn't have been down there at all, so when she got into the way of Stan (the guy in charge of the area we were all working in), he demanded to know who'd brought her down there.

"I'm with Judy," Bertha answered defiantly.

When Judy showed up a few minutes later, Stan accused, "*You're* the one who brought her down."

"Oh, yes," Judy cheerfully replied. "Isn't she a great worker? We all adore Bertha."

Magical. At that moment, Judy was able to take Stan's description of herself as an outlaw, or at least an incompetent manager who was responsible for this breach in protocol and efficiency, and instantly redefine the situation with the words "Isn't she a great worker?"

"Yeah, she's been working very hard, but . . . ," Stan continued.

"You know, she's always been a great worker!" Judy exclaimed.

This is a pure and positive example of how describing brings into being. Stan was hell-bent on describing a catastrophe—he was ready to go to town, read Judy the riot act, and bring out the tar and feathers. The situation had "turf war" written all over it . . . until Judy instantly turned it around and made it work *for* her. Sure, Stan kept trying to make his little inroads and forays, but Judy kept him relentlessly focused on Bertha being a hard worker.

❧ ❧ ❧

While describing problems as opportunities can serve to diffuse negativity, negative descriptions of neutral situations can create problems where none would normally exist. That's one lesson we can all learn from Steve.

I went to a massage place because I've been having back problems. Well, the masseuse rubbed me in places I didn't think

*were appropriate. I told my wife of eight years about it because
I felt so bad and we have a very honest and open relationship.
Now my wife thinks I cheated on her because I didn't jump off
the table or tell the masseuse to stop. What do you think?*

— Steve, 35, Tallahassee, FL

All you had to do, Steve, was keep your big mouth shut. You created this problem, either out of a guilty conscience due to your inability to tell the masseuse no, or because you were hoping your wife would laugh the whole thing off or punish you. This isn't even about the stupidity of confession or knowing that there are some things that don't make a whole lot of sense to tell each other. This is about *describing* something as "sinful" when it was just plain stupid!

In talking about this as if it were something worthy of confession, you made it a larger issue than it really was. For example, if your secretary came to work wearing a really low-cut shirt and you thought, *Whoa, baby!* hopefully, you'd be smart enough not to tell your wife. It's not that you're lying to her, Steve, it's just that while it's okay for you to notice another woman's cleavage, talking about it to your wife just makes a big deal out of nothing. Similarly, if your wife takes a tennis lesson and her instructor has great buns and seems to be flirting with her, hopefully, she'll just enjoy it and leave it at that. I hope she'd be smart enough not to talk about it with you because all that would do is make you miserable. Steve, I think you single-handedly proved that some things are better left unsaid. Please memorize this, along with the rule about confession, and live a wholesome, sensible life with nothing to even tempt you to confess.

What you need to do now is get a male masseuse and tell your wife, "I don't want to keep apologizing for this because it makes it bigger than it should be. It wasn't adultery—it was stupidity on my part. I was caught unawares, and it will never happen again. From now on, let's get massages together and move on from all this."

Tool #8: Expectation Is the Death of Serenity

Expectations say a *huge* amount about us and *nothing* about other people. This is because expectations are primarily unspoken, unstated demands. Disappointment is often a foregone conclusion. The classic example is of a woman who picks out an engagement ring, a honeymoon destination, a china pattern, and a baby name— after she's been out on one date with a guy! Meanwhile, the groom-to-be is out whooping it up with Bachelorette Number Three. Talk about superimposing our template on somebody else's motives, goals, and perspective!

Most of us happily impose our expectations on others, while being absolutely unwilling to accept them ourselves. When somebody says, "I expected you to do it," we say, "Who the hell are *you* to expect anything of *me?*" And that's the point: In the end, thwarted expectations cause disappointment, disagreement, hurt, and hostility. Expectations that are specific, open, and negotiable (such as when a parent says to their child, "I'll pay for your college education *if* you maintain a 3.0 grade point average"), or the expectations we have of ourselves (such as expecting to get healthier by sticking to an exercise regimen) are much less troublesome than those "Read my mind and do what I want you to do without my ever having to ask" jobs. With such expectations, there are only two things do: (1) Recognize and understand them; or (2) drop them.

If you can stop expecting anything of anyone other than yourself, then you can ease up on other people and get on with the business of living your life, figuring out who you are, what you want, and what makes you happy. All those questions and answers are in that secluded, serene, innermost sanctum of yourself. Go visit—quietly and often.

🥀 🥀 🥀

Unrealistic expectations can be the cause of discontent, but for Carl, they're a by-product of a larger issue.

My wife and I have been married for ten years, but lately we've been having some problems. The other day, she made a comment that went way over my head. She said, "If you give me a compliment or do something nice for me, you shouldn't expect anything in return." I guess this means that if she has to say "Thank you" or "Jeez, that was nice," then the compliment wasn't given unconditionally. Can you clarify that? Am I wrong to expect something in return?

— Carl, 46, Cheyenne, WY

You both have a point, Carl. You feel that it's nice to be acknowledged when you've done something because it increases the probability that you'll do it again, while she feels that a compliment isn't a contract—it should be given freely and with no strings attached.

Truth be told, Carl, it sounds like the two of you have an underlying issue that you're ignoring—neither of you is feeling very cherished by the other one. If this is just a symptom of the problem rather than the problem itself, you could spend a lot of time deciding who's right and still not get any closer to a solution. So, it's time to problem-solve here. The problem isn't that someone should say "Thank you" if you open the door for them or "Gee, you look nice"—that's just good manners. My point is that you're ignoring the fact that neither of you is feeling very happy with one another in your relationship.

Instead of focusing on whether she should acknowledge you if you pay her a compliment, concentrate on creating a context where she feels that you love and respect her, and that the compliment isn't meant to elicit anything else. What she's really saying is: "You expect that you can ignore me for long periods of time or be nasty to me, and then everything will be okay as soon as you come up with a compliment—then you'll wanna have sex with me, or you'll want me to be nice to you, and that makes me feel used." Your expectation is that as long as you're still around, she should realize that you love her. *That's* what's really going on here—you know that, I know that, and she knows that. So rather than focus on who's right, who's wrong, and what you do or don't have a right to expect after paying your wife a compliment, you're better off trying to solve the real problem with your relationship. Maybe both of you should stop expecting to be hurt, abandoned, or used . . . and try being more loving with each other.

Tool #9: Attitude Is Everything

There's an old joke about twins, one an optimist, the other a pessimist. One day, their father decides to test them: He takes the pessimistic one into a room full of candy, toys, and games, and the kid says, "Is this all there is?" Then, he takes the optimist into a room full of horse manure and watches as the kid happily begins to dig. Shocked, the father asks him what he's doing, and the kid says: "Well, there's got to be a pony in here somewhere."

There are people in this world who are never happy, even if wonderful things happen to them. Either they expected more, or their brother has more, or it's not what they envisioned at all. By the same token, there are those who are content and happy with very little. The moral of this story is that we aren't responsible for what *happens* to us, but we're absolutely responsible for how we *respond*—and how we respond is our *attitude*.

Attitude, more than any other single factor, determines our lives. If you wake up in the morning and decide it will be a good day, then it will; if you decide it will be a lousy day, then it will be just that. You can win the lottery and still manage to say, "Yeah, but I gotta pay taxes," or "Yeah, but it wasn't a Superball," or "Yeah, but I gotta split it with three other people." (Or as author Wayne Dyer puts it, "You can wake up in the morning and gripe, 'Good God, it's another day!' or smile and say, 'Oh, good, God, it's another day.'")

Cranky folks like to describe themselves as realists, but whose reality? Realists like to view life as mean, brutish, and short . . . umm, that's not reality. "If I'm a pessimist, I'll never be disappointed" translates to: "I'm always disappointed and determined to be miserable!"

Happiness is a choice, but so is misery. Perpetual misery may be a safeguard against disappointment, but it also protects against happiness. Pessimists, I can hear you muttering, "Yeah, her first name is Joy, what do you expect her to say?" Don't buy what I'm saying sight unseen. Try test-driving happiness: Decide to be happy for the next hour; if that works, you can try it for the day. This is your life. *You* are the one in charge. You can choose to be happy. You really can.

❧ ❧ ❧

Attitude is more than just about being happy or miserable. Some of us have hard-working attitudes, some of us are more leisurely; some have a thrifty attitude, and others spend like there's no tomorrow. Ray's attitude is that he's a big spender, which has caused a financial crisis for him and his wife.

> *I've been having a big problem with credit cards. I've run up my bills to where it's really bad—I owe $15,000, and I net $1,900 a month. I think I'll get some money from my father and pay those cards off, but I'm afraid that my wife and I aren't disciplined enough to have credit cards. I want to cut them up, but what do you think I should do if my wife starts running them up again?*
>
> — Ray, 45, Las Vegas, NV

Wow! Basically, Ray, your attitude is clearly that spending money will make you happy, but it doesn't mesh with expecting your dad to bail you out or being "afraid" of not being disciplined. Your attitude is childish: "I'll act on impulse, and Daddy will bail me out." Ray, you're 45 years old—time for an attitude adjustment, since at this point, even if you didn't spend any money on rent, you still wouldn't be able to pay off your credit card bills this year. You and your wife shouldn't have credit cards at all. That means no "emergency card" either, because you'll use it and then you'll be up a creek when you really do have a crisis.

Forget credit cards and try to start saving. What you may decide to do is get a debit card for emergencies because it's only as good as the amount of money you have in the bank, and you can always put more money in. The advantage to having a bank account is that you actually *get* interest on it, as opposed to having to *pay* interest on the money you owe on your credit card. You two don't have the temperament for credit cards—you have a spending problem. Get rid of the plastic and don't even use the debit card that much. Use cash, because using credit cards is very easy, whereas parting with real twenties isn't. It's time to change your view of yourself from, "I'm a guy who doesn't care about money" to one that says, "I need to prove to myself that I'm a grown-up who doesn't need Daddy to bail me out."

Tool #10: Bribery Works

"Bribery" has gotten a bad reputation, when it's just the fine art of showing why it's in someone's best interest to do it your way. In fact, bribery is the essence of positive reinforcement, which is the idea that when someone does something we like, we give them a reason to do it again. Negative reinforcement, on the other hand, punishes someone for disappointing us to discourage them from doing it again. And in study after study, positive reinforcement has been proven to be the more effective technique.

I saw the value of bribery firsthand when my friend's daughter was in the second grade. Although she was getting straight A's, she was spending half of her time in the nurse's office because she liked the individual attention. My friend was worried that her daughter was getting the wrong message as to how the world works—she didn't want her thinking she could excel with no effort. So she said to her daughter, "Listen, if you try as hard as you can for six weeks, you'll get the reward of your choice." My friend subsequently ended up with two kittens, as well as a second grader who was neither slacking off nor resenting Mom for making her study.

In a way, bribery touches on our discussion of expectations being the death of serenity. Expecting people to do what we want, especially when what they want is altogether different from what we want, is the definition of *unrealistic*. A bribe, however, can be that wonderful peace offering that establishes the fact that *you* matter, your response matters, and your opinions matter.

❧ ❧ ❧

In Miguel's case, a bribe is just what the doctor ordered.

I've had a problem with my mom this past summer about how much time I spend on the phone. We kept track yesterday, and I spent 2 hours and 23 minutes throughout the day on the phone talking to my friends. Mom says she'd rather see me working or doing something productive. What should I do?

— Miguel, 14, Alexandria, VA

Miguel, what's irritating your mom is that she has to pay that phone bill, not to mention doing the cooking, the cleaning, the laundry, you name it, while you sit around and burn up the phone lines. She views you as getting a free ride, and it's irritating.

If you were 16 or 17, I'd say, "Miguel, get a clue, a job, and your own phone." Right now, though, you can't afford your own phone, so make the deal with your mom. Say to her, "Mom, draw up a list of chores that you want me to do. Then we'll sit down and estimate how long these will take me to do, and for every two minutes of chores, I'd like one minute of phone time." That way, you'll be able to use the phone and she won't nag you. She'll love you for this idea, Miguel. This really is the model for how to deal with your mom, your dad, or any adult who has more power than you do—figure out what they want from you, and offer it to them in exchange for what you want. Works every time!

Tool #11: Beware of All or Nothing

Human beings don't tolerate ambiguity very well. We love to see the world as black and white, right or wrong—we don't like gray. We like our decisions to be yes or no, such as: "Do I spend my bonus on a pair of shoes or put it in the bank?" But our decisions are much more likely to be: "Do I spend $500 on the shoes I really want, and then eat nothing but Spam for the next month, or do I spend $50 on these not-so-great shoes, but still eat like a human being?" (**Author's note:** For the record, I don't eat Spam [no offense intended, Spam-lovers], nor have I ever spent anywhere near $500 on shoes [hmmm, a Spam-eating Imelda Marcos, what an image].)

Most decisions fall into a gray area, although we have a tendency to try to make them black or white, right or wrong, good or evil, so that we can lower the anxiety and risk involved in possibly making the wrong choice. This is neither effective nor realistic. If you see the world as "my way or your way," you're going to lose a lot of maneuvering room and a lot of possibility for negotiation, cooperation, learning, and creative solutions.

Do you spend Christmas with your family as usual, or with your new wife's family? This is too black or white—somebody (maybe even everybody) is unhappy. Compromise can be found in the gray area—maybe you could spend Christmas Eve with one family and Christmas Day with the other; or Christmas with your family and New Year's Eve with your wife's, or vice versa; or alternate where you go every year; or get both families to your house for the holidays. If you see the possibilities of gray—negotiation and cooperation—and not black and white, you're increasing your options.

❦ ❦ ❦

Options can feel scary because choice means the possibility of choosing wrong. That's why all-or-nothing situations are so common. Todd's attempt at problem solving exemplifies this strategy.

*My sister-in-law, June, is having an affair with the hus-
band of my wife's best friend. June has ruined this family's
life; consequently, my wife no longer wants to hear from her
sister. Is it okay for us to cut her off completely?*

— Todd, 42, Louisville, KY

Todd, I understand your problem only too well, but your solution
leaves a lot to be desired. Major-league disapproval is to be expected,
but unless June is a toxic person on all counts, I don't see why you
have to shut her out of your lives. No one is saying that you should
embrace June and all her shortcomings with open arms, but why not
find a middle ground that allows you to maintain this key familial
relationship while keeping a moral distance?

This is a classic all-or-nothing situation, and it doesn't have to be.
You and your wife can easily explain to June that, while you don't want
to sever your relationship with her, the two of you have no interest in
hearing about her new relationship. Strike a deal—you'll still talk to
her and have her over for dinner, but she won't mention your wife's
best friend or the husband she snatched away from her.

While we're on the subject, focusing all of your anger on June is
an easy way out. When you say that "June has ruined this family's life,"
you seem to be neglecting one very important party—the husband.
After all, it's *his* wife and kids whose lives have been most affected
here. I understand your wife's frustration and embarrassment, but
these feelings alone aren't sufficient grounds for disowning a sister.
You and your wife don't have to mention June when the best friend is
around, and you can continue to communicate your disapproval of
June's relationship to her by refusing to discuss it. Cutting June out of
your lives isn't going to solve anything, so what's the point?

Tool #12: Prepare for Change—It's Inevitable

Human beings love routine and hate change. Routine may be
boring, but it's also peaceful and stable; while change is exhilarating,
it's also frightening and disorienting. Who cares if we're bored out

of our minds if the road to boredom is calm and smooth? Why bother to do something new and exciting if the path to such an adventure is scary and rough? The problem with this philosophy is that change is going to happen, whether you're ready or not. We expend tons of energy trying to keep everything the same rather than anticipating and preparing for change, thus making it less shocking to our change-averse system.

Ignorance isn't much fun, but it's a fact of life. Routine can lull us into a false sense of security, permanence, and immortality. Somehow, we believe that we can continue to show up at the same office at 9:00 A.M., drink our second cup of coffee at 10:00, have lunch at one of three predetermined restaurants at noon, gossip by the watercooler at 2:00 P.M., and play Free Cell at 4:30 for the rest of our livelong days. You need only recall your reaction to the news that one of your favorite products had been discontinued by the manufacturer to see that for humans, the idea of change is upsetting on a great many levels.

Death and taxes aren't the two certainties—death and *change* are. It's no wonder that we find change so terrifying, because in essence, change and death are one and the same. When you do something new, like alter a personality trait, move to a new city, or even invest in a new set of pajamas, a small part of you gets left behind. Suddenly, you're no longer Shy Sally, or Seattle Sally, or Sally who Sleeps in a Syracuse University Sweatshirt. Now, you're Outgoing Sally, or Chicago Sally, or Sally who Sleeps in a Nightgown. You have a different view of yourself, who you are, what you can do, how others see you, and a bit of that person you once were no longer exists. It's only natural that we try to hold on as long as possible to the person we've come to know and love before letting bits go and facing the mourning period.

❦ ❦ ❦

Tom's problem appears to be a family issue, but all he's really doing is resisting the natural change that comes with growing up.

I haven't been getting along with my parents lately. My father is an alcoholic, but my mom is only focusing on what she thinks is wrong with me. I'm going to junior college and getting decent grades—but my mom just kicked me out of the house and told me to find my own place to live because I came home late. I need money for school, and I don't know how I'm going to afford it if I have to pay rent. What should I do?

— Tom, 19, Cincinnati, OH

Tom, you're going through a process that everyone has to go through at some point in their lives. It's called "self-reliance." In your case, it's happening sooner rather than later, but eventually, everyone you know is going to be "kicked out" of their parents' home and forced to make their own way. Don't look at this as a difficult time with your parents, but as your time to leave the nest.

At 18, you probably view yourself as an adult, and emotionally, you are, but financially, you're not. Tom, get thee to the financial aid office and see what they can do for you. You might be eligible for scholarships and grants, student loans, or work-study programs. If not, you can go to school part-time and work part-time, or go to school at night and work during the day. Of course, this is going to be more difficult than relying on your parents, but no one ever said that growing up was going to be easy. And that's the point: You'll be a stronger, more mature adult for the experience.

That major change from kid to adult can happen at 18, 28, or 88. But since it's one of the most significant changes you're ever going to go through, the fact that it's happening for you now is good—that way, you'll get used to the idea that change is a normal, frequent, often upsetting, sometimes exciting, but inevitable part of life.

Playing Doctor

See if you can help Linda and Jerry figure out which of the 12 tools we've discussed works best for their problems.

My co-worker and I went out on two dates in two weeks, and then he started cancelling on me. Yesterday, I found out he's had a girlfriend all along. Should I confront him?

— Linda, 37, Durango, CO

1. What tool would you use to help guide Linda?

   (a) Expectations are the death of serenity.
   (b) Don't confess.
   (c) By describing we bring into being.
   (d) Listen to the Universe's voice.

Choice "a" is the correct response. Choices "c" and "d" are partially right, in that they can help to change Linda's attitude toward her co-worker. By redefining the situation (option "c") she can let go of her indignation and be flattered that when her co-worker wanted to test the dating waters, he chose to ask her out. Option "d" is also a good way for Linda to diffuse some of her disappointment. Of course, had Linda simply kept her expectations in check, she wouldn't have to redefine the situation or try to be philosophical about being blown off. Choice "b" is wrong because it has nothing to do with the matter at hand—confession and confrontation are not one and the same. Linda's main problem is that she allowed her expectations to get ahead of reality. Unmarried individuals are allowed to date different people, and it doesn't sound like her co-worker did anything wrong.

2. How would you respond to Linda's question regarding confronting her co-worker?

   (a) Yes, make a big scene right in the office.
   (b) No, let it go.
   (c) No, confront his girlfriend instead.
   (d) I'll say! While you're at it, you might also think about filing a sexual-harassment suit.

The correct response is "b." As we saw in our response to question number 1, this co-worker has not done anything wrong. He's neither married nor engaged, so he's entitled to ask out anyone he chooses. Making a scene, confronting his girlfriend, and filing a sexual-harassment suit all fall under the "fatal attraction" category. Unfounded expectations are dangerous precisely because we tend to overreact when we're disappointed.

❧ ❧ ❧

Three years ago, my wife died, leaving me with two boys who are now 11 and 12. Last year, I met someone whose husband had died several years before and who had kids the same age as mine. After about a week of dating, we all moved in together. While it's been a great experience, she seems a bit too hung up on money, and it's irritating me. I mean, just yesterday, she told the kids that they couldn't all go out for ice cream because it was too expensive. It's just ice cream! What should I do?

— Jerry, 41, Tucson, AZ

1. Of the 12 tools we covered in this chapter, which do you think applies to Jerry?

   (a) Do good.
   (b) Attitude is everything.
   (c) Beware of all or nothing.
   (d) Listen to the Universe's voice.

Choice "d" is the most applicable to Jerry's particular case. The money hang-up is just the universe telling Jerry that perhaps he rushed this relationship. The things that brought him and girlfriend together were feelings of bereavement, sexual needs, and kids. But they don't know each other. They moved too fast and now they have to rewind.

2.   How would you suggest that Jerry proceed?

   (a) Break up.
   (b) Move out and start dating each other exclusively.
   (c) Enroll in couples therapy.
   (d) Listen to your girlfriend and stop being such a spendthrift.

Choice "a," is too drastic after an entire year of relatively happy cohabiting. Choice "d" would mean ignoring the irritation that Jerry feels, a clear warning sign that all is not right with the living arrangement. Choice "c" may be premature considering that this is a pair that has never made a truly conscious decision to stay together or focused on what they have in common other than mutual grief. I would consider this option primarily because of the four kids involved. Even though choice "b" is more difficult, it's the most sensible—even though it's difficult. Moving out and returning to dating mode will help Jerry and his girlfriend get to know each other for who they truly are as opposed to who they want and need each other to be. It also gives the kids some breathing room. As y'all probably know, I am *not* a fan of cohabiting when there are kids involved.

Shrink Wrap

The way we think about what happens to us is almost entirely responsible for how we feel about ourselves and the world around us. This chapter has been about viewing ourselves as part of a larger whole. We're not alone in this world, and the following tools go a long way toward making our jobs as components of the ecosystem easier:

- **The Universe's voice** reminds us that there's something larger than the immediate.

- **When one door closes, another one opens.**

- **Blurring our perspective** allows us to understand that we don't know it all.

- **"Do good"** is grammatically incorrect, but it's moral, ethical, and fulfilling, too.

- **Confession doesn't right a wrong.**

- **Tolerating differences** is key to learning and growing.

- **When we describe, we bring into being.**

- **Expectation is the death of serenity.**

- **Attitude makes all the difference.**

- **Bribes are a sign of respect** for both your views and those of others.

- **All or nothing isn't a workable approach to life.**

- **Prepare for change; it's inevitable.**

STEP 8:
❧ INTERACTIONS ❧

Two years ago, I got a divorce, and for the next six months, I wasn't able to see my now 17-year-old son and 15-year-old daughter. Access became a problem when my ex-wife sent them off to an orthodox religious school and constantly bad-mouthed me to them. So I filed for custody and put in a motion to have my son for the summer. While he was staying with me, we went to look at a new high school. During a hearing for temporary custody, he told the judge that he really liked the school. But now that it's become an issue of permanent custody, he's saying he's not interested anymore. What do I do?

— Norman, 44, Concord, MA

Norman, you and your ex-wife don't seem to be doing a very good job of letting your kids have much emotional space. They must feel as if they're wishbones, and each of their parents is grabbing a leg and yanking. If you and your ex don't want to be married to each other, so be it, but you can't make the kids choose which one of you they love best—yet that's what both of you are trying to do.

Right now, the best thing to do is tell your children, "I love you dearly. Wherever you're most comfortable is fine with me. If you're with your mom, I want to make arrangements to see you. If you're with me, obviously we'll arrange for you to see your mom. But know that I love you, and this isn't a popularity contest. I know it's hard for you guys, but it's a hard time for me, too. You can love me *and* your mom, you can live wherever you choose, and both of us will still be a presence in your life no matter where you are physically."

The bottom line is that you guys have got to lay off of the high-pressure tactics. Taking your son to schools, bad-mouthing each other, dragging them into court . . . your kids are gonna have ulcers, and that's not fair! Since most courts will allow children of this age to have a say in determining their living arrangements, you may as well accept their decision about where they want to live—even if you think it may have been made under duress.

As for your son, yes, he might have told you and the judge one thing, but he may have told his mother something else. You could talk to your lawyer about this and go to court, but first try to be a bit more understanding. Maybe the kid changed his mind, maybe he found a girlfriend, maybe Mom said she'd buy him a car, or maybe he tells both of you what he thinks you want to hear. I don't know what went on (after all, 17-year-olds aren't exactly known for their reliability), but my point is that your son isn't a trophy. He'll be fine living with either of you, since he'll spend most of his time in school and with his friends anyway. If you and his mother don't make this a battleground, then he'll probably emerge from adolescence okay. You don't want your child feeling like no matter what he does, he's going to disappoint a parent. But that's what you're doing and *you have to stop it.*

At this moment, I'd let him be. I would affirm to him how much you love him, how difficult you know the choice is for him, and that you'll still love him no matter what. Cut him some slack on this— after all, we're not talking about the rest of anybody's life here. All we're talking about is trying very hard to not damage a child, and I don't think you're working hard enough at it. I know your feelings are hurt, Norman, but this is *not* the way to handle things.

❧ ❧ ❧

Jean-Paul Sartre once said, "Hell is other people." Now, while I wouldn't exactly second that motion, Norman's example does illustrate the difficulty that competing agendas present in our lives. So, in this chapter, we're going to focus on *interactions*. Now that you've absorbed the first seven steps in this book, you're not locked in the past, you know who you are, you have perspective, and you understand where you're going as well as how to get there. So it's time to take this show on the road—and that means dealing with other people.

The first thing you have to understand about interaction is that it's a two-way street. You know your own motives and intentions, but to get where and what you want in life, you'll have to understand that other people have their own set of motives and intentions, too. I know I've spent a lot of time encouraging you to not read other people's minds, but you have to understand that you're not the only one with an agenda if you're to bypass the kind of conflicts that can keep you stuck. Step 8 deals specifically with issues related to smoothing the course of interactions, which are the following:

- People do things for a reason.

- Positive reinforcement works.

- You need to pick your battles.

- If you have nothing to spare, you have nothing to share.

- Apologies, overtures, and forgiveness are crucial life tools.

People Do Things for a Reason

The basic rule of interaction is that we all do things for a reason. But unless you give the people in your life a highlighted copy of this book, they may not be as self-aware as you are right now. Still, you're going to be much better off if you make the assumption (and you know how much I hate assumptions) that you're like other people in the sense that you're acting from motive and intent and so are they.

If someone's actions seem illogical, then you should suppose that you're missing a piece of the puzzle. Logic just means "internal consistency," which we all have. Thinking *I'm the only logical person around here* is a big mistake. For example, the statement "You're overreacting" is ridiculous and patronizing, for there's no such thing as an overreaction—people always act consistently with their motives, intent, experience, or understanding.

I'm asking you to do a very tricky thing, which is to keep in mind what your reasons are on the one hand, but understand that other people *also* have reasons, which may or may not be consistent with yours. Therefore, when you bump into conflict, instead of blaming, try to unravel what your motives and intents are first; then attempt to help the other person understand what theirs are. This way, both of you can see exactly what you're trying to accomplish, where your goals meet, where they part ways, and where the middle ground lies.

What Do You Want?

I'm going to clue you in to one of the secrets of the universe: We all take bad stuff personally. If something's going wrong, our first assumption is that we're somehow responsible. If our team loses, it's because we didn't root hard enough. If a colleague gets fired, it's because we spent too much time chatting with them and kept them away from their work. Blame is a knee-jerk reaction, precisely because we feel that our terrible secret has come out—we're not perfect after all, and someone's going to point the finger at us. But before they even get a chance to do that, we'll point our own finger and try to deflect the blame onto someone else.

A very powerful way of understanding another person's agenda when you're in conflict with each other is to ask, calmly and gently and without sarcasm, anger, or frustration, "What do you want?" This doesn't mean that you have to go along with it, but you need to clarify and understand the situation for yourself. Asking, "Okay, in your fantasy, how would this play out?" will focus the other person on their motives and intent. You can then listen to their answer and begin matching your own motives to theirs.

For example, let's say that one morning your co-worker comes in to work and he's visibly distraught. You gently comment that he doesn't seem too happy, and he mumbles under his breath that he's fine. But then you go on to ask him if there's anything you can do to make the situation better. Now, the moment you start asking him questions, several things can happen. Perhaps you misread him, but since you're being open and really trying to help, he'll say, "I really appreciate your concern, but I'm fine." He might even ask you why you thought he was upset.

If he wasn't unhappy and you just misread the signals, you'll now be better informed about what's going on. Better still, in the process of clarification, you've both gained from the interaction because two great things have happened: (1) You're feeling better because he's not unhappy; and (2) he's feeling better about you because you've shown him you cared.

If your co-worker really is unhappy, you can ascertain if he's unhappy with *you* or with someone else. If someone else is upsetting him, then your concern has opened the door to conversation. He might decide to tell you: "My girlfriend is driving me crazy, but I really don't want to talk about it right now."

Again, you've both won. If he does take you up on the offer to talk about it, you can find out what's wrong. In the end, he'll feel better and so will you. You will have been helpful to him, and he will have seen your kindness. Even if he doesn't take the opportunity to share, he'll probably still feel good because you were so concerned about him, and you'll feel good because you're not taking his bad mood personally. So far, you're on a roll.

But what if he is, in fact, unhappy with you? Well, you can either become defensive and hostile, or ask him what you're doing that's causing him concern—or if you don't want to make him feel self-conscious about it, you could ask, "If the situation could be anything you want it to be, what would you make it?"

If you decide to react defensively, then you have no business asking your co-worker what's bothering him. However, having read this book and thereby being armed with a strong grasp of your motives, you are now able to understand that two people can disagree and it doesn't mean that either of them is wrong—sincere, nice people actually can disagree. Equipped with this understanding, you can get to the heart of the matter and begin problem-solving by giving your co-worker the power to make a wish and turn the situation into anything he wants, giving him enormous power without making him feel defensive.

Presumably, this approach will enable him to sort out his feelings and figure out what's bothering him. Maybe he'll say, "If I was in charge of the world, you'd show up on time," or "We could have better communication if we meet weekly." Hopefully, he'll be smart about it and realize that you haven't given him an invitation to rip you to shreds. In the end, anything you sort out together is a win-win situation because you've made him feel comfy, safe, and cared for, and he's supplied the information that you were after.

Mutual satisfaction is the goal of all human interaction, but since people have different motives and intentions, we have to put some effort into figuring out what these drives are so that we can arrive at a resolution that's acceptable to all involved.

Get Me to the Point

The question "What do you want?" is a great focusing tool, because information is the only way to get to a resolution. It can cut through a lot of blather and be incredibly effective when coupled with a smile. Tone of voice matters a *lot*. Your question needs to sound sincere and heartfelt—the subtext has to be, "I want to know. I'm interested." Anger is a response to the feeling that attention isn't being paid; that no one's listening, no one cares, and that we're not important. So asking somebody what they want can make a big difference.

But beware—folks are sometimes reluctant to unravel their tangled webs and get to the point. I'm allowed a huge privilege on the radio that most of us don't have in day-to-day life: I have the leeway to actually ask people, "Can you get me to the point on this?" Although this technique is incredibly useful, it can be a bit bloody sometimes. So, you should only use it if you've reached the end of your rope with somebody.

Again, remember that your tone of voice is crucial. Before you say, "Can you get me to the point here," try buffering the potential blow with phrases such as "I'm getting a little lost in the details" or "I'm a simple person and I'm not exactly sure where you'd like me to focus." This way, you're shouldering the responsibility *and* helping the other person to focus and bring you closer to a happy resolution.

❧ ❧ ❧

Janine's problem is that she can't relate to her father because she refuses to accept that he has a reason to do what he's doing.

> *Recently, my father has been acting very strange. The man is 62 years old, and he's started dating an "exotic dancer" who can't be a day over 30. He bought a Ferrari, left his legal practice, and is building a cabin in the mountains so that he can have privacy and inspiration to write a book about his life. I think he's getting senile. What do you think?*
>
> — Janine, 33, Portland, OR

Janine, I don't think senility is your father's problem. It seems like your dad is having a ball, and *you're* the one with the problem. Although you may not agree with some of his choices, he's clearly earned the right to do as he pleases, since he's worked long and hard all his life.

I understand that it's uncomfortable to see your heretofore stable and reliable father going a bit haywire on you. He's acting out in a way that's not at all in keeping with the person you've come to know and love. Suddenly, everything he does seems to contradict what you took to be his values and principles. But have you really stopped to think about *his* needs, goals, and dreams? Have you two ever talked about what he sees for himself in his future? Do you know if he loved his job or if he was just doing it out of a sense of obligation? Did he hate the family station wagon, enjoy the law, or wear thong underwear? Okay, scratch the last question, but you do see my point, right?

It sounds like it's time for an open and honest discussion with your dad. Ask him questions such as, "Where would you like to see this relationship with Fifi La Rue go?" "Do you see yourself ever going back to work?" "What's really crucial to you?" or "What about me? Will I have a place in your new life?" Instead of focusing on how to best serve your own motives and intents (whatever those may be), really listen to what your father is saying—and remind yourself that his actions have nothing to do with how he feels about you. If he's experiencing a kind of rebirth, it's not because *you've* disappointed him, nor does it necessarily mean that he's been living a lie his entire life. In other words, taking his behavior personally is missing the point. This is about *him*, not *you*.

Janine, think of your father as a bus driver and of yourself as a passenger sitting way in the back of the bus. Your father is steering, trying to get around pedestrians, bicyclists, and cars and avoid a traffic jam. From where you're sitting, though, all you can see is that the bus isn't moving along as fast or as steadily as the other cars on the street. You're in a hurry, the pressure is on, and your body heat is rising. You'd probably be thinking, *This driver is incompetent!* But the truth is, your father is allowed to run his own life— it's *his* bus, and his perspective is different from yours. Janine, maybe it's time to move to the front of the bus and see what traffic looks like from his point of view . . . just be sure to stay behind that white line, please.

Reinforcing the Positive

It's extraordinary how much time with the people in our lives— such as our children, our employees, and our significant others—is spent on catching them doing something wrong. This is a counterproductive approach that sends the message that the people we care about are constantly being judged and being found wanting. All of us respond very poorly to the notion that there's something wrong with us because, as we've talked about before, that's precisely what we already feel. The feeling that no matter what we are, it's wrong, is the downside to our society, So anytime you catch someone doing something wrong, you reinforce all of their insecurities, which constantly reminds them that they're not okay.

Now then, how do you go about modifying others' behavior to suit your best interests? Well, just as we discussed in the last chapter, positive reinforcement is a technique that works whether you're dealing with your lover, employee, child, or friend. When you reinforce the positive, you're saying, "This is what you're good at; I value this about you," and it moves people away from that black hole of insecurities that are within us all.

Instead of tearing people apart, positive reinforcement helps people find a positive way of behaving. If you ignore the negative and reinforce the positive, you'll be working on the *useful* assumption that past the age of two, most people know right from wrong. And if you let someone deal with their own conscience, then you're letting them sort things out for themselves.

This reminds me of a client I once had. She came in and announced, "I need to find a job."

"What do you want to do?" I asked.

"I really don't want to be a secretary," she said.

"What *do* you want to do?"

"Well, I hate typing and I really hate filing."

"Okay . . . what would you *like* to do?"

"I can't stand having someone else tell me what to do."

Ugh! All this woman could think about specifically was the negative stuff—she couldn't focus on anything other than what she *didn't* want. So we ended up spending a lot of time talking about the power of specificity, and how if we describe it, we bring it into being. The same principles hold true in interactions—if you describe and reinforce the positive, you're giving someone a very specific way of thinking about their behavior. (I'd add "sincere" here, too, because if all your praise sounds the same regardless of person or situation, it will have no value whatsoever.)

❦ ❦ ❦

Lois's son is just crying out for some positive reinforcement.

I'm having a problem with my 17-year-old son. This year, he went away to boarding school because he thought it was a better educational opportunity. But because he was on his own for the first time and was exposed to a wide range of people, we're having a reentry problem now that he's back at home with me, his dad, and his brother. For example, last night he said, "Everyone else is smoking, drinking, and doing drugs, and I don't feel I'm being rewarded for not doing these things." How are we supposed to respond to that?

— Lois, 47, Richmond, VA

Lois, why not ask the obvious question: "What kind of reward do you want?" Your son is legitimately pointing out that the way to get attention in our society and in his age group is to make a mess of things, to use drugs, to get somebody pregnant, to drive a car too fast, and to bad-mouth your parents. He's not doing any of that, and he seeks a little applause. So when he says, "I'd like a reward," ask him what he wants. Because if nothing else, you'll get some insight into his exact thinking. You won't be promising compliance, just curiosity.

Don't worry about what will happen if he asks for something exorbitant. You'll cross that bridge if and when you ever get to it. My guess is that he's just saying, "I want some attention," which isn't unreasonable. But do be prepared if he says, "I want a Porsche"—of course you can also say, "Well that's nice, *I'd* like a Porsche, too"— but at least you'll have a starting point for discussion (or shopping!).

Lois, at this point, your son is essentially saying, "Pay attention to me! I don't want to feel like I'm a nice guy and nice guys finish last. I also don't want to be taken for granted." I'm sure you can understand how that feels, right?

Choose Your Battles

No matter how evolved you are and no matter how much you reinforce the positive, conflicts will inevitably arise in your interactions—which could be because the other person isn't as evolved as you are, has a different perspective, or just isn't you. Slipups and complaints are a fact of life, but it's important to pick your battles. If you're always sniping at somebody, then you're going to be out of ammunition when it's time to tackle the complaint that really matters.

Choosing your battles is the flip side to reinforcing the positive. Sometimes, not paying attention can be a very powerful tool—so be judicious, close your eyes to the minor transgressions for the greater good, and realize that people would rather be praised than punished— and they'd rather be punished than ignored. In other words, don't jump on every little thing, and don't lash out!

In families and relationships, the best way to avoid sniping at each other is to pick one day a week to talk about what's going on. That way, you'll be assured that six days is the longest you'll ever have to wait to be heard. You can take that time to get a pen and paper and write down all the instances of the negative behavior, as well as to figure out how important your complaint is and whether or not you can let it go.

Weekly gripe sessions allow issues to be examined at regularly scheduled times, so the "You always; you never" trap can be avoided. Problems are solved when they're still fresh, never more than a week old. Sniping is no longer necessary, events are current—what happened ten years ago doesn't have any relevance because if the problem is ongoing, it can be resolved now, and if it's no longer an issue, why bother discussing it?

❦ ❦ ❦

Marla has chosen a useless battle, and she's winding up missing the forest for the trees in the process.

I need some insight and reassurance about my 15-year-old son's behavior. He's recently started wearing his hair spiked— he puts gel and beeswax in it. He's really a good kid, but he seems to like attention. I'm a little concerned about the hair, though. It looks awful! Can I place restrictions on it? I told him that he can't wear it that way to school.

— Marla, 44, Concord, NH

Look around, Marla—your son's look is very hip! Don't you remember *your* mother saying that bell-bottoms made you look funny and exposed your navel, or that tie-dye didn't suit you? How about the way our parents used to hate long hair on guys? Older men would say, "We can't tell if it's a boy or a girl from the back," and it was like, *Hello?! That's what we're trying to do here.* This is the same thing. Yes, Marla, you've officially become your mother. Every generation has to find a way to drive the previous one nuts, and hair is certainly one of the ways to do it. Today's boys *and* girls are wearing their hair all kinds of ways (or they're shaving their heads), which of course, drives their parents wild. Your son is just saying, "Mom, I'm not your little boy anymore; I'm my own person." And he's picked a relatively benign way of doing it. After all, he doesn't have a pink mohawk or messages shaved in his scalp—which he may still decide to do—but he has come up with a way to set himself apart from you and his dad.

School is *his* business, Marla. Of course you can say, "You can't wear it that way when we go visit Grandma" . . . but all you'll do is give him a good excuse not to visit Grandma. The same goes for church, your friends, and your niece's wedding.

If you're asking me, "Do kids want to look naughtier than they are?" Sure, nobody wants to look like a goody two-shoes . . . you wanted to look like a harlot when you were a virgin, and he wants to look like a tough homie, even though he's a middle-class suburban kid. That's normal. But I would definitely lay off this, Marla. Choose your battles. If you fight this one, that means that you're going to lose sight of some of the more important things related to your son—such as the fact that he does well in school, he's respectful, he's not doing drugs, and he's not a wild kid—he just has a wild hairdo. What you can do is spike *your* hair or have your husband spike his . . . and see how fast Junior stops. After all, if you guys do it, how hip can it be? And if nothing else, a few years from now, you'll look back on that Christmas card with the strange hairdo and get a lump in your throat remembering the years he was still living at home and driving you nuts.

If You Have Nothing to Spare, You Have Nothing to Share

There are times in every relationship when we're just flat-out unavailable—we're sick, sad, tired, stressed, or some combination of these factors. And it happens to the people we love as well. These are tricky times in a relationship because, just as you can't invite anyone over for dinner if your pantry is bare, you can't share *yourself* if you have no emotion and energy to spare.

Luckily, most people are perfectly willing to occasionally accept this behavior because they've been there themselves, especially if we let them know of our mood ahead of time . . . unfortunately, we don't always know ahead of time. The thing to do when you bump into this type of situation is to not be embarrassed about it, just admit it. Simply divulging that you didn't even realize until this moment how stressed you were or how upset the argument you had with your mom made you can work miracles. If you can tell somebody what set you off, they won't take it personally—and if you promise to make it up to them so that they've got something to look forward to, most people are willing to cut you some slack.

❦ ❦ ❦

Doug's girlfriend sounds as if she's about had it with his couch-potato ways.

> *I have a very tough job that keeps me in the office up to 15 hours a day. Sometimes I don't have the energy to entertain my girlfriend, and she gets really mad at me. She says that if I'm going to be tired and stressed out, I shouldn't invite her over. But I miss her and want to see her. What should I do?*
>
> — Doug, 27, Chicago, IL

Doug, listen to what your girlfriend is saying. She not only has a valid point, but a specific prescription, too. Even if she'd only planned to spend the evening watching TV in her pajamas, coming over to your place to watch you mope or nod off is not her idea of a good time. It's not that she doesn't love you or enjoy spending time with you, but decreasing the *quantity* of time you spend together might improve the *quality* of your time.

It's more than a little insulting for you to assume that any time *with* you is better than time *without* you. It's not that your girlfriend is asking you to entertain her, but she would like you to put forth some effort. Now, if energy is the last thing you have after putting in a grueling day at the office, then maybe you should let her know in advance that you're not going to be good company and that you need a rain check. That way, she doesn't wind up doing her hair, polishing her nails, choosing her outfit, and wasting perfectly good perfume on a boyfriend who won't even notice, since all he really wants is a warm body to pass out next to.

Doug, I think you might be worried that breaking a date will upset her, but trust me when I tell you that she'll appreciate your consideration if you promise to wine and dine her like a movie star come the weekend. You might also want to think about not making plans on Monday nights or other times when you know you'll be tired—that way, she won't spend her entire day anticipating a fun time only to hear about how beat you are, how your boss is a moron, and how you're the company's most unappreciated genius. You might say, "This is an extremely busy week at the office, so I need to focus all my energy on getting the job done. I want to see you very much, but I'm not going to be a good date until this weekend." Then you'll probably find that she'll be receptive to the arrangement. And if she decides to come over anyway, that's okay, because you'll have been honest, she'll know what to expect, and both of you will be able to relax.

Apologies, Overtures, and Forgiveness

Since none of us are perfect creatures, we need to learn how to properly apologize. Again, this goes back to motive and intent, because understanding someone else's motives can help you figure out what you did wrong, how to apologize for it, and how to behave differently next time.

An apology has to be sincere and specific, but it doesn't have to include an explanation. The following, for example, are *not* authentic apologies:

- "I'm sorry you feel that way."

- "Well, I'm sorry—I guess it's always my fault."

- "I suppose you want an apology from me."

- "You misunderstood what I meant."

- "You brought this on yourself."

In addition, be sure that you know the difference between an apology and an overture. An overture is, in essence, asking a favor of someone. You're asking the person to forgive you without taking responsibility—while an apology takes responsibility. An apology says, "I'm laying myself on the line here. I care enormously about you, and I want to make this problem go away. I know how to do it because I know where the problem lies. I messed up, I blew it, and I take responsibility for the mistake as well as for the rehabilitation." An overture, on the other hand, says, "I don't like this feeling, and I want to make it okay, but I have no idea how to do it. Please tell me what to do."

If someone refuses to accept your apology, telling them to "Get over it already!" is unwise, futile, and inappropriate. When you've hurt someone's feelings, it isn't up to *you* to tell them how long it's going to take to feel okay. Furthermore, the apology should fit the offense. The tangible aspect of an apology plays a vital role in this, which is why I'm such a fan of the "grovel bouquet." For example, if you stood someone up at their mother's house for dinner, a simple "Gee, I'm sorry" isn't going to work. Not only did you stand them up, which is insulting enough, but you did it in front of their mother! This is flowers, chocolates, and ticker-tape parade time! Serious groveling needs to be done here, and that's okay.

Everybody has a difficult time saying "I'm sorry" because it makes us feel vulnerable. It brings us face-to-face with the fear that our terrible secret (that we're not perfect) is going to be exposed. But the truth is that it's almost as difficult to accept an apology as it is to offer one. That's why it's important to try to be as gracious as possible when receiving an apology.

In accepting the apology, it's perfectly okay to say, "I'm willing to forgive you if you do this [such as clean the house for a month, promise never do it again, and so forth]." Unless you're prepared to go through life always bearing a grudge, it's not a bad idea to think through what it would take for this relationship to heal. Even if you don't want it to be remedied, you're still better off treating your psyche as a magic slate—just erase that grudge. Since letting go is much easier said than done, here are a few techniques to help you:

1. Close your eyes and breathe deeply. What you're trying to do is break up that logjam, so try to remember a time when you felt loved and cared for. Allow your intellect to dissolve, and break up that big lump of anger or sadness that you

have inside you. Then look around and see if you can take your situation a little less personally by asking, "Has this happened to anyone else?"

2. Understand that even if you've bashed heads with someone, it doesn't mean that everything is over forever. When we don't get what we want, there's naturally a part of us that feels unworthy, hurt, lost, and sad, so if you can remind yourself that this is just a lousy feeling and there's no factual basis to it, you can choose not to feel that way. You can say, "What if I decided to *not* feel this way, to *not* take this personally? What if I decided to move forward?" Victimization is about passivity, so if you can ask, "What are my needs? Are there other ways of dealing with this?" then you're finally taking control.

3. Revisit the grudge in a way that allows you to float above it by playing "Be a Martian, Be Thy Neighbor, or Be a Browne." Then you can use a technique that I use on the air all the time. Someone will call in and say, "So-and-so hurt my feelings," and I'll ask, "Well, do you think *you've* ever hurt anybody's feelings?" And of course, they have. So if we can understand our own motives at the time we hurt someone else's feelings, then by forgiving ourselves, we can forgive them, or vice versa.

4. Even if you're not actively harboring a grudge at this very moment, you can still benefit by thinking about the important role *forgiveness* plays in our lives. Grudges sludge up our systems by taking little parts of our psyche and occupying them with negative energy. But they can also take a toll on our self-esteem. When people keep going back to their grudges and focusing on them, they can end up with a self-image that sounds a lot like this: "Well, ever since I was two, people kept hurting my feelings. There was the time my

teacher took me out of the school recital, the time my next-door neighbor broke my skateboard, the time that no one wanted to sit next to me on the school bus . . . I guess there's something about me that makes people want to hurt me. I'm weak, I'm ugly, and everybody hates me." Whew! Forgiving others is a gift to self and forgiving others allows for generosity to others.

A wound will heal by itself unless you keep picking at it. A grudge keeps a wound open, infected, and damaged. We *can* choose to heal and let go. A grudge doesn't have to be permanent—you can write it on a piece of paper and burn, bury, flush, or shred it. Or you can try this technique that a friend showed me during a sad moment in my life—she told me to hold out my hand (palm facing upward), bring my hand to my mouth, and blow on my fingers. In other words, *blow it off.* It works. Concentrate on whatever pain, sadness, or loss is weighing you down, and blow it off.

Playing Doctor

Test your knowledge of interactions on Jodi.

My 5-year-old thinks he's 16! When he was young, I made the mistake of not disciplining him, and now he thinks he runs the house. For instance, if I ask him to follow me so I can give him his bath, he'll refuse because he's watching TV. Or, I'll ask him to pick up his toys, and then I'll check back and it still won't be done. Is it too late to get him to behave himself?

— Jodi, 32, Lahaina, HI

1. What two principles of interactions apply in Jodi's case?

   (a) "Choose your battles," *and* "If you have nothing to spare, you have nothing to share."

(b) "Reinforce the positive," *and* "Apologies, overtures, and forgiveness."

(c) "Pick your battles," *and* "Apologies, overtures, and forgiveness."

(d) "People do things for a reason," *and* "Reinforce the positive."

Choice "d" is the correct response. Jodi isn't giving her son any reason to do as she says. Since, as I've mentioned, just about everyone past the age of two knows the difference between right and wrong, Jodi's son is refusing to do as he's told for a reason, and he's getting attention for what he knows is negative behavior. Jodi needs to reinforce positive behavior with sufficient consistency to convince her son to behave. Choices "a," "b," and "c" are incorrect because they have little to do with Jodi's immediate concern. This is one battle that Jodi must choose if she wants her son to grow up and become a productive member of society.

2.   What advice would you give Jodi for how to deal with her son in the future?

(a) Reason with him and praise his good behavior.

(b) Spare the rod, spoil the child.

(c) Refuse to speak with him whenever he does something "bad."

(d) Bribe him with toys and field trips if he takes his bath.

The best response is choice "a," because at this point, Jodi's son has no understanding of why he needs to do what she says. Jodi seems to think that *If he loves me, he'll do what I say,* but the reality is that he's going to do what he wants, which is why Jodi has to give him options. It's important to explain why he should do what she tells him: "You can keep watching TV and get a bath later, but then there won't be a story. Or you can come take a bath now and then you'll get a bedtime story." And, when she approves of her son's behavior, Jodi needs to be vocal about it so that the little cherub understands that he's doing something right.

Choice "b" won't work, for as we've already seen, punishment comes in a distant second to positive reinforcement in the realm of behavior modification, not to mention that it mostly teaches a child that hitting is okay when you're frustrated—it's not. Choice "c" is better than a spanking, but it also focuses on the negative instead of celebrating the positive. As for "d," well, that can get ruinously expensive—both financially and psychologically—when you're dealing with an unruly five-year-old, because the child is likely to figure out that the more he acts out, the better chance he'll have of being rewarded when he does do something right. With her help, Jodi's son can understand the positive feelings that occur when Mom catches him doing something right, and both can celebrate what a good boy he is.

Shrink Wrap

Many, many books have been devoted to improving your interactions, winning friends, and influencing people. But you don't need to read the entire body of literature devoted to this stimulating field— just follow the five simple steps laid out in this chapter:

- Understand that **we all do things for a reason.**

- **Reinforce the positive to achieve satisfying interactions.**

- **Choose your battles** and don't lash out at everything.

- Be aware that **if you have nothing to spare, you have nothing to share.**

- **Learn the difference between making an overture and an apology,** practice forgiveness, and let go of grudges.

❧ CONCLUSIONS ❧

Conclusions? Already?! It seems like it was only moments ago that I was explaining the ideas behind time-shifting, the first step to getting unstuck. We've covered a great deal of territory since those pages, and hopefully, this book has equipped you with the tools you need to think as a problem-solving free spirit rather than a stuck-in-the-past, self-pitying, self-righteous blamer or pity-party host. And since this is *your* book, margin markings (I know, I was taught to *never* write in a book, too, but you have my permission), dog-eared pages, and underlined passages are all kosher, as is going back to review any techniques or insights that you found particularly helpful or difficult to understand—especially as you encounter specific problems in your life.

Since we've already summed up every chapter's key points in our handy-dandy "Shrink Wrap" sections, this won't be your typical end-of-the-book recap. The conclusions discussed here are more like parting thoughts and useful exercises, proving once again that it's never too late (even in a book) to learn something new and important!

Think of this chapter as my parting gift to you, a little goodie bag full of party favors and pleasant surprises. It's my way of making sure that you don't leave empty-handed.

I've divided the chapter into two sections: "Things to Think About," and "Things to Do."

Things to Think About	Things to Do
• Don't panic, take your time.	• Write it down.
• Resist the blame game.	• Practice square breathing.
• Don't start wars.	• Visualize and relax.
• Choose to be happy.	• Use your magic wand.

Don't Panic

Panic can be helpful in life-or-death situations, but it's a dangerous day-to-day emotion. It's as if your motor's being revved while it's still in neutral—which means that you're overtaxing the system without actually going anywhere or accomplishing anything. Panic releases adrenaline, which is speed without direction, energy without focus, and movement without plan.

A problem requires you to be your best—caring, thoughtful, considerate, and rational. Our society admittedly places great emphasis on doing things quickly, but in reality, how *fast* you do something is important only in relation to how *well* you do it. The rush to come up with an instant solution, and the tendency to react rather than think, are extremely expensive. Taking the time to be thorough and careful, will allow you to pick up the pace with practice.

If somebody asks you a question and you don't know the answer, it's okay to say, "Let me get back to you on that." Taking the time—whether it's a few minutes, hours, or days—to sort through is usually a good investment, as long as your actions are appropriate, they seldom need to be immediate. Especially for the impulsive among us, allowing 24 hours to respond is calming, focusing, even relaxing, and it's often much more effective. So the next time you're puzzled about something, sleep on it before making your decision.

❦ ❦ ❦

Panic is usually associated with real or imagined stress. However, we also tend to act without thinking of consequences because we want our anxiety to go away so that we'll feel better immediately. For instance, I recently got a call from Shawna, who, after not hearing from her date in three days, decided to leave a message on his answering machine. Shawna really wanted this guy to call her, but she jumped the gun because she was uncomfortable waiting for him, and she wanted the ball to be in his court. Unfortunately, there are a number of problems with this approach: (1) While not inherently obvious, it's always better to have the ball in your court (within your control) than in someone else's (where they have the power); (2) non-machines (this means any *living* thing) should *never* make a date with a machine; (3) in order to temporarily escape some discomfort, Shawna actually ended up acting as if she would prefer that the whole thing be over and done with rather than deal with the ambiguity and anxiety of waiting for a call; and (4) worst of all, her behavior gained her squat—she was *still* waiting for him to call! Three days really isn't very long—she could have either diverted herself temporarily or been willing to tolerate the old "Will he or won't he?"—and in the end, she would have been much better served to just cool her heels for a bit.

When we panic, we want to rid ourselves of uncomfortable feelings, but this often turns out to be counterproductive. Tolerating occasional and mild discomfort not only teaches us patience, but it allows us to avoid impulsive, irrational responses. Life isn't always fun, and *panic* by definition is a quick but short-lived response, so learning to wait out an uncomfortable situation is a crucial life skill. I'm not talking about suffering for any length of time, but testing our own limits gives us a sense of mastery, courage, strength, and self-knowledge . . . not a bad tuition for such crucial lessons. The anxiety or catalyst doesn't have to be anything major—the problem can be as mundane as flunking an exam because studying and worrying about the test questions felt miserable; or deciding, *If it's not going perfectly, I'm out of there* when a relationship goes through a rough patch. Working through your relationship's problems or mastering a course may involve the icky feeling that you're not in complete control and that even though you're working toward a really important goal, it may not come to fruition.

In theory, the immediate and unreasoned response to any challenge is to fight or run to escape the discomfort—in other words, to panic. Accepting discomfort, learning diversionary tactics, thinking through alternatives, rereading this book—anything that will keep you from acting on a panic-induced impulse—are important skills to master.

Panic only offers short-term solutions to long-term problems. The short-term solution to almost any problem is to cut and run. If somebody confronts you, punch him out or flee. If you don't like your job, quit. If you're unhappy in your relationship, leave. But in the long run, you're not actually solving the problem at all, and you wind up with this big black cloud of unresolved issues following you around like your own personal Greek tragedy.

So, when you're tempted to go for the quick fix, stop and take the time to figure out if this is a solution you can live with down the line, or if it's just a knee-jerk reaction. Of course, running may turn out to be a perfectly good solution for the long term, but make sure you've thought it through before you decide to bolt.

Don't Blame

In life, stuff happens and things go awry. Unfortunately, we rarely have a diabolical villain to blame for all of our problems. But somehow, we still manage to find people to blame—they're called "scapegoats." The problem with the blame game is that it gives away all our power because, instead of looking for solutions, we look for bad guys. Then we focus on making ourselves feel better by punishing the evildoers instead of actually solving our problems.

Sandy, a 28-year-old woman who called my radio program, immediately announced that her life had been ruined. A year before, a doctor had misdiagnosed her acute condition (bacterial endocarditis), and she's never been the same since. She had a laundry list of complaints: She's had to have open-heart surgery; she's no longer the positive, athletic person she used to be; she's in constant pain; she got fired from her job because her supervisor said that Sandy was always at doctors' appointments, and she was in the process of suing her doctor for malpractice, which required countless depositions. Sandy felt that *somebody* had to pay for her misery.

"So what's your question?" I asked.

"Well, I've actually got two: Number one—should I sue my boss? And number two—how do I get back to who I used to be?"

"Sandy, part of you is more or less on the right track, but the other part is dragging you to Blame City, which is a really nasty place. I'm afraid you're about to mortgage your present and future to your past," I told her. "You're alive *and* you're only 28 years old. I understand that you've had a really lousy time lately, but I want you to move on as quickly and strongly as possible. Doctors are human beings. They sometimes make mistakes, and yours was a tricky diagnosis. Since your next deposition is in two weeks, take that time to focus on everything about your situation, including your misery, your court battle, your surgery, and your unemployment. At the end of two weeks, turn everything over to your lawyer, because you'll either get money out of this or you won't—it will be over one way or another. Obsessing about it isn't going to do anybody any good."

"Well, what about suing my company?" Sandy asked.

"If I hear you correctly, you're telling me that you've spent most of the last year at one doctor's appointment or another, and you've been sick and unhappy," I said. "It sounds as if your company's complaint that you were never there was legitimate, so I'm not sure what suing them would accomplish. Maybe it's time to accept that the last year was the Universe trying to teach you Humility 101, or that some wonderful new chapter of your life is about to begin. Rather than focus any more on what sounds like a truly horrible year, let your lawyer deal with your suit, while *you* deal with your new life, including finding a new job."

Sometimes, even when rotten stuff happens, there simply isn't anyone to blame. Sandy was looking for a scapegoat when she should have been looking for solutions. Bacterial endocarditis is a difficult diagnosis and it can progress very quickly; so even if her physician had diagnosed her earlier, she may still have had to have the surgery. At this moment, Sandy's physically stable, but I'm worried about her soul. She could very well spend the rest of her life blaming "bad guys" for what's wrong with her life. I tried to make her see that by giving up the ability to realize that her life is ahead of her, instead of languishing on a hospital chart somewhere, Sandy was making a misdiagnosis of her own.

❦ ❦ ❦

Dividing the world into "good guys" and "bad guys" is a mistake, because when something goes wrong, it leaves us in a lousy place (the past) with a powerful opponent (our enemy), but *becoming* the bad guy is just as dumb and pointless. Telling people things they already know (invariably something negative) will make you the bad guy. For example, men call me up all the time to say, "My wife's put on weight, and when I tell her, she gets mad." Umm . . . *duh!* These guys are lucky that their wives don't go Hannibal Lecter on them and rip their faces off.

Have you ever noticed that when we tell somebody, "I'm only being honest," we're invariably telling them something bad? For example, I recently visited one of my sisters (who shall remain nameless), and she said, "I really don't like your hair that way."

"Why would you say that?" I asked.

"I'm just being honest," she said.

Being who I am, I told her, "Look, there are only two possibilities here. The first is that I like my hair, so who are you to tell me that you don't like it? It's my hair and I didn't ask for your opinion. The second possibility is that I got a bad haircut and I hate it, too—so why do I need you telling me that I don't look good? No matter how you look at it, if I haven't asked you what you thought about my hair, why would you volunteer the information, especially when you're being negative?"

Most of us live in a land of mirrors, so we know when we've put on weight, when our haircut isn't flattering, or when we look tired. So telling somebody something negative under the guise of, "Hey, I'm only being your friend," "I just thought you'd wanna know," or "I'm just being honest" is tacky, adds to the world's misery quotient, and is definitely not okay.

Don't Start Wars

Even when you're dealing with somebody who's completely screwy, you still have a choice: You can choose to be a peacemaker or a warmonger. I'm not saying that you have to appease totally irrational people, but you *can* find a way to set some limits that would enable peaceful coexistence without compromising your personal integrity.

Take Naomi, for instance. She called and told me that her husband had committed serial adultery over the course of their five-year marriage. She finally tossed him out, and mentioned that her best friend, Kirsten, had been instrumental in helping her through this. Recently, however, Kirsten had embarked upon an affair with a married man herself, and Naomi was not amused.

"Naomi, do you really want to start a war?" I asked her. "You don't need to have it out with Kirsten about her affair if you set limits with each other. Make a deal with her—tell her that you'll promise not to complain to her about how wretched you feel if she promises not to tell you how happy she is."

It was clear to me that every time Naomi complained about how miserable she was, Kirsten viewed this as Naomi's way of laying a guilt trip on her. And every time Kirsten told Naomi about what a great time she was having with the married guy, Naomi was reminded of her husband's affairs with other women. Although both women have legitimate points of view in the friendship (I've never been a fan of adultery, but we're talking about a long-term friendship, not a recitation of the Ten Commandments), and can easily choose to go to war with one another, they can also choose to put forth some effort, work to preserve their friendship, and avoid an emotional bloodbath by setting some limits.

Choose Happiness

Happiness is a choice, and there's no better proof of this than what happened after September 11, 2001. Ever since the terrorist attacks, thousands of people have called me with myriad fears, such as, "What about anthrax? Should I fly? What about smallpox? What about an atomic bomb in a suitcase?"

And I keep telling them, "Just try to commit suicide by terrorist, and then tell me how easy it is."

First of all, to succeed at dying this way, you have to be in the right city, at the right time; you also need to be in the right building, on the right floor. Believe it or not, on September 11, more than 95 percent of the people in the Twin Towers actually escaped. As for planes, you have to be on the right flight, on the right day, at the right time, because out of the 30,000 or so planes that fly every day, only four crashed on September 11. And there were less than 300 people total on those four flights. As for anthrax, you have to make sure you get the right kind—because if you get the skin-contagion form and you wash your hands, it's all over. You're fine. There have been only *six* individuals who have died of anthrax in the United States, which is a country of *280 million.* So, if you're really feeling suicidal, your best odds are to get in a car and neglect to buckle your seat belt. That's where true risk of death and dismemberment comes from—not from terrorists.

If you're still intent on feeling like an endangered species, then the way you deal with your fear is everything. Say that you knew you were going to die in 24 hours. Would you rather spend that time cowering in your house and worrying what was going to happen next, or would you like to be on a beach, playing in the surf with the people you love? Your choice determines your stated of mind—you can choose to make yourself happy, or you can choose to be miserable. If nothing else, the

World Trade Center tragedy certainly separated the world into those who know how to opt for happiness and those who don't.

Write It Down

As you've probably noticed, I'm a great fan of paper and pen—when in doubt, whip 'em out! There's nothing like a blank piece of paper to help us get really focused, since all of us have been talking a lot longer than we've been writing. Although typing (on a computer or typewriter) is okay, it's an entirely different level of feedback and hand-eye coordination, and it even engages different parts of the brain. On your computer, you can delete, get caught up with the spell checker, choose a font, divert to Free Cell, accidentally erase everything (I really don't want to talk about that one, trust me) . . . it's a different experience from picking up a pen and writing.

A journal is a great gift *of* yourself *to* yourself. No need to go out and buy one of those fancy, vellum, leather-bound numbers—a plain spiral notebook will do just ducky. Keeping a log not only gets your thoughts out of your head and onto paper, but it can:

- help you get to sleep at night;

- provide you with a way of charting your own progress;

- give you a place to streamline and clarify your decision-making (that old pro-and-con list); and

- enable you to go back and read who you were a long time ago.

It's *your* thing, and you can use it for anything you desire. Writing things down is a very personal, private experience—if you want to communicate with someone, talk to them face-to-face. And don't do the cowardly, passive-aggressive trick of leaving your journal around so that the people in your life will understand how you *really* feel.

That's not going to fly. *Keep it private.* Whether you're using your journal to sing the praises of your newest love or to purge your soul of all negative thought, don't leave it around for other people to read. The best way to keep your journal a secret is to use a plain spiral notebook. People will be much less tempted to open a boring old notebook than something that says in big, block letters: "MY MOST PRIVATE THOUGHTS AND OTHER COOL THINGS."

❧ ❧ ❧

Now let's look at the ABC's of effective, active, get unstuck, get moving, problem-solving behavior.

Practice Square Breathing

Square breathing is an incredibly valuable technique that can control our body's fight-or-flight response, which is an instantaneous reaction to real or imagined danger. We inherited this instinct from our cave-dwelling ancestors, for those who had it lived long enough to pass their DNA on to us.

Naturally, these days we aren't facing any mastodons, but our bodies still respond to stress by preparing to run or do battle, which means getting oxygen to large muscles in a hurry. Luckily, the body has a very effective system of doing just that by *hyperventilating,* a 50-cent word that basically means "over-breathing." Hyperventilating manifests itself as:

- increased heart rate;

- narrowed bronchial passages;

- tingling in the fingers and lips;

- cold sweats;

- gastrointestinal distress (including upset stomach, nausea, or the need to urinate or defecate);

- dizziness and light-headedness; and

- *piloerection* (a fancy term for "goose bumps").

These symptoms don't occur randomly; but are quite functional. For example, the heart rate increases to get the blood pumping faster. The bronchial passages close down to ensure that oxygen effectively finds its way to the lungs. Tingling in fingers and toes occurs because pooled, stored blood is moved to large muscles, ASAP. Gastrointestinal symptoms are brought on because the body is moving blood and oxygen to large muscle groups, and away from nonessential areas (such as the head, the stomach, and the hands and lips)—food can be digested later, assuming there is a later. Sweat releases heat resulting from rapidly metabolizing muscles, since the human body can only tolerate a limited range of temperature. Dizziness and light-headedness are the result of moving blood away from the head. Both can be confused with fuzzy vision, caused by pupillary dilation, which allows for the maximum amount of light and information—at this point, you don't care what's farther down the road, you care what's right in front of you. In our ape ancestors, goose bumps were hair follicles which fluffed up, making for a big and dangerous look. All in all, these were very useful responses if a saber-toothed tiger was viewing you as dinner.

Fast-forward to today: Your boss has just called you in for review, and these symptoms aren't helping you at all. Your cramping stomach, inability to catch your breath, racing heart, sweaty palms, goose bumps, and dizziness aren't exactly dressing you for success. But you *can* use that adrenaline to make the present moment immediate, razor sharp, and vital.

Square breathing is the way to channel these biological responses to your advantage so that you can focus. Hyperventilation means that you're actually breathing too much, so what you want to do is decrease the amount of oxygen you're taking in, without turning blue.

It's actually useful to practice hyperventilating because then you can learn how to instantly calm yourself down. To practice, sit on the edge of your bed and pant like a puppy dog for about three minutes in front of a clock with a second hand. To alleviate all seven symptoms, you can inflate a brown paper sack like a megaphone, put it over your nose and mouth, and rebreathing the carbon dioxide you're exhaling. Then, as your body's carbon dioxide/oxygen ration changes, your symptoms will subside.

Since most of us don't carry brown paper sacks around with us and don't relish the idea of whipping out the old bag in public, square breathing is a terrific alternative. Under ordinary circumstances, we parallel breathe—exhaling and inhaling about 15 to 17 times per minute. When we're hyperventilating, the increase can be dramatic and sudden, or subtle and insidious. By increasing respirations at the rate of one or two per minute, we'll suddenly find ourselves in the middle of a full-fledged panic attack after about an hour or two.

Square breathing, on the other hand, slows everything down by dropping the old parallel breathing mode in favor of squaring off:

1. Inhale to a count of four.

2. Hold to a count of four.

3. Exhale to a count of four.

4. Hold again a the count of four.

5. Repeat the first four steps as many times as necessary.

Square breathing is the technique used in Lamaze classes for prepared childbirth and by athletes for concentration. Whether you're about to give a speech, ask your boss for a raise, or you just feel claustrophobic in the subway, this technique *really* works. Square breathing focuses and relaxes you in any awkward or uncomfortable situation. (I got to the point where I could actually hold to the count of 22—now *that's* relaxing.) Through practice, you can also increase those intervals, slow everything down, and learn to attain a sense of inner calm, even in the most stressful of circumstances. Closing one nostril with your index finger and just breathing out of the open one will also work.

So now you've got three options—choose the one that works best for you. I like square breathing for its flexibility and because it's not so obvious that anyone else will know what you're doing.

Visualize and Relax

Square breathing is a reliable standby during stress, but being able to feel relaxed, happy, and content is a cool tool that can head anxiety off at the pass. I didn't invent this technique, but I've taught and practiced guided relaxation and visualization for years. Want to try it? Just follow these instructions, step-by-step:

1. Turn off your phone, TV, computer, radio, pager—anything that can make noise.

2. Make sure the room is comfortable—not too hot or cold, and not too bright or dim.

3. Sit in a comfortable seat that supports your back, arms, and legs.

4. Gently close your eyes so you're focusing on your "third eye" (that space between your eyes).

5. Envision your favorite place—it may be a beach, a forest, the home you grew up in, your grandparents' house, a warm bath . . . wherever you feel most comfortable.

6. Allow yourself to view that place in very specific detail. Smell the smells, feel the warmth, hear the sounds, and see the sights.

7. See yourself entering that place.

8. Now visualize someone entering that place to be with you, somebody who, whether dead or alive, loves you and you love back. They sit calmly across from you and look into

your eyes. There's no need for words, for you're both able to communicate everything that's in each other's heads and hearts. All the thoughts that you both have always wanted to share (and maybe had a difficult time communicating in real life) are all transmitted without words. You understand each other perfectly—all the love, affection, and respect you have for each other is obvious to both of you. You feel seen, known, and loved.

9. A white light appears in your space. It starts off as just a little pinpoint, but it begins to get larger and larger until it fills the entire space with you and your beloved. The light fills you with complete contentment, happiness, and relaxation. You feel loved, warm, and relaxed.

10. When you're ready for them to go, the person you're with slowly leaves. You have no sense of loss, abandonment, or sadness, because you know that they'll be back with you whenever you wish. You feel content and peaceful as they slowly depart.

11. The white light slowly begins to recede and grows smaller until it fades away.

12. Now you decide to leave the safe and wonderful place you've chosen, knowing that you can return whenever you wish, for it will always be there waiting for you.

13. You're back in your chair with your eyes still closed. You allow yourself to feel heavy, relaxed, and warm in that chair.

14. Sit quietly, enjoying the total relaxation.

15. Slowly rub your thumb along your fingers and wiggle your toes before slowly opening your eyes.

16. Give yourself a moment to enjoy the sensations of your body before you reenter your world.

A sense of relaxation, contentment, focus, inner peace, and increased energy are often the benefits of this powerful technique, which can be used before work *or* sleep, when you're really angry, or whenever you're feeling a need to refocus. Like square breathing, this is a method that allows you to override the quick response impulse of your sympathetic nervous system by invoking a completely different part of your brain and your awareness.

❀ ❀ ❀

A compatible technique to assert your will over your body (or your intellect over your emotions) is a stylized relaxation exercise. If you're trying to go to sleep, this is a wonderful technique to do in bed; if you want to relax before a date, a day at the office, or a speech, it works better in a chair.

Whether you're sitting or lying down, start with your feet and work your way up. Repeat each step twice—holding the contraction for two to three seconds and then relaxing—before moving on to the next muscle group. Remember, this exercise isn't about flexibility or skill, just body awareness. It's not a competition or a race, it's just you becoming more attuned to how to relax your tense little old self.

1. Make a "fist" of your foot by curling your toes and heels under so that the toes and heels are almost touching. Then slowly unclench your foot.

2. Tense your ankles by rotating your feet to the left and then to the right. Relax.

3. To get at your calf muscles, point your toes to the ceiling for three to four seconds, point them to the floor, and then relax.

4. To flex your thigh muscles, raise and lower your leg (no high kicks, please). Once you know how your quadriceps feel, you'll be able to tense them without raising or lowering your legs.

5.   Clench your buttocks and then release.

6.   When you get to your internal organs, there's an activity
     for women called "Kegel exercise," which uses the muscle
     you utilize when stopping urination (but guys can try this,
     too). Tense this muscle without clenching your buttocks,
     then release.

7.   Flex your stomach muscles by turning your "tail" under
     (gently tilting your pelvis toward the ceiling), then relax.

8.   As you get to your arms, start with your shoulders, where
     most of us carry huge amounts of tension. Bring them all the
     way up to your ears, and then slowly lower them. As you're
     doing this, press your shoulders down and back toward your
     spine, so you can really feel the tension move out.

9.   Make a bicep muscle and slowly release it.

10. Clench your hands into fists and then shake the fingers out,
     since a lot of tension can build up in the hands.

11. When you get to your face, clench your jaw and then loosen it.

12. Move your tongue to the roof of your mouth, then lower it.

13. Scrunch your face into a scary mask, then relax all your
     facial muscles.

14. Roll your eyeballs into the back of your head and then
     forward again.

15. Raise your eyebrows, then lower them.

16. Feel your eyebrows melting off your face.

17. For every muscle group, clench tightly, hold for two or
     three seconds, unclench, and then clench again so that
     all of your major muscles contract and then relax. This

releases muscular tension, but it also enables the blood to circulate vigorously, which helps to relax and gets rid of stored toxins. By the time you're rolling your eyeballs around, you should feel fairly relaxed. If you don't, start again. Don't stress out if there are certain muscle groups you can't clench—if you can't wiggle your ears, no sweat. *Relaxation* is the point here, not trying to follow some routine "perfectly."

Use Your Magic Wand

I love magic wands. I personally own several, and I think everybody should have at least one. A magic wand is a tangible symbol that helps us ask, "If I could make the situation turn out the way I want it to, what would happen next?"

Figuring out what you *do* want—in the next five minutes, five hours, five months, or five years—moves you out of your emotions and into your intellect. This forces you to be specific, which "magically" increases the probability of getting what you want.

Wands are really quite helpful. You can make your own, which embodies whatever magic you wish. It's always good to have a bit of magic close at hand. Since I own a batch of wands, I've been known to lend one out for a day or two in an emergency. When people in my life are trying to make a decision, I encourage them to borrow one of my wands temporarily and figure out what they really want. I'm repeatedly told that my wands are indeed "magic," for they seem to help everybody they touch!

Shrink Wrap

There's a reason this book is called *Getting Unstuck*: I want you to be able to float like a butterfly, soar like an eagle, and enjoy your life, instead of trying desperately to raise one foot out of the muck while simultaneously trying to keep yourself from falling face down in it.

People call me when they're stuck, and I help them find a way out by changing from the passive, whiney, blaming mode to the active, unencumbered, logical, nonjudgmental, creative, even happy problem-solving mode. Sometimes the solutions are straightforward and obvious; sometimes they aren't. But even when the answers are simple, they're rarely easy.

Life wasn't invented to be easy—we'd all be pretty bored if it was. Life is interesting, fun, terrible, silly, exciting, trivial, important, thought-provoking, sinister, heartwarming, and heartbreaking—but it's certainly not effortless or problem free. Having difficulty in some area doesn't mean that you're a bad person, that you're unlovable, or that you need antidepressants. *Problems just happen.* Don't make them obstacles or value judgments about your life or worth. Problems are indeed a normal part of everyday life—and *we all have them.*

Problems are the knots between pearls, which keep the stones from shifting and scarring each other. They also keep the entire necklace from unraveling, should one pearl get damaged or lost. This ultimately makes a really good necklace. Problems enrich and define the pearls that are strung together to make the beauty of your life. Just don't get tied up with or in the knots—go for the pearls.

View problems as learning experiences, challenges, lessons, and the way to know you're alive and kicking. Just remember to *keep moving.* Pay tuition to Life for Humans 101 without complaint, remember what you've learned, and get on with your life. You already possess the skills you need—this book is about recovering, uncovering, and discovering that ability in yourself. So get going! You've got everything you need to live your life—stop, look, listen, and go for it. You now have all the tools you need to remain unstuck, so get moving and *live* your life!

Self-Help Resources

The following list of resources can be used to access information on a variety of issues. The addresses and telephone numbers listed are for the national headquarters; look in your local yellow pages under "Community Services" for resources closer to your area.

In addition to the following groups, other self-help organizations may be available in your area to assist your healing and recovery for a particular life crisis not listed here. Consult your telephone directory, call a counseling center or help line near you, or contact:

AIDS

(United States)

CDC National AIDS Hotline
(800) 342-2437

Caring for Babies with AIDS
P.O. Box 35135
Los Angeles, CA 90035
(323) 931-9828
www.caring4babieswithaids.org

Children with AIDS (CWA)
Project of America
P.O. Box 23778
Tempe, AZ 85285
(800) 866-AIDS (24-hour hotline)
www.aidskids.org

Elizabeth Glaser Pediatric AIDS
Foundation
2950 31st St., #125
Santa Monica, CA 90405
(888) 499-HOPE (4673)
www.pedaids.org

The Names Project Foundation—
AIDS Memorial Quilt
P.O. Box 5552
Atlanta, GA 31107
(800) 872-6263
www.aidsquilt.org

Project Inform
205 13th St., Ste. 2001
San Francisco, CA 94103
(800) 822-7422 (treatment hotline)
(415) 558-9051 (S.F. and Int'l)
www.projectinform.org

Spanish HIV/STD/AIDS Hotline
(800) 344-7432

TTY (Hearing Impaired) AIDS Hotline
(CDC National HIV/AIDS)
(800) 243-7889

(United Kingdom)

National AIDS Helpline
0 800 567123
www.healthwise.org.uk

National AIDS Trust
New City Cloisters
196 Old Street
London EC1V 9F4
020 7814 6767
www.nat.org.uk

(Canada)

Canadian AIDS Society
4th Floor- 309 rue Cooper Street
Ottawa ON K2P 0G5
(613)230-3580

Health Canada
HIV/AIDS
www.aidsida.com

ALCOHOL ABUSE

(United States)

Al-Anon Family Group Headquarters
1600 Corporate Landing Parkway
Virginia Beach, VA 23454-5617
(888) 4AL-ANON
www.al-anon.alateen.org

Alcoholics Anonymous (AA)
General Service Office
475 Riverside Dr., 11th Floor
New York, NY 10115
(212) 870-3400
www.alcoholics-anonymous.org

Children of Alcoholics Foundation
164 W. 74th St.
New York, NY 10023
(800) 359-COAF
www.coaf.org

Mothers Against Drunk Driving (MADD)
P.O. Box 541688
Dallas, TX 75354
(800) GET-MADD (438-6233)
www.madd.org

National Association of Children of Alcoholics (NACoA)
11426 Rockville Pike, #100
Rockville, MD 20852
(301) 468-0985
(888) 554-2627
www.nacoa.net

National Clearinghouse for Alcohol and Drug Information (NCADI)
P.O. Box 2345
Rockville, MD 20847
(800) 729-6686
www.health.org

National Council on Alcoholism and Drug Dependence (NCADD)
20 Exchange Pl., Ste. 2902
New York, NY 10005
(212) 269-7797
(800) NCA-CALL (24-hour hotline)
www.ncadd.org

Women for Sobriety
P.O. Box 618
Quakertown, PA 18951
(215) 536-8026
www.womenforsobriety.org

(United Kingdom)

Alcohol Concern
020 7922 8667
www.alcoholconcern.org.uk

Alcoholics Anonymous
General Service Office
PO Box 1, Stonebow House
Stonebow YO1 7NJ
(44) 01904-644026
www.alcoholics-anonymous.org.uk

Healthwise Drinkline
0800 917 8282
www.healthwise.org.uk

(Canada)

Alcoholics Anonymous
www.aa.org/index.html

Al-Anon/Alateen
(800) 714-7498 (for information and materials)
(800) 443-4525 (for meeting locations)

Canadian Center on Substance Abuse
75 Albert Street, Suite 300
Ottawa ON K1P 5E7
(613) 235-4048
www.ccsa.ca

Canadians for Safe and Sober Driving
P.O. Box 397
Station "A"
Brampton ON L6V 2L3
(905) 793-4233
www.add.ca

ALZHEIMER'S DISEASE

(United States)

Alzheimer's Association
919 N. Michigan Ave., Ste. 1100
Chicago, IL 60611
(800) 272-3900
www.alz.org

Alzheimer's Disease Education and Referral Center
P.O. Box 8250
Silver Spring, MD 20907
(800) 438-4380
adear@alzheimers.org

Eldercare Locator
330 Independence Ave., SW
Washington, DC 20201
(800) 677-1116
www.eldercare.gov

(United Kingdom)

Alzheimer's Society
Gordon House
10 Greencoat Place
London SW1P 1PH
020 7606 0606
www.alzheimers.org.uk

(Canada)

Alzeheimer Society of Canada
20 Eglinton Avenue W., Suite 1200
Toronto ON M4R 1K8
(800) 616-8816
www.alzheimer.ca

CANCER

(Unites States)

National Cancer Institute
(800) 4-CANCER
www.nci.nih.gov

(United Kingdom)

CancerHelp UK
Institute for Cancer Studies
University of Birmingham
Edgbaston
Birmingham B15 2TA
www.cancerhelp.org.uk

(Canada)

Canadian Cancer Society
(888) 939-3333
www.cancer.ca

CHILDREN'S ISSUES

Child Molestation

(United States)

Childhelp USA/Child Abuse Hotline
15757 N. 78th St.
Scottsdale, AZ 85260
(800) 422-4453
www.childhelpusa.org

Prevent Child Abuse America
200 South Michigan Ave., 17th Floor
Chicago, IL 60604
(312) 663-3520
www.preventchildabuse.org

(United Kingdom)

Childline
Royal Mail Building, 2nd Floor
Studd Street
London N1 OQW
0800 1111 (helpline)
0800 400 222 (text phone service)
www.childline.org.uk

National Society for the Prevention of Cruelty to Children (NSPCC)
Weston House
42 Curtains Road
London EC2A 3NH
020 7825 2500 (administration)
0808 800 5000 (helpline)

(Canada)

Child Abuse Hotline
(800) 387-5437

Kids Help Phone
(800) 668-6868
http://kidshelp.simaptico.ca

The Canadian Society for the Prevention of Cruelty to Children
Box 700, 356 First Street
Midland ON L4R 4P4
(705)526-5647

Crisis Intervention

(United States)

Girls and Boys Town National Hotline
(800) 448-3000
www.boystown.org

Children of the Night
14530 Sylvan St.
Van Nuys, CA 91411
(800) 551-1300
www.childrenofthenight.org

Covenant House Hotline
(800) 999-9999
www.covenanthouse.org

Kid Save Line
(800) 543-7283
www.kidspeace.org

Youth Nineline
(referrals for parents/teens about drugs, homelessness, runaways)
(800) 999-9999

(United Kingdom)

Barnardo's
Tanner's Lane
Barkingside
Ilford IG6 1QG
020 8550 8822
www.barnardos.org.uk

Childline
Royal Mail Building, 2nd Floor
Studd Street
London N1 OQW
0800 1111 (helpline)
0800 400 222 (text phone service)
www.childline.org.uk

The Prince's Trust
18 Park Square East
London NW1 4LH
020 7543 1234
www.princes-trust.org.uk

Safe in the City
020 7922 5710
www.safeinthecity.org.uk

(Canada)

Covenant House
575 Drake Street
Vancouver BC V6B 4K8
(604) 685-7474
www.covenenthousebc.org

Covenant House
20 Gerrard Street East
Toronto, ON M5B 2P3
(416) 598-4898
www.covenanthouse.org

Kids Help Phone
(800) 668-6868
http://kidshelp.simpatico.ca

Missing Children

(United States)

Missing Children . . . HELP Center
410 Ware Blvd., Ste. 710
Tampa, FL 33619
(800) USA-KIDS
www.800usakids.org

National Center for Missing
& Exploited Children
699 Prince St.
Alexandria, VA 22314
(800) 843-5678 (24-hour hotline)
www.missingkids.org

(United Kingdom)

National Missing Persons Helpline
0500 700 700
www.missingpersons.org

UK Missing and Exploited Children
http://uk.missingkids.com

(Canada)

Child Find Canada
1-1808 Main Street
Winnipeg MB R2V 2A3
(204) 339-5584
www.childfind.ca

Missing Children Society of Canada
Suite 219, 3501 - 23 Street NE
Calgary AB T2E 6V8
(800) 661-6160
www.mcsc.ca

Children with Serious Illnesses
(fulfilling wishes):

(United States)

Brass Ring Society
National Headquarters
551 E. Semoran Blvd., Ste. E-5
Fern Park, FL 32730
(407) 339-6188
(800) 666-WISH
www.worldramp.net/brassring

Make-a-Wish Foundation
3550 N. Central Ave., Ste. 300
Phoenix, AZ 85012
(800) 722-WISH (9474)
www.wish.org

(United Kingdom)

Make-a-Wish Foundation UK
01276 24127
www.make-a-wish.org.uk

Starlight Foundation
11-15 Emerald Street
London WC1N 3QL
020 7430 1642
www.starlight.org.uk

(Canada)

Make a Wish Foundation of Canada
2239 Oak Street
Vancouver BC V6H 3W6
(888) 822-9474
www.makeawish.ca

CO-DEPENDENCY

Co-Dependents Anonymous
P.O. Box 33577
Phoenix, AZ 85067
(602) 277-7991
www.codependents.org

Co-Dependents Anonymous
World Service, Inc.
PO Box 7051
Thomaston, GA USA 30286-0025
(706) 648-6868
www.wscoda.org

DEATH/GRIEVING/SUICIDE

(United States)

AARP Grief and Loss Programs
(202) 434-2260
(800) 424-3410
www.aarp.org/griefandloss

Grief Recovery Institute
P.O. Box 6061-382
Sherman Oaks, CA 91413
(818) 907-9600
www/grief-recovery.com

National Hospice and Palliative Care
Organization
1700 Diagonal Rd., Ste. 300
Alexandria, VA 22314
(703) 837-1500
www.nhpco.org

Parents of Murdered Children
(recovering from violent death
of friend or family member)
100 E 8th St., Ste. B41
Cincinnati, OH 45202
(513) 721-5683
(888) 818-POMC
www.pomc.com

SIDS (Sudden Infant Death Syndrome)
Alliance
1314 Bedford Ave., Ste. 210
Baltimore, MD 21208
(800) 221-7437
www.sidsalliance.org

Suicide Awareness Voices of Education
(SAVE)
Minneapolis, MN 55424
(952) 946-7998

Suicide National Hotline
(800) 784-2433

(United Kingdom)

The Compassionate Friends
53 North Street
Bristol BS3 1EN
0117 953 9639 (helpline)
0177 966 5202 (administration)
www.compassionatefriends.org.uk

Winston's Wish
The Clara Burgess Centre
Gloucestershire Royal Hospital
Great Western Road
Gloucester GL1 3NN
+44 (0) 1452 394377 (general inquiries)
0845 20 30 40 5 (family line)
www.winstonswish.org.uk

(Canada)

Canadian Hospice Palliative Care Association
43 Bruyère St., Ste. 131 C
Ottawa, ON K1N 5C8
(800) 668-2785
www.cpa.net

Seasons Centre for Grieving Children
4 Alliance Boulevard, Unit 7
Barrie ON L4M 5J1
(705) 721-5437
www.seasonscentre.com

Suicide Information and Education Centre
#201 1615-10th Avenue SW
Calgary AB T3C 0J7
www.suicideinfo.ca

DEBTS

(United States)

Consumer Credit Counseling Service
Credit **Referral**
(800) 388-CCCS

Debtors Anonymous
General Service Office
P.O. Box 920888
Needham, MA 02492-0009
(781) 453-2743
www.debtorsanonymous.org

DIABETES

(United States)

American Diabetes Association
(800) 342-2383
www.diabetes.org

(United Kingdom)

Diabetes UK
10 Parkway
London NW1 7AA
020 7424 1000
www.diabetesuk.org

(Canada)

Canadian Diabetes Association
(800) 226-8464
www.diabetes.ca

DOMESTIC VIOLENCE

(United States)

National Coalition Against Domestic Violence
P.O. Box 18749
Denver, CO 80218
(303) 831-9251
www.ncadv.org

National Domestic Violence Hotline
P.O. Box 161810
Austin, TX 78716
(800) 799-SAFE (24-hour hotline)
(800) 787-3224 (TTY)
www.ndvh.org

(United Kingdom)

Women's Aid
PO Box 391
Bristol BS99 7WS
08457 023 468 (helpline)
0117 944 441 (administration)
www.womensaid.org.uk

Victim Support
0845 30 30 900 (helpline)

(Canada)

Evolve (KLINIC)
870 Portage Avenue
Winnipeg, MB MR3G 0P1
(204) 784-4090
www.klinic.mb.ca

National Domestic Violence Hotline
(800) 363-9010

Safe Home
(888) 926-0301

DRUG ABUSE

(United States)

Cocaine Anonymous National Referral Line
(800) 347-8998

National Helpline of Phoenix House
(cocaine abuse hotline)
(800) 262-2463
(800) COCAINE
www.drughelp.org

National Institute of Drug Abuse (NIDA)
6001 Executive Blvd., Rm. 5213
Bethesda, MD 20892-9561
Parklawn Building
(301) 443-6245 (for information)
(800) 662-4357 (for help)
www.nida.nih.gov

World Service Office, Inc. (CA)
3740 Overland Ave., Ste. C
Los Angeles, CA 90034-6337
(310) 559-5833

(United Kingdom)

National Drug Helpline
0800 77 66 00
www.ndhl.org.uk

The Centre for Recovery
Cyswllt Ceredigion Contact
49 North Parade
Ceredigion SY23 2JN
01970 626470
www.recovery.org.uk

Narcotics Anonymous—UK Region
020 7730 0009
www.ukna.org

(Canada)

Canadian Assembly Narcotics Anonymous
CANA/ACNA
PO Box 25073 RPO West Kildonan
Winnipeg MB R2V 4C7
www.cana-acna.org

Canadian Centre on Substance Abuse
75 Albert Street, Suite 300
Ottawa ON K1P 5E7
(613) 235-4048
www.ccsa.ca

EATING DISORDERS

(United States)

Overeaters Anonymous
National Office
P.O. Box 44020
Rio Rancho, NM 87174-4020
(505) 891-2664
www.overeatersanonymous.org

(United Kingdom)

Eating Disorders Association
103 Prince of Wales Road
Norwich NR1 1DW
0845 634 1414 (adults)
0845 634 7650 (youth)
www.edauk.com

(Canada)

National Eating Disorder
Information Center
CW 1- 211 Elizabeth Street
Toronto, ON M5G 2C4
(866) 633-4240
www.nedic.ca

GAMBLING

Gamblers Anonymous
International Service Office
P.O. Box 17173
Los Angeles, CA 90017
(213) 386-8789
www.gamblersanonymous.org

Gamblers Anonymous UK
PO Box 88
London SW10 0EU
08700 50 88 80
www.gamblersanonymous.org.uk

Gamblers Anonymous Canada
(by Province)
www.gamlersanonymous.org.mtgdirCAN.html

HEALTH ISSUES

(United States)

American Chronic Pain Association
P.O. Box 850
Rocklin, CA 95677
(916) 632-0922
www.theacpa.org

American Holistic Health Association
P.O. Box 17400
Anaheim, CA 92817
(714) 779-6152
www.ahha.org

The Chopra Center at
La Costa Resort and Spa
Deepak Chopra, M.D.
7321 Estrella Del Mar
Carlsbad, CA 92009
(760) 931-7524
www.chopra.com

The Fetzer Institute
9292 West KL Ave.
Kalamazoo, MI 49009
(616) 375-2000
www.fetzer.org

Hippocrates Health Institute
(A favorite annual retreat for Louise Hay)
1443 Palmdale Court
West Palm Beach, FL 33411
(800) 842-2125
www.hippocratesinst.com

Hospicelink
190 W. Brook Rd.
Essex, CT 06426
(800) 331-1620

Institute for Noetic Sciences
101 San Antonio Rd.
Petaluma, CA 94952
(707) 775-3500
www.noetic.org

The Mind-Body Medical Institute
110 Francis St., Ste. 1A
Boston, MA 02215
(617) 632-9530 (press 1)
www.mbmi.org

National Health Information Center
P.O. Box 1133
Washington, DC 20013-1133
(800) 336-4797
www.health.gov/NHIC

Optimum Health Institute
(Louise loves this place!)
6970 Central Ave.
Lemon Grove, CA 91945
(619) 464-3346
www.optimumhealth.org

Preventive Medicine Research Institute
Dean Ornish, M.D.
900 Bridgeway, Ste. 2
Sausalito, CA 94965
(415) 332-2525
www.pmri.org

(United Kingdom)

National Health Service (NHS) Direct
0845 4647 (24 hour nurse advice line)
www.nhsdirect.nhs.uk

UK Health Centre
www.healthcentre.org.uk

(Canada)

Health Canada
Minister's Office
Brooke Claxton Bldg., Tunney's Pasture
PL 0906C
Ottawa, ON K1A 0K9
(613) 952-1154 (fax)
www.hc-sc.gc.ca

HOUSING RESOURCES

(United States)

Acorn
(nonprofit network of low- and moderate-income housing)
739 8th St., S.E.
Washington, DC 20003
(202) 547-9292

(United Kingdom)

The Abbeyfield Society
(for elderly people)
The Abbeyfield House
53 Victoria Street
St Albans
Herts AL1 3UW
01727 857536
www.abbeyfield.com

Centrepoint
(for young people)
Neil House
7 Whitechapel Road
London E1 1DU
020 7426 5300
www.centrepoint.org.uk

Shelterline
0808 8000 4444
www.shelter.org.uk

(Canada)

Abbeyfield Houses Society of Canada
Box 1, 427 Bloor Street West
Toronto, ON M5S 1X7
(416) 920-7483
www.abbeyfield.ca

Canada Mortgage and Housing Corporation
700 Montreal Road
Ottawa, ON K1A 0P7
(613) 748-2000
www.cmhc-schl.gc.ca

IMPOTENCE

(United States)

Impotence Institute of America
8201 Corporate Dr., Ste. 320
Landover, MD 20715
(800) 669-1603
www.impotenceworld.org

(United Kingdom)

The Impotence Association
PO Box 10296
London SW17 9WH
020 8767 7791
www.impotence.org.uk

MENTAL HEALTH

(United States)

American Psychiatric Association of America
1400 "K" St. NW
Washington, D.C. 20005
(888) 357-7924
www.psych.org

Anxiety Disorders Association of America
11900 Parklawn Dr., Ste. 100
Rockville, MD 20852
(301) 231-9350
www.adaa.org

The Help Center of the American Psychological Association
(800) 964-2000
www.helping.apa.org

The International Society for Mental Health Online
www.ismho.org

Knowledge Exchange Network
www.mentalhealth.org

National Center for Post-Traumatic Stress Disorder (PTSD)
(802) 296-5132
www.ncptsd.org

National Alliance for the Mentally Ill
2107 Wilson Blvd., Ste. 300
Arlington, VA 22201
(800) 950-6264
www.nami.org

National Depressive and Manic-Depressive Association
730 N. Franklin St., Ste. 501
Chicago, IL 60610
(800) 826-3632
www.ndmda.org

National Institute of Mental Health
6001 Executive Blvd.
Room 8184, MSC 9663
Bethesda, MD 20892
(301) 443-4513
(301) 443-8431 (TTY)
www.nimh.nih.gov

(United Kingdom)

Depression Alliance

Mind (The National Association for Mental Health)
15-19 Broadway
London E15 4BQ
020 8519 2122
www.mind.org.uk

Sane
1st Floor
Cityside House
40AdlerStreet
London E1 1EE
020 7375 1002
0845 767 8000 (saneline—open noon–2 a.m.)
www.sane.org.uk

(Canada)

Canadian Mental Health Association
2160 Yonge Street, 3rd Floor
Toronto, ON M4S 2Z3
(416) 484-7750
www.cmha.ca

Mood Disorders Association of Canada
4-1000 Notre Dame Avenue
Winnipeg, MB R3E 0N3
(800) 263-1460

PET BEREAVEMENT

(United States)

Bide-A-Wee Foundation
410 E. 38th St.
New York, NY 10016
(212) 532-6395

Grief Recovery Hotline
(800) 445-4808

Holistic Animal Consulting Centre
29 Lyman Ave.
Staten Island, NY 10305
(718) 720-5548

(United Kingdom)

Animal Samaritans
52 Verdant Lane
London SE3 1LF
020 8852 9132
www.animalsamaritans.org.uk

(Canada)

Pet Therapy Society of Northern Alberta
330, 9768 170 Street
Edmonton, AB T5T L54
(780) 413-4682
http://paws.shopalberta.com/PTRemember.htm

RAPE/SEXUAL ISSUES

(United States)

Rape, Abuse, and Incest National Network
(800) 656-4673
www.rainn.org

SafePlace
P.O. Box 19454
Austin, TX 78760
(512) 440-7273

National Council on Sexual Addictions and Compulsivity
P.O. Box 725544
Atlanta, GA 31139
(770) 541-9912
www.ncsac.org

Sexually Transmitted Disease Referral
(800) 227-8922

(United Kingdom)

Rape Crisis Federation of Wales and England
7 Mansfield Road
Nottingham NG1 3FB
0115 934 8474
www.rapecrisis.co.uk

Rape and Sexual Abuse Counseling
01962 848018 (administration)
01962 848024 (helpline for women)
01962 848027 (helpline for men)
http://rasc.org.uk

(Canada)

Canadian Association of Sexual Assault Centres
77 East 20th Avenue
Vancouver BC V5V 1L7
(604) 876-2622
www.casac.ca

Let's Protect
(list of resources for women in Canada and the US)
www.letsprotect.com

SMOKING

(United States)

Nicotine Anonymous World Services
419 Main St., PMB #370
Huntington Beach, CA 92648
(415) 750-0328
www.nicotine-anonymous.org

(United Kingdom)

Quit
0800 00 22 00
www.quit.org.uk

(Canada)

Lung Association
3 Raymond Street, Suite 300
Ottawa ON KR1 1A3
(613) 569-6411
www.lung.ca/smoking

STRESS REDUCTION

(United States)

The Biofeedback & Psychophysiology Clinic The Menninger Clinic
P.O. Box 829
Topeka, KS 66601-0829
(800) 351-9058
www.menninger.edu

New York Open Center
(In-depth workshops to invigorate the spirit)
83 Spring St.
New York, NY 10012
(212) 219-2527
www.opencenter.org

Omega Institute
(a healing, spiritual retreat community)
150 Lake Dr.
Rhinebeck, NY 12572-3212
(845) 266-4444 (info)
(800) 944-1001 (to enroll)
www.eomega.org

The Stress Reduction Clinic
Center for Mindfulness
University of Massachusetts Medical Center
55 Lake Ave. North
Worcester, MA 01655
(508) 856-2656

(United Kingdom)

International Stress Management Association
PO Box 348
Waltham Cross EN8 8ZL
07000 780430
www.isma.org.uk

TEEN HELP

ADOL: Adolescent Directory Online
Includes information on eating disorders, depression, and teen pregnancy.
www.education.indiana.edu/cas/adol/adol.html

Al-Anon/Alateen
1600 Corporate Landing Parkway
Virginia Beach, VA 23454-5617
(888) 425-2666
(888) 4AL-ANON
www.al-anon.alateen.org

Focus Adolescent Services: Eating Disorders
(877) 362-8727
www.focusas.com/EatingDisorders.html

Future Point
A nonprofit organization that offers message boards and chat rooms to empower teens in the academic world and beyond.
www.futurepoint.org

Kids in Trouble Help Page
Child abuse, depression, suicide, and runaway resources, with links and hotline numbers.
www.geocities.com/EnchantedForest/2910

Planned Parenthood
810 Seventh Ave.
New York, NY 10019
(212) 541-7800
(800) 230-PLAN
www.plannedparenthood.org

SafeTeens.com
Provides lessons on online safety and privacy; also has resources for homework and fun on the Web.
www.safeteens.com

TeenCentral.net
This site is written by and about teens. Includes celebrity stories, real-teen tales, an anonymous help-line, and crisis counseling.
www.teencentral.net

TeenOutReach.com
Includes all kinds of information geared at teens, from sports to entertainment to help with drugs and eating disorders.
www.teenoutreach.com

Hotlines for Teenagers

(United States)

Girls and Boys Town National Hotline
(800) 448-3000

Childhelp National Child Abuse Hotline/Voices for Children
(800) 422-4453
(800) 4ACHILD

Just for Kids Hotline
(888) 594-5437
(888) 594-KIDS

National Child Abuse Hotline
(800) 792-5200

National Runaway Hotline
(800) 621-4000

National Youth Crisis Hotline
(800) 448-4663
(800) HIT HOME

Suicide Prevention Hotline
(800) 827-7571

(United Kingdom)

Alateen
(for teens with alcohol concerns)
020 7403 0888

Anti Bullying Campaign
(counseling and advice)
020 7378 1446

Careline
(counseling and advice)
020 8514 1177

Family-line UK (for families in crisis)
0845 756 7800

National Association for Children of Alcoholics
0800 567123

(Canada)

AIDS/ Sexually Transmitted Diseases Info
(800) 772-2437

Gambling Help Line
(800) 665-9676

Kid's Help Phone
(800) 668-6868

ABOUT THE AUTHOR

Dr. Joy Browne is a licensed clinical psychologist, proud mom, and the host of her own internationally syndicated daily radio show. Every day, millions of listeners in the U.S., Canada, and on Armed Services Radio worldwide hear her give advice on everything from cheating boyfriends to the best new plays on Broadway. She has won numerous awards for her work, including the American Psychological Association's President's Award and the *TALKERS Magazine* award for Best Female Talk Show Host two years in a row. In addition to radio, Dr. Browne has hosted her own television show and has been a guest on *Oprah, Montel, Larry King Live,* and more.

This is Dr. Browne's eighth book. Her other titles include *The Nine Fantasies That Will Ruin Your Life* and the bestselling *Dating for Dummies.* Before finding her way to the airwaves, Dr. Browne was a teacher, archeologist, and engineer on the U.S. space program. Joy keeps herself inspired by dancing, hot-air ballooning, and practicing yoga. She is a proud resident of New York City.

Other Hay House Titles
of Related Interest

❧ ❧ ❧

We hope you enjoyed this Hay House book.
If you would like to receive a free catalog featuring additional
Hay House books and products, or if you would like information
about the Hay Foundation, please contact:

Hay House, Inc.
P.O. Box 5100
Carlsbad, CA 92018-5100

(760) 431-7695 or (800) 654-5126
(760) 431-6948 (fax) or (800) 650-5115 (fax)
www.hayhouse.com

❧ ❧ ❧

Published and distributed in Australia by:
Hay House Australia Pty Ltd, P.O. Box 515,
Brighton-Le-Sands, NSW 2216 • *phone:* 1800 023 516
e-mail: info@hayhouse.com.au

Distributed in the United Kingdom by:
Airlift, 8 The Arena, Mollison Ave., Enfield, Middlesex,
United Kingdom EN3 7NL

Distributed in Canada by: Raincoast, 9050 Shaughnessy St.,
Vancouver, B.C., Canada V6P 6E5

❧ ❧ ❧